PEVERELLY'S NATIONAL GAME

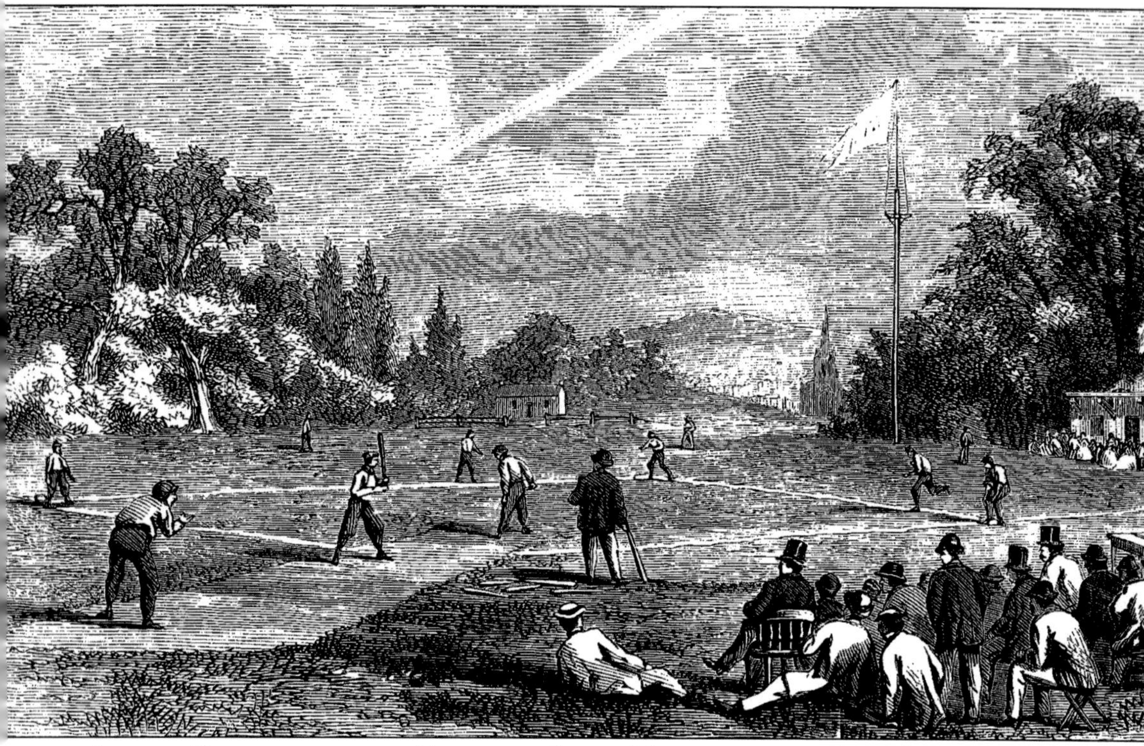

ACTUAL PICTURE FROM THE PEVERELLY BOOK. This engraving is the only picture in the original publication of Peverelly's *American Pastimes*. The scene is typical of the ball game as witnessed by men and women alike in the Civil War era of the 1860s. Off in the distance, you can see a tented area. This was meant for the ladies. Baseball—or "base ball" as it was more commonly written at the time—was popular with women from the very beginning. They found it more exciting than cricket. Only horse-racing was close to being as popular as baseball, as an outdoor sport. The book doesn't mention where this game is being played or the members of the opposing "crack" nines. Baseball clubs would send out their best nines when competing against other clubs. Some of the older clubs that started in the 1840s and '50s had dozens of active members, even hundreds in some cases, by the time Charles Peverelly wrote *American Pastimes* in 1866. The field is likely the Elysian Fields, "The Birthplace of Baseball," where top New York nines flooded the fields across the river in Hoboken, New Jersey. Only the images remain of this grand, green cathedral. Life, and base ball, were much simpler then . . . (Source: American Pastimes, Charles Peverelly, 1866.)

(coòer) The images that you see on the cover are all classic examples of the beauty within this ancient, simple game. On the front cover, baseball's first superstar, Jim Creighton, shows us the pitching stance of the 1860s. Tragically, Creighton died after rupturing an organ while swinging a bat—he was 21 years old. On the back cover is a very early photograph of a game being played by the Hudson River BBC, at Newburgh, New York. Most early images of baseball are portraits or staged sittings. And the large background image is from Frank Leslie's *Illustrated Newspaper*, c. 1865. The picture shows a game being played in the middle. It also has the ghostly image of Jim Creighton looking down upon the game. The players that adorn the page are stars of the day.

Peverelly's National Game

John Freyer and Mark Rucker
With an Introduction by John Thorn

ARCADIA
PUBLISHING

ISBN 978-0-7385-3404-6

Published by Arcadia Publishing
Charleston, South Carolina

Printed in the United States of America

Library of Congress Control Number: 2005923153

For all general information, please contact Arcadia Publishing:
Telephone 843-853-2070
Fax 843-853-0044
E-mail sales@arcadiapublishing.com
For customer service and orders:
Toll-Free 1-888-313-2665

Visit us on the Internet at www.arcadiapublishing.com

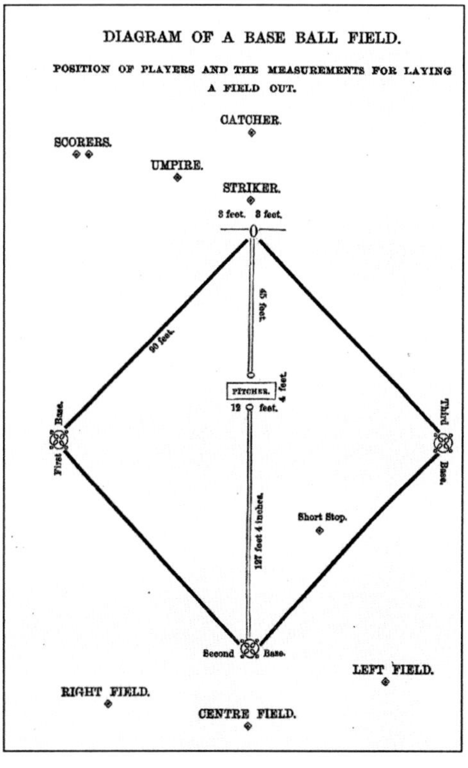

PEVERELLY BASEBALL DIAGRAM. This diagram of a baseball field with players' positions was the only other image in the original book. Notice that the second baseman played at the bag. Baseball of this period was still a simple game. Pitchers were just discovering the value of speed as a means to getting a batter out. The earliest forms of the game catered to the striker (batter). The ball was pitched or lobbed to the plate, underhand. Balls (1964) and strikes (1858) were not called with any consistency. Batters could wait for their pitch, or wait for the runners on base to move up all the way to third base, before knocking them in. This had a lot to do with the high scoring affairs that characterized early "base ball." (Source: American Pastimes, Charles Peverelly, 1866.)

Contents

ACKNOWLEDGMENTS

American Pastimes was written in 1866 by Charles Peverelly. It covered the history of baseball, cricket, rowing, and yachting clubs in the United States. In his own words, "Charles A. Peverelly . . . has been engaged in the reporting of Out-Door Sports for several New York Journals for more than twenty years." Peverelly self-published his book after the 1866 baseball season.

The sole purpose of adapting his classic chapter on baseball, "The National Game," is to make the historical information within it available to modern readers. The original text—Peverelly's words—have not been altered, but line spacing and indentation have been altered in places to fit the present volume. Also, contemporary images with brief commentary (italicized) have been added throughout, bringing to life the game as it was played and witnessed in Peverelly's time. This book has something for everyone: for the baseball researcher, information that once was only available on microfiche; for the vintage base ball player, an insight into the game as it was played some 140 years ago; and for the fan, images and information about baseball that have not been seen by the public in more than a century.

The transcription of this book has sought to preserve the quality of content as it is presented in the original book. Misspelled words, imaginative punctuation, and bad grammar are all a part of this transcription. If something looks out of place, it's there because it has been so since the first publication.

Peverelly's section on baseball appears to be a compilation of sorts. As part of his process of gathering information for the book, one can assume that letters were sent out to clubs; Peverelly would print the direct correspondences from clubs that responded. This gives the book a "patchwork" feel, with no consistent flow. When teams didn't respond, Peverelly would fill in the information with scores of contests and general information about the team.

Some glaring omissions in his book include teams like the Putnam Club, who disbanded in 1860, and junior clubs like the Star, Mohawk, Young America, Fly Away, and Harmony. Peverelly's focus seems to have been towards the East Coast clubs that would form the National Association. The book does not represent the imminent explosion of baseball that was occurring in the years 1866 and 1867. By reading this book alone, one would get the feeling that baseball was not popular inland, while just the opposite was true. By 1867, baseball was a "National Game," being played from coast to coast. There were established teams in Detroit, Chicago, Saint Louis, Cincinnati, Louisville, and San Francisco—as early as 1859.

The present volume adds images and boxscores to help convey the simplicity of the game. Images in the book, outside of the author's collection, were provided by several sources. Mark Rucker of Transcendental Graphics has a passion for baseball imagery, exceeded only by his passion for baseball itself. Box scores, outside of the author's collection, were furnished by Charles "Newt" Weaver, who has an incredible collection of box scores from early baseball history.

Baseball historian John Thorn has helped shape and polish this book, adding helpful criticism and years of knowledge to this project.

This book could not have been done without the help of Ted Hathaway of Rational Pastimes, who sent me a copy of Peverelly several years ago. From the first time I saw the book, it has been stuck in my mind to do this project ever since.

Other's who get a thank you include Priscilla Astifan, Coot Hunkele, Dean Thilgen, Angus McFarland, Joanne Hulbert, Tom Gilbert, Fred Ivor-Campbell, Tom Shieber, Paul Wendt, and Larry McCray.

And last but not least, my wife Carrie and my son, Jack, who are my two favorite cheerleaders, and my best friends.

INTRODUCTION

On September 24 and 25, 1844, at the St. George Cricket Club Grounds along the East River in Manhattan, the first international cricket match took place between the United States and Canada. The American team was drawn from several New York, Philadelphia, Washington City, and Boston clubs, all hotbeds of cricket. The match drew over 20,000 spectators, according to contemporary reports, many of them with a gambling interest in the outcome.

A year later, almost to the day—September 22, 1845—a four-oared regatta was held at Hoboken's Elysian Fields, a pleasure ground for New Yorkers, especially the legions of country lads who had streamed into the city looking for work. Rowing was America's first modern sport, in that competitions were marked by record keeping and prizes yet also provided spectator interest for those with no pecuniary interest. The first boat club to be organized in the United States was named the Knickerbocker, in 1823.

It may not have been a coincidence when on the day following the regatta some New York City gentlemen who were already playing the new game of baseball at the Elysian Fields organized themselves into a club, which they called the Knickerbockers. The game had been played earlier, of course. Recent finds have substantiated that a game called baseball had been played as early as 1823 in New York and 1791 in Pittsfield, Massachusetts. But the Knickerbockers claimed the palm for being the first true club not because they were first to play the game; they knew that the New York Club had played the game before them. Rather, like their upstanding brothers of the scull, sail, and wicket, the Knicks created a constitution, had regular days for play and practice, admitted members upon due consideration, and conducted themselves in accordance with written rules. Also, in what has been a neglected consideration, they were accorded pioneer status because their name left no doubt as to the heritage upon which they were based: the universally applauded Dutch rather than the reviled British.

It is this fluid state of American sport that Charles A. Peverelly sought to document in 1866 with his *Book of American Pastimes, Containing a History of the Principal Base Ball, Cricket, Rowing and Yachting Clubs of the United States*. The author had witnessed the explosion of interest in baseball over the previous ten years, but he could not have known how soon cricket would forever lose all claim to being an American pastime. Nor could he have anticipated the tertiary role that yachting and rowing would come to have in his own lifetime.

What John Freyer and Mark Rucker have done in extracting the baseball content of Peverelly's book is commendable and overdue. Apart from *Peverelly's National Game*, as it is now retitled, being the first baseball book (not counting paperbound annual guides and other ephemera), this book has been unavailable for so long that much of its information has become lost to researchers and aficionados of the early game. What did the early team uniforms look like? Where were their playing grounds located? Who were their officers, year by year since their founding? Those features alone, plus the extensive treatment of such pioneer clubs as the Knickerbocker of New York and the Olympic of Philadelphia, make the republication of Peverelly's baseball section a watershed event. But there is more, so much more, for those with eyes to see and ears to hear. Through an act of historical imagination, the reader may place himself in the years immediately following the Civil War, for which he will be richly rewarded with a thousand glittering prizes.

Yes, Peverelly's prose is arch and, though typical of the period, sometimes even more indigestible than that of his peers: "Dodworth's Band was in attendance to enliven the scene, and all the arrangements were exceedingly creditable to the taste and liberality of the committee who had charge of the festive occasion." As a sportswriter Peverelly was exceedingly fastidious, more Felix Unger than Oscar Madison. And yes, the book is not a page-turner, driven by a strong narrative; it is a book to peruse, to consult, to take pleasure in knowing it resides on your shelf.

Study the original Knickerbocker Rules. "[Rule] 9th.—The ball must be pitched, and not thrown, for the bat." So why is that fellow on the mound today called a pitcher and not a thrower? ("Pitcher" is just a vestigial relic of the old game, as is the phrase "McGillicuddy was knocked out of the box.") "[Rule] 10th.—A ball knocked out the field, or outside the range of the first or third base, is foul." Does that mean that what we would call a home run was a foul ball? (Yes. The Knicks' playing ground was along the North [Hudson] River and they couldn't afford to lose any of their expensively handmade baseballs.) "[Rule] 11th.—Three balls being struck at and missed and the last one caught, is a hand out; if not caught is considered fair, and the striker bound to run." Is this the same rule that survives today and once made Mickey Owen infamous? (Yes. It's as old as three strikes and you're out, and maybe even older, as it echoes the rules of town ball, in which there was no foul territory.)

Note that each detail in Peverelly's ledger may extend to a story you know or one day will. "On the 13th of August [1855]," the author writes of the Knickerbockers, "the uniform of the club was again regulated. Blue woolen pants, white flannel shirt, with narrow blue braid, mohair cap, and belt of patent leather. With the exception of a change of cap, the uniform has ever since remained the same. On the 27th of August the first flag staff was raised, and the Knickerbocker banner unfurled." That banner, a triangular pennant with a "K" in a circle on a background of a red panel and a blue one, went to the grave with James Whyte Davis, a Knick since 1850 who kept it on his dresser after the club disbanded in 1882, and insisted that he be wrapped in it upon burial. In 1899 he was.

Born in the Boston area in 1821 or 1822, Peverelly moved to New York as a young man and worked as a bookkeeper and clerk while scribbling a few sports reports, but he led an active social life. In 1846 he had been a committee member of the Young Bachelors' Society, and thus may have had something to do with staging the annual Bachelor's Ball, a Valentine's Day institution in New York since 1827. In 1848 he became a charter member of the Atalanta Boat Club, which lasted nearly a century, and through his reporting of boat races he soon became recognized as one of the nation's experts. A New York Herald story of June 25, 1869 states that a race on the Hudson was won by a boat named for the "veteran aquatic authority Charles A. Peverelly." By this time he had abandoned baseball reporting because his eyes were weakening. When he died in his 84th year on November 7, 1905, at his son-in-law's home in Brooklyn, Peverelly was the oldest living member of the Atalanta.

Who likes to read in an Introduction that the book he is about to commence may not be good but instead is good for him? Yet that may be said of any book approached incorrectly. One does not curl up in bed with the *Encyclopaedia Britannica.* And one does not look for helpful information about house repair in *Gone with the Wind. Peverelly's National Game* has lain unread for so long that it is like a treasure chest with an obdurate lock. But the key, dear reader, is in your hand.

John Thorn

National Game:

Peverelly's Original Text

The game of Base Ball has now become beyond question the leading feature of the out-door sports of the United States, and to account for its present truly proud position, there are many and sufficient reasons. It is a game which is peculiarly suited to the American temperament and disposition; the nine innings are played in the brief space of two and one half hours, or less. From the moment the first striker takes his position, and poises his bat, it has an excitement and *vim* about it, until the last hand is put out in the ninth innings. There is no delay or suspense about it, from beginning to end; and even if one feels disposed to leave the ground, temporarily, he will generally waive his desire, especially if it is a close contest, from fear of missing some good point or clever effort of the trial.

An American assemblage cannot be kept in one locality for the period of two or three hours, without being offered something above the ordinary run of excitement and attraction. They are too mercurial and impulsive a race not to get drowsy and dissatisfied with anything which permits their natural ardor to droop even for a brief space of time. Hence their congeniality with, and partiality for Base Ball, which game caters to their inclinations and desires to a nicety; in short, the pastime suits the people, and the people suit the pastime.

It is also, comparatively, an economical recreation; the uniform is not costly, the playing implements, colors, and furnishing of a neat club-room, need not occasion an extravagant outlay when divided, pro rata, by the members of a full club. In aquatic organizations, either of Yachting or Rowing (both glorious sports), the expenses are necessarily heavy. The uniforms, boathouses, and boats, all necessitate liberal disbursement, and not unfrequent renewal. Base Ball does not demand from its votaries too much time, or rather, too great a proportion of the day. In the long sunshiny days of summer, games are frequently commenced at four and even five o'clock in the afternoon, and completed some time before sunset. Consequently the great mass, who are in a subordinate capacity, can participate in this health-giving and noble pastime.

The game stands to-day in a proud and fairly-won position- scarcely requiring eulogy from any source. Dating from the years when the old Knickerbocker Club, closely followed by the Gotham, Eagle, and Empire, gave their colors to the breeze as rallying points for the lovers of the game to muster at, it has grown with giant strides until its organizations are the pride of numberless villages, towns, and cities, all over the land. Wherever established, it has quickly had the sentiment and good feeling of the community with it, and with scarcely an effort, achieved solid popularity. Having no debasing attributes, and being worthy of the presence of the good and the refined, it has everywhere been countenanced and encouraged by our best citizens; and of the thousands who gather at important matches, we have always noted with sincere gratification that the ladies constituted an honored proportion.

The game originated in Great Britain, and is familiarly known there as the game Rounders. We quote a description of the game. The reader will observe that it is the merest outline of what is now termed by the American press and public The National Game.

"Rounders.—This game is played with a ball and bats, or sticks something of the form of a policeman's truncheon. A hole is first made, about a foot across and half a foot deep. Four other stations are marked with pegs stuck into the ground, topped with a piece of paper, so as to be readily seen. Sides are then chosen, one of which goes in. There may be five or more players on each side. Suppose that there are five. One player, on the side that is out, stands in the middle of the five-sided space, and pitches the ball towards the hole. He is called the feeder. The batsman hits it off, if he can; in which case he drops the stick, and runs to the nearest station, thence to the third, and all around if the hit has been a far one. The other side are scouting, and trying to put him out, either by hitting the batsman as he is running, or by sending the ball into the hole, which is called 'grounding.' The player at the hole may decline to strike the ball, but if he hits at it, and misses twice running, he is out. When a player makes the round of the stations back to the hole, his side counts one towards the game. When all the players are out, either by being hit or the ball being grounded, the other side get their innings. When there are only two players left, a chance is given of prolonging the innings, by one of them getting three balls from the feeder; and if he can give a hit such as to enable him to run the whole round, all his side come in again, and the counting is resumed. The feeder is generally the best player on his side, much depending on his skill and art. The scouts should seldom aim at the runners from a distance, but throw the ball up to the feeder or to some one near, who will try to hit or to ground, as seems the most advisable. A caught ball also puts the striker out."

We commence our sketches of the clubs of the National Association with a carefully prepared and interesting history of the pioneer Knickerbocker Club, of New York.

KNICKERBOCKER BASE BALL CLUB

During the years of the 1842 and '43, a number of gentlemen, fond of the game, casually assembled on a plot of ground in Twenty-seventh street—the one now occupied by the Harlem Railroad Depot, bringing with them their bats, balls, etc. It was customary for two or three players, occasionally during the season, to go around in the forenoon of a pleasant day and muster up players enough to make a match. The march of improvement made a "change of base' necessary, and the following year they met at the next most convenient place, the north slope of Murray Hill, between the railroad cut and Third avenue. Among the prominent players were Col. James Lee, Dr. Ransom, Abraham Tucker, James Fisher, and W. Vail, the latter better known in later years of the Gotham Club, as "*Stay-where-you-am-Wail.*" In the spring of 1845 Mr. Alex Cartwright, who had become an enthusiast in the game, one day upon the field proposed a regular organization, promising to obtain several recruits. His proposal was acceded to, and Messrs. W.R. Wheaton, Cartwright, D.F. Curry, E.R. Dupignac, Jr., and W.H. Tucker, formed themselves into a board of recruiting officers, and soon obtained names enough to make a respectable show. At a preliminary meeting, it was suggested that as it was apparent they would soon be driven from Murray Hill, some suitable place should be obtained in New Jersey, where their stay could be permanent; accordingly, a day or two afterwards, enough to make a game assembled at Barclay street ferry, crossed over, marched up the road, prospecting for ground on each side, until they reached the Elysian Fields, where they "settled." Thus it occurred that a party of gentlemen formed an organization, combining together health, recreation, and social enjoyment, which was the nucleus of the now great American game of Base Ball, so popular in all parts of the United States, than which there is none more manly or more health giving.

The parent Knickerbockers claim for themselves the original organization, from the succeeding clubs derived their rules of playing, and which was always ready to foster, encourage, and promote the pleasure of all who were desirous of enjoying the game. Its members have from its inception been composed mostly of those sedentary habits required recreation, and its respectability has ever been undoubted. The same standard still exists, and no person can obtain admission in the club merely for his capacity as a player; he must also have the reputation of a gentleman; and hence arises one of the causes of its not being what is called a match-playing club.

The organization bears date the 23d of September, 1845. Its first officers were: President, Duncan F. Curry; Vice-President, Wm. R. Wheaton; Secretary and Treasurer, Wm. H. Tucker.

CURRY'S SIDE.	Runs	Outs	JOHNSON'S SIDE.	Runs	Outs
Curry	1	3	Johnson	4	2
Neibuhr	5	2	Cartwright	5	0
J. O'Brien	4	0	Turney	2	2
Drummond	4	2	Smith	2	2
Hart	3	2	Turk	3	2
Bogart	4	1	Birney	2	1
Moncrief	3	2	W. O'Brien	3	1
Dupignac	2	1	Wheaton	4	1
Broadhead	1	1	Morgan	2	1
De Witt	0	1	O'Brien	1	0
Totals	27	15	Totals	28	12

RUNS EACH INNING.

Curry's Side	3	6	4	7	7	27
Johnson's Side	3	5	6	4	10	28

J. W. O'Brien was fined six shillings for swearing in this game. He also played "Jack on both sides," there being an odd number of members on the field. On October 28, in a *practice* game, Cartwright was fined six shillings for disputing the umpire's decision. What primitive days these were to be sure. On Nov. 18 a *ten-inning game was played between sides* chosen by Tucker and Wheaton, which the latter won by 51 aces to 42 in ten innings' play. Wheaton's side included Dr. Adams, Cone, Tolman, Turney, Dupignac, Morgan, Turk, Jones and Smith. Tucker's side had Moncrief, W. O'Brien, Cartwright, Birney, Niebuhr, Curry, De Bost, Suydam and I. O'Brien. Wheaton made ten runs in this game, Dr. Adams nine and *Niebuhr seven. This was the last* practice game of 1845.

When the Knickerbockers began their summer practice on the Hoboken fields the ordinary summer visitors to that charming locality, with its shady walks and quiet country surroundings, and its rambles along the riverside, used to watch the ball tossers with surprised and incredulous looks, as if astonished to find that grown men could be found to engage in what they thought boys' play. But after a while the ball games of an afternoon at the *Elysian Fields became quite an attractive feature of* the place, and at times two or three hundred people would be found looking on at the games. But how the office worked merchant and business men did enjoy participating in those field gatherings of an afternoon once a week, and how much they slept, with what improved appetite they sat down to their home tables *after their afternoon's* game at Hoboken. That first years' experience of the Knickerbocker club of the charms of ball playing at the Elysian Fields of a summer afternoon, never left the memory *of a solitary member of the* club, until death wiped out the record.

BOXSCORE OF ONE THE LAST KNICKERBOCKER PRACTICE GAMES. *The Knickerbockers played several practice games amongst club members in the fall of 1845. This was several months before there first organized game in June of 1846 versus the New York Club, who later became the core group of the Gotham club. Recent research has shown that there is solid evidence that the game was being played on a regular basis as early as 1837, according to Randall Brown's article "How Baseball Began" in SABR's The National Pastime Magazine (Number 24). The roster's of this practice game reads like a who's who of early incubators of the fledgling game. Alexander Cartwright, the "Father of Baseball," scored five runs, without making an out. Based on that stat, you can assume he was a decent base ballist. (Source:* Vintage Ballist.*)*

RULES OF THE KNICKERBOCKER BASE BALL CLUB, ADOPTED SEPTEMBER 23, 1845.

1st. Members must strictly observe the time agreed upon for exercise, and be punctual in their attendance.

2d. When assembled for exercise, the President, or in his absence the Vice-President, shall appoint an Umpire, who shall keep the game in a book provided for that purpose, and note all violations of the By-Laws and Rules during the time of exercise.

3d. The presiding officer shall designate two members as Captains, who shall retire and make the match to be played, observing at the same time that the players put opposite to each other should be as nearly equal as possible; the choice of sides to be then tossed for, and the *first in hand* to be decided in like manner.

4th. The base shall be from "home" to second base, forty-two paces; from first to third base, forty-two paces, equidistant.

5th.—No stump match shall be played on a regular day of exercise.

6th..—If there should not be a sufficient number of members of the Club present at the time agreed upon to commence exercise, gentlemen not members may be chosen in to make up the match, which *shall not be broken up* to take in members that may afterward appear; but, in all cases, members shall have the preference, when present, at the making of a match.

7th.—If members appear after the game is commenced they may be chosen in if mutually agreed upon.

8th.—The game to consist of twenty-one counts, or aces; but at the conclusion an equal number of hands must be played.

9th.—The ball must be pitched, and not thrown, for the bat.

10th.— A ball knocked out of the field, or outside the range of the first or third base, is foul.

11th.—Three balls being struck at and missed and the last one caught, is a hand out; if not caught is considered fair, and the striker bound to run.

12th.—If a ball be struck, or tipped, and caught, either flying or on the first bound, it is a hand out.

13th.—A player running the bases shall be out, if the ball is in the hands of an adversary on the base, or the runner is touched with it before he makes his base; it being understood, however, that in no instance is a ball to be thrown at him.

14th.—A player running who shall prevent an adversary from catching or getting the ball before making his base, is a hand out.

15th.—Three hands out, all out.

16th.—Players must take their strike in regular turn.

17th.—All disputes and differences relative to the game, to be decided by the Umpire from which there is no appeal.

18th.—No ace or base can be made on a foul strike.

19th.—A runner cannot be put out in making one base, when a balk is made by the pitcher.

20th.—But one base allowed when a ball bounds out of the field when struck.

WILLIAM R. WHEATON,
WILLIAM H. TUCKER,
Committee on By-Laws.

At a meeting held at Mc Carty's Hotel, Elysian Fields, May 5, 1846, the following officers were elected for the year:—Duncan F. Curry, President: Daniel L. Adams, Vice-President; William H. Tucker, Treasurer; A.J. Cartwright, Secretary.

On June 5, 1846, the first honorary members were elected, viz. James Lee and Abraham Tucker. At the same meeting Curry, Adams and Tucker were appointed a committee to arrange the preliminaries, and conclude a match with the New York Base Ball Club. From all the information the writer has been able to gather, it appears that this was not an organized club, but merely a party of gentlemen who played together frequently, and styled themselves the New York Club. However, the match was played at Hoboken on June 19, 1846, it being the first the Club engaged in, and the particulars are certainly not creditable as far as runs are concerned. But four innings were played, as it will be remembered the game was won by the parties making twenty-one aces, or over, on even innings.

Knickerbocker.—Turney, 1 o. 0 r.; Adams, 1 o. 0 r.; Tucker, 2 o. 0 r.; Birney, 1 o. 1 r.; Avery, 0 o 0 r.; H. Anthony, 2 o. 0 r.; D. Anthony, 2 o. 0 r.; Tryon, 2 o. 0 r.; Paulding, 1 o. 0 r.—Total, 12 o. 1 r.

New York.—Davis, 1 o. 3 r.; Winslow, 2 o. 2 r.; Ransom, 2 o. 3 r.; Murphy, 0 o. 4 r.; Case, 0 o. 4 r.; Johnson, 1 o. 2 r.; Thompson, 2 o. 2 r.; Trenchard, 2 o. 1 r.; Lalor, 2 o. 2 r.—Total, 12 o. 23 r.

At a meeting held at McLean's Hotel, 54 Walker street, November 7, 1846, a resolution was passed authorizing a present to Mr. McCarty of ten dollars. It would appear by this that no sum was paid for the use of the ground at Hoboken. At the same meeting a committee was appointed to provide a grand dinner at the end of the season, to take place on the 26th of November.

The third annual meeting was held at McLean's Hotel, 54 Walker street, April, 1847, and the following gentlemen elected officers:—D.L. Adams, President; A.J. Cartwright, Vice-President; A.H. Drummond, Secretary; C.H. Birney, Treasurer.

The fourth annual meeting was held at "Schwartz's" Hotel, 14 Dey street, on the 1st of April, 1848.

The rule was adopted, that the player running to the first base was out, if the ball was held by an adversary on that base before the runner reached it. The previous rule applied to all the bases. The officers elected for 1848, were: D.L. Adams, President; A.J. Cartwright, Vice-President; Eugene Planchet, Secretary; F.C. Niebuhr, Treasurer. Directors—A.H. Drummond, B.C. Lee, Wm. H. Tucker. At a meeting held Nov. 17, 1848, a resolution was passed, that the annual dinner be given on the 30th of November. The fifth annual meeting was held at Abell's, 474 Broadway, on the 7th of April, 1849. The officers elected for the year, were: D.L. Adams, President; Ed. W. Talman, Vice-President; Eugene Plunkett, Secretary; F.C. Niebuhr, Treasurer. Directors—E.R. Dupignac, A.H. Drummond, B.C. Lee. At a meeting held April 24, 1849, a uniform was adopted for the club, viz. Blue woollen pantaloons, white flannel shirt, chip (straw) hats; and it may here be mentioned that the blue and white has ever since remained the costume of the club. The straw hats were abolished some years later.

The annual meeting for 1850, was held on the 6 th of April, at Smith's, 35 Howard street. The resignation of W. H. Tucker was received with deep regret. He was one of the founders of the institution, always evincing a lively interest in its welfare. The following officers were elected: E.W. Talman, President; F.C. Niebuhr, Vice-President; Eugene Plunkett, Secretary; Wm. Bunker, Treasurer. Directors—A.H. Drummond, B.C. Lee, James Moncrief.

During the year 1850, twelve members were elected, and Charles S. DeBost was one of the number, having been reelected. His name in the annals of Base Ballwill always be remembered with pleasure. He was very active and full of good-humor, always creating much amusement upon the ball field; as a catcher he held the first rank for many years, and it may be asserted that he has never had a superior in that position.

It was in September of that year Jas. Whyte Davis was elected, and who has been a continuous member to the present date, and the only one of the old members that remains upon its roll. This gentleman is yet an active player, and evinces the same interest and retains the same desire for the sport that he has for the last sixteen years. The annual meeting for 1851 was held at Smith's, 35 Howard street, on the 5th April. The following officers were elected: F.C. Niebuhr, President; A. H. Drummond, Vice-President; Eugene Plunkett, Secretary; H.T.

Anthony, Treasurer; D. L. Adams, Geo. Brown, Wm. L. Talman, Directors. The second match of the Club was played with the Washington Club, at the Red House, Harlem, on the 3d of June, 1851, and was won by the Knickerbockers, 21 aces to 11.

The only particulars that can be found of this game are the number of runs made in each innings, viz.:

Knickerbocker—1st innings, 0 r.; 2d, 3 r.; 3d, 3 r.; 4th, 3 r.; 5th, 5 r.; 6th, 0 r.; 7th, 1 r.; 8th, 6 r.—Total 21 r.

Washington—1st innings, 2 r.; 2d, 5 r.; 3d, 1 r.; 4th, 0 r.; 5th, 1 r.; 6th, 2 r.; 7th, 0 r.; 8th, 0 r.—Total 11 r.

The return match was played at the Elysian Fields, on the 17th of June, 1851. 10 innings

Knickerbocker—Tucker, 5 outs, 2 runs; Adams 4 o. 3 r.; Plunkett, 3 o. 4 r.; Talman, 6 o. 0 r.; Stevens, 4 o. 2 r.; De Bost, 3 o. 3 r.; Dick, 1 o. 5 r.; Murray, 3 o. 2 r.; Davis, 1 o. 2 r.—Total, 30 o. 22 r.

Washington.—W. H. Vancott, 5 outs, 1 run; Trenchard, 5 o. 2 r.; Barnes, 2 o. 2 r.; Burns, 3 o. 2 r.; Davis, 3 o. 2 r.; Winslow, 4 o. 2 r.; Case, 2 o. 4 r.; Jackson, 4 o. 2 r.; T. Vancott, 2 o. 3 r.—Total, 30 o. 20 r.

Umpire for Knickerbocker, G.A. Brown. Umpire for Washington, J. Murphy. J. Hone, Referee.

Mr. C.V. Anderson was President of the Washington Club. An entertainment was given after play at McCarty's Hotel, Elysian Fields. The annual dinner of the Club took place at Sinclair's, corner Broadway and Eighth street, on the 25th of November.

The annual meeting for 1852 was held at Smith's, 35 Howard street, on the 3d of April. The following officers were elected: F.C. Niebuhr, President; A.H. Drummond, Vice-President; Eugene Plunkett, Secretary; H.T. Anthony, Treasurer; Geo. A. Brown, D.L. Adams, Peter S. Henderson, Directors. The following members celebrated the 4th July, 1852, by proceeding to Bath, L.I., on the 5th of July to enjoy dinner and a game of ball: Adams, Davis, Curry, DeBost, McDonald, Ladd, Greenleaf, Dick, Clancy, Stevens, Brotherson, Dillon, Murray and Birney.

During this year, 1852, there must have been two matches played with the Gotham Club, which had just organized, consolidating with the Washington Club of the previous year. In these two matches the Knickerbockers must have been the victors, as it appears by the minutes of June, 1854, a record was made that the match played at that time was the first they won out of five. There were two played in 1853; and the two in 1852, and the one in June, 1854, would make five.

If the above suppositions are wrong, and there were no matches played in 1852, then the record made that the match in June, 1854, was the first the Gothams won out of five, must have embraced the first two played in 1851 with the Washingtons, and which were looked upon as the same, nearly all the same party of Washington, having merged in the Gothams.

The annual meeting for 1853, was held at Smith's, 25 Howard street in April; the following officers were elected: F.C. Niebuhr, President; A. H. Drummond, Vice-President; Jno. Clancy, Secretary; Geo. A. Brown, Treasurer; D.L. Adams, E. H. Birdsall, C.S. De Bost, Directors.

On the first of July, 1853, a match was played at Hoboken, with the Gotham Club, and from some cause, not stated, but two innings were played, the Gothams making two runs, and the Knickerbockers making nine runs. The match was concluded on the 5th of July. Knickerbocker, twenty-one runs; Gotham, twelve runs. Hone, Umpire for Gothams; Brown, Umpire for Knickerbockers; Curry of Knickerbockers, Referee.

On the 14th of October, the return match was played at the Red House, terminating in a victory for the Knickerbockers. Knickerbocker, twenty-one runs; Gotham, fourteen runs.

Moncrief, of Knickerbockers, Referee.

At a meeting held November 19,1853, a communication was received from the Eagle Club, asking for a committee to join them in arranging a set of rules for playing, and Dr. Adams, Curry and Tucker were appointed.

The annual meeting, for 1854, was held at Smith's, 35 Howard street, on the 1st of April. The committee on rules presented the following as having been arranged to govern the three clubs, viz. The Knickerbockers, Gotham and Eagle.

1. The bases shall be "Home" to second base, forty-two paces; and from the first to third base, forty-two paces, equidistant; and from Home to pitcher not less than fifteen paces.
2. The game to consist of twenty-one counts, or aces; but at the conclusion an equal number of hands must be played.
3. The ball must be pitched, and not thrown, for the bat.
4. A ball knocked outside the range of the first or third base, is foul.
5. Three balls being struck at and missed, and the last one caught, is a hand out; if not caught is considered fair, and the striker bound to run.
6. A ball being struck, or tipped, and caught, either flying or on the first bound, it is a hand out.
7. A player must make his first base after striking a fair ball, but should the ball be in the hands of an adversary on the first base before the runner reaches that base, it is a hand out.
8. Players must make the bases in order of striking, and when a fair ball is struck and the striker not put out, the first base must be vacated as well as the next base or bases if similarly occupied; players may be put out, under these circumstances, in the same manner as when running to the first base.
9. A player shall be out, if at any time when off a base he shall be touched by the ball in the hands of an adversary.
10. A player who shall intentionally prevent an adversary from catching or getting the ball, is a hand out.
11. If two hands are already out, a player running home at the time a ball is struck, cannot make an ace if the striker is caught out.
12. Three hands out, all out.
13. Players must take their strike in regular rotation; and after the first inning is played the turn commences at the player who stands on the list next to the one who lost the third hand.
14. No ace or base can be made on a foul strike.
15. A runner cannot be put out in making one base, when a balk is made by the pitcher.
16. But one base allowed if the ball, when struck, bounds out of the field.
17. The ball shall weigh from five and a half to six ounces, and be from two and three-quarters to three and a half inches in diameter.

The officers elected for the year 1854, were: President, F.C. Niebuhr; Vice-President, A H. Drummond; Secretary, James Whyte Davis; Treasurer, G.A. Brown; Directors, D.L. Adams, C.S. De Bost, W.F. Ladd.

In May of this year Mr. Samuel H. Kissam was elected. He has been a continuos member to the present time; one of the very few left of the old members, and who has been one of the most active and attentive, and still retains his love of the sport and attachment to the old club.

On the 30th of June the Knickerbockers played with the Gothams, at the Red House, Harlem, the game occupying three hours. Sixteen innings were played before the twenty one aces were made. Knickerbocker, sixteen; Gotham, twenty-one. Wm. G. Tucker, of Gotham, Referee.

On the 20th of September the return match was played with the Gotham Club at the Elysian Fields, occupying two and a quarter hours, with nine innings; Knickerbockers, twenty-four; Gothams, thirteen. Wm. Cotheal, of Eagle Club, Referee.

One of the most exciting and interesting games ever played was the closing one for 1854, at the Red House, Harlem, occupying two hours, with twelve innings and twelve runs each, which could not be concluded for want of daylight. Knickerbocker, twelve; Gotham, twelve. Umpire for Knickerbocker, G.A. Brown; Umpire for Gotham, G. Vancott; Armfield, of Eagle Club, Referee.

The first match with the Eagle Club was played at Hoboken on the 10th of November, 1854, barring six of the first nine of the Knickerbockers; five innings were played in one hour. Eagles scored twenty-one runs, and Knickerbockers, four runs. A. H. Drummond, Umpire for Knickerbockers; John W. Mott, Umpire for Eagles; W. H. Vancott, of Gothams, Referee.

On the 17th of November the return match with the Eagles was played at Hoboken in one hour and a half; five innings played; Eagles scored twenty-two runs and Knickerbockers twenty-one runs. A.H. Drummond, Umpire for Knickerbockers; John W. Mott, Umpire for Eagles; T.G. Vancott, of Gothams, Referee.

A grand dinner was given on the 15th of December, at Fijux's 11 Barclay street, by the Knickerbocker, Eagle and Gotham Clubs. An equal delegation was present, and an excellent bill of fare presented. The utmost hilarity prevailed, and everything passed off in a happy manner. A song, composed for the occasion by J.W. Davis, of the Knickerbocker Club, was so well received that the Eagle Club had it printed. It was entitled "Ball Days," and abounded in witty allusions to the principal players of the three Clubs.

The annual meeting for 1855 was held on the 7th of April. The following officers were elected for the year: A.H. Drummond, President; E.R. Dupignac, Jr., Vice-President; Jas. W. Davis, Secretary; Geo. A. Brown, Treasurer. Director— D. L. Adams, C. S. De Bost, Wm. B. Eager, Jr.

On the 1st of June, played with the Gotham Club, at Red House, Harlem, the game occupying 2 1/4 hours with 11 innings. Gothams, 21 runs; Knickerbockers, 12 runs. Wm. F. Ladd, Umpire for Knickerbockers; John Hone, Umpire for Gothams, Armfield, of Eagle Club, Referee.

On the 5th of June, played with the Eagle Club, at Hoboken. Time, 1 1/4 hours, 4 innings. Eagles, 14 runs. Knickerbockers, 27 runs. W.F. Ladd, Umpire for Knickerbockers; J. W. Mott, Umpire for Eagles. W.H. Van Cott, of Gothams, Referee.

On the 13th of August, the uniform of the club was again regulated. Blue woollen pants, white flannel shirt, with narrow blue braid, mohair cap, and belt of patent leather. With the exception of a change of cap, the uniform has ever since remained the same. On the 27th of August the first flag staff was raised, and the Knickerbocker banner unfurled.

On the 13th of September, played with the Gotham Club, at the Elysian Fields, Hoboken; time 1/4 hours, with 5 innings. Knickerbockers, 22 runs. Gothams, 7 runs. A.H. Drummond, of Knickerbockers, Umpire; John Hone, of Gothams, Umpire. Armfield, of Eagles, Referee.

On the 20th of September, played with the Eagle Club at the Elysian Fields; time 1 1/4 hours, 6 innings. Knickerbockers, 21 runs. Eagles, 10 runs. A.H. Drummond, Umpire for Knickerbockers; J.W. Mott, Umpire for Eagles. G. Van Cott, of Gothams, Referee.

The annual meeting for 1856 was held on the 5th of April. The officers elected for the season were: D.L. Adams, President; H.T. Anthony, Vice-President; B.K. Brotherson, Secretary; Jas. W. Davis, Treasurer. Directors—Wm. B. Eager, Jr., Wm. F. Ladd, R.F. Stevens.

On the 22d of May, a married and single match was played, 6 innings; the Bachelors winning by a score of 23 to 21. On the 30th of August, a very interesting match was played at Hoboken, with the Empire Club, occupying 3 1/4 hours, with 8 innings, resulting in a tie, both clubs scoring 21 runs. T.G. Voorhis, Umpire for Empires; G.A. Brown, Umpire for Knickerbockers. T.G. Van Cott, of Gothams, Referee.

On the 5th of September, the last match was played with the Gotham Club, at the

Red House, Harlem; 7 innings; the Gothams winning by a score of 21 to 7. D.F. Curry, Umpire for Knickerbockers; G. Van Cott, Umpire for Gothams. A.J. Bixby, of Eagles, Referee.

On the 19th of September, played with the Eagle Club, at Hoboken; 3 innings; Eagles winning by a score of 24 to 17. Umpires: A. H. Drummond, of Knickerbockers, and J. W. Mott, of Eagles. C. Sniffin, of Atlantic, Referee.

On the 25th of September, played with the Empire Club, at Hoboken, with 7 innings, the Knickerbockers winning by a score of 21 to 12. W. H. Grenelle, Umpire for Knickerbockers; T.G. Voorhis, Umpire for Empire. M. E. Gelston, of Eagles, Referee.

On the 9th of October, played with the Eagle Club, at Hoboken; 6 innings; the Eagles winning by a score of 21 to 10. W. H. Grenelle, Umpire for Knickerbockers; J.W. Mott, Umpire for Eagles. A. D. Teed, of Gothams, Referee.

At a meeting held at Smith's, 462 Broome street, on the 6 th of December, the President stated that the object to be the propriety of altering the By-Laws, and of calling a general Base Ball Convention. This seems to be the first step which originated the present "National Association of Base Ball Players."

Mr. Davis offered the following resolution, which was carried. "That Messrs. Adams, Grenelle, and Wadsworth be appointed a committee on the part of the Club to call a convention of the various Base Ball Clubs of this city and vicinity." Mr. Wadsworth moved the above resolution be published in *Porter's Spirit of the Times, and the Sunday Mercury*, together with the following:—

Pursuant to the above resolution the various Base Ball Clubs of this city and vicinity are requested each to select three representatives to meet at 462 Broome street, in the city of New York, on Thursday the 22d day of January next, at half-past seven o-clock P.M.

A special meeting was held at Smith's, 462 Broome street, on March 7, 1857, for the purpose of adopting the new rules. Dr. Adams reported from the Base Ball Convention Committee, presenting the rules and regulations adopted by that body.

Mr. Davis moved, " that we accept the reports of the committee, and that we also accept the rules of the game as adopted by that body, only so far as to govern this club in playing matches with other clubs," which was carried.

The rules adopted by said convention included the one of catching the ball on the bound, which the Knickerbocker Club did not conform to "except for matches with other clubs." The "fly" game was originated by Mr. Davis, who worked hard to induce the Knickerbockers to adopt it, and finally succeeded. Repeated attempts were made in later years to pass the same in convention, and the "fly " game rule was adopted at the meeting of 1865.

The annual meeting for 1857 was held on April 4. The following were elected officers for the year: D. L. Adams, President; H.T. Anthony, Vice-President; N. B. McLaughlin, Secretary; Jas. W. Davis, Treasurer; F.C. Niebuhr, W.H. Grenelle, William H. Tucker, Directors. At a meeting, held June 1, Mr. W.A. Woodhull was elected Treasurer in place of J. W. Davis, declined. William F. Ladd was elected honorary member. Walter Avery, one of the first members of the Club, was reelected, and still remains upon the roll, one of its active members.

On June 8 played with the Eagle Club at Hoboken; five innings; resulting in a victory for the Eagles by a score of twenty-five to seventeen. John W. Mott, Umpire for Eagles; H.T. Anthony, Umpire for Knickerbockers; A. D. Teed, of Gothams, Referee. This was the first season that the rules required the playing of nine innings; but a game might be decided at the end of five. Rain prevented the playing of nine innings on this occasion. On June 24 played with the Empire Club; nine innings; the Knickerbockers winning by a score of thirty-seven to twenty-three. William H. Grenelle, Umpire for the Knickerbockers: T.G. Voorhis, Umpire for the Empires; M.E. Gelston, of Eagles, Referee. On September 10 played with the Empire Club nine innings; the Empires winning by a score of twenty-eight to seventeen. William H. Grenelle, Umpire for the Knickerbockers: Bloomfield, Umpire for Empires; A. J. Bixby, of Eagle Club; Referee. On September 15 played with the Eagle Club; nine innings; the Knickerbockers winning by a score of eighteen to seventeen. John W. Mott, umpire for Eagles; W. H. Grenelle, Umpire for Knickerbockers; Hoyt, of Empire, Referee.

At a meeting held January 30, 1858, at Fijux's, a communication was received from the Empire Club requesting the Knickerbockers to call a convention of all regular organized Base Bal Clubs, and the President was empowered to confer with the other presidents in the matter.

At a meeting held February 27, 1858, Messrs. D. L. Adams and W.H. Grenelle were appointed delegates to the first convention of Base Ball Clubs, to be held on the 10th of March, 1858, and the following clubs represented by two delegates each: Knickerbocker, Gotham, Eagle, Empire, Putnam, Baltic, Excelsior, Atlantic, Harlem, Eckford, Continental, Union, Metropolitan, Columbian, Osceola, Oriental, Stuyvesant, Hamilton, Pastime, Liberty (of New Brunswick), Monument, Amity, St. Nicholas, Nassau and Mutual. A resolution was adopted declaring the Convention a permanent organization, and a committee of three was appointed to prepare and submit a Constitution and By-Laws. The committee reported, adopted the same, and the "National Association of Base Ball Players" was duly organized thereunder. The first annual meeting was held at Cooper Institute on the 9th of March, 1859.

The annual meeting for 1858 was held on the 3d of April. The officers elected for the year were: James W. Davis, President; Alfred Vredenburgh, Vice-President; Beverly Clarke, Secretary; Wm. A. Woodhull, Treasurer; F. C. Niebuhr, N.M. Welling, Wm. H. Tucker, Directors.

On the 8th of July, the first game was played with the Excelsior Club, of South Brooklyn, on their grounds near Carroll Park, with whom the most cordial relations have ever since existed. Excelsior thirty one runs; Knickerbocker, thirteen runs; nine innings. F. S. Wells, Scorer for Excelsiors; W. A. Woodhull, Scorer for Knickerbockers. S. Yates, of Eagle Club, Umpire. After the game the Excelsiors escorted the Knickerbockers to Montague Hall, where a fine entertainment awaited them.

On the 29th of July, played with the Eagle Club at Hoboken nine innings; won by the Eagle, whose score was forty-five to eighteen. John Grum, of Eckfords, Umpire.

On the 20th of August the return match was played with the Excelsior Club on the grounds of the Gotham Club, at Elysian Fields, which was one of the finest games ever played; the score standing, at the end of nine innings, fifteen, to fourteen in favor of the Excelsiors. After the close of this match, the Excelsior Club was escorted to Odd Fellows' Hall, Hoboken, by the Knickerbocker Club, and entertained in splendid style, covers being laid for over two hundred gentlemen. Dodworth's Band was in attendance to enliven the scene, and all the arrangements were exceedingly creditable to the taste and liberality of the committee who had charge of the festive occasion.

The home-and-home match with the Empire Club occurred on the 22d of September, at Hoboken; the game was closed on the eighth innings, on account of darkness, resulting in a score of twenty-one runs each.

OFFICERS FOR 1859.— James Whyte Davis, President: Walter T. Avery, Vice-President; James F. Wenman, Secretary; L.J. Belloni, Jr., Treasurer.

June 30.— First fly game with Excelsiors, at Hoboken. Time, two hours; Excelsiors, 26; Knickerbocker, 22. A. J. Bixby, of Eagle Club, Umpire.

August 2.—Return game on the fly on Excelsior grounds, South Brooklyn. Time, one hour forty-five minutes; Excelsiors, 20; Knickerbockers, 5. Peter O'Brien, of Atlantic Club, Umpire.

August 11,—Match with Empire Club, on the fly, at Hoboken. Time, three hours. Knickerbockers, 60; Empire, 33. A. J. Bixby, of Eagle, Umpire.

August 22.—Muffin match with Excelsiors, on the fly, on their grounds, foot of Court street, Brooklyn. Time, three hours. Excelsiors, 41; Knickerbockers, 37; seven innings.

September 12.— Return Muffin match with the Excelsiors, on the fly, at Hoboken. A. G.

Pearsall, of Excelsiors, Umpire. Excelsiors, 56; Knickerbockers, 47.

September 26.—First and only game with the Star Club (Juniors), at Hoboken. Star, 33; Knickerbockers, 11. A. J. Bixby, of Eagles, Umpire.

OFFICERS FOR 1860.— James White Davis, President; Walter T. Avery, Vice-President; James F. Wenman, Secretary; D.B. Keeler, Jr., Treasurer.

August 25.— Fly game with Excelsiors, on their grounds, Brooklyn. Time, three hours thirty-five minutes. Excelsiors, 32; Knickerbockers, 9. Burtis, of Gotham, Umpire.

OFFICERS FOR 1861.—Daniel L. Adams, President; Walter T. Avery, Vice-President; Anson S. Palmer, Secretary; Henry A. Thomas, Treasurer. No matches played by the club in 1861.

OFFICERS FOR 1862.—William P. Bensel, President; Alonzo Slote, Vice-President; James Whyte Davis, Secretary; Thomas J. O'Brien, Treasurer. The Knickerbocker Club did not engage in any game in 1862.

OFFICERS FOR 1863.— William P. Bensel, President; Alonzo Slote, Vice-President; James Whyte Davis, Secretary; William L. Taylor, Treasurer.

September 3.—Friendly game with the Excelsior Club at Hoboken. Knickerbocker, 22; Excelsior, 20. Henry L. Slote, Scorer for both clubs; Alonzo Slote, of Knickerbockers, Umpire.

September 22.—The return game was played on the Excelsiors ground. Knickerbockers, 56; Excelsiors, 45.

October 12.— A third of these friendly series was played at Hoboken. Excelsiors, 42; Knickerbockers, 13. H. Chadwick, scorer for both clubs; Thomas Dakin, of Excelsiors, Umpire.

OFFICERS FOR 1864.—William P. Bensel, President; Walter T. Avery, Vice-President; James Whyte Davis, Secretary; William L. Taylor, Treasurer.

July 11.—A friendly game was played with the Excelsiors at Hoboken; time, two hours fifteen minutes. Excelsiors, 36; Knickerbockers, 27. H.P. Boswick, of Excelsiors, Umpire.

July 21 .—A Friendly game played with the Excelsiors, on the ground at Brooklyn. Excelsiors, 85; Knickerbockers, 39.

September 22.—The last of these friendly games for the season was played at Hoboken. Excelsiors, 53; Knickerbockers, 48. W.H. Young, of Excelsiors, Umpire.

OFFICERS FOR 1865.— Williams L. Taylor, President: James E. Vail, Vice-President; Thomas Grierson, Secretary; R.H. Hinsdale, Treasurer.

July 6.—A friendly game was played with the Excelsiors at Hoboken, with eleven innings. Excelsiors, 29; Knickerbockers, 25.

July 25.—A friendly game with the Excelsiors at Capitoline ground, Brooklyn. Excelsiors, 60; Knickerbockers, 45.

August 17.—Played with the New York Club, at Sixty-fifth street. New York, 58; Knickerbockers, 13.

September 11.— Played with the Greenburgh Club (of Dobbs' Ferry), at Hoboken. Greenburgh, 26; Knickerbockers, 23. Isaac Evans, of Mutual, Umpire.

September 21.— A friendly game with the Excelsiors at Hoboken. Time, one hour forty-five minutes. Knickerbockers, 22; Excelsiors, 17.

October 5.—Played a match with the New York Club at Hoboken., New York, 28; Knickerbockers, 11.

October 20.—Played a match with the Eclectic club, resulting in a tie, score of thirty-one runs each; seven innings.

OFFICERS FOR 1866.— William L. Taylor, President; James E. Vail, Vice-President; C.A. Righter, Secretary; R.H. Hinsdale, treasurer.

May 25.—Played a friendly game with the Excelsiors at the Capitoline Grounds, Brooklyn. Excelsiors, 56; Knickerbockers, 42.
June 4.—The return friendly game was played at Hoboken. Excelsiors, 27; Knickerbockers, 39. M. Humphrey, of Eclectic, Umpire.
July 14.— Played a friendly game with the Palisade Club at Englewood; Knickerbocker, 39; Palisade, 17.
August 30.—The return game with the Palisade Club was played at Hoboken. Palisade, 37; Knickerbockers, 28.
September 29.— The third game with the Palisade Club was played at Englewood, N.J. Time, two hours thirty-five minutes. Palisade, 42; Knickerbockers, 27.

EXCELSIORS AND KNICKERBOCKER PANORAMIC PHOTOGRAPH. *The Knickerbocker Base Ball Club of New York City and the Excelsior BBC of Brooklyn were among the earliest and strongest organizations in the nation at the time this panoramic photo was taken in 1859. The only players that might have recognizable baseball names in the group were early Knickerbockers D. L. Adams and C. S. DeBost, Harry Wright, and Asa Brainard, who pitched for the Cincinnati Red Stockings in 1868 and '69. (Source: Transcendental Graphics.)*

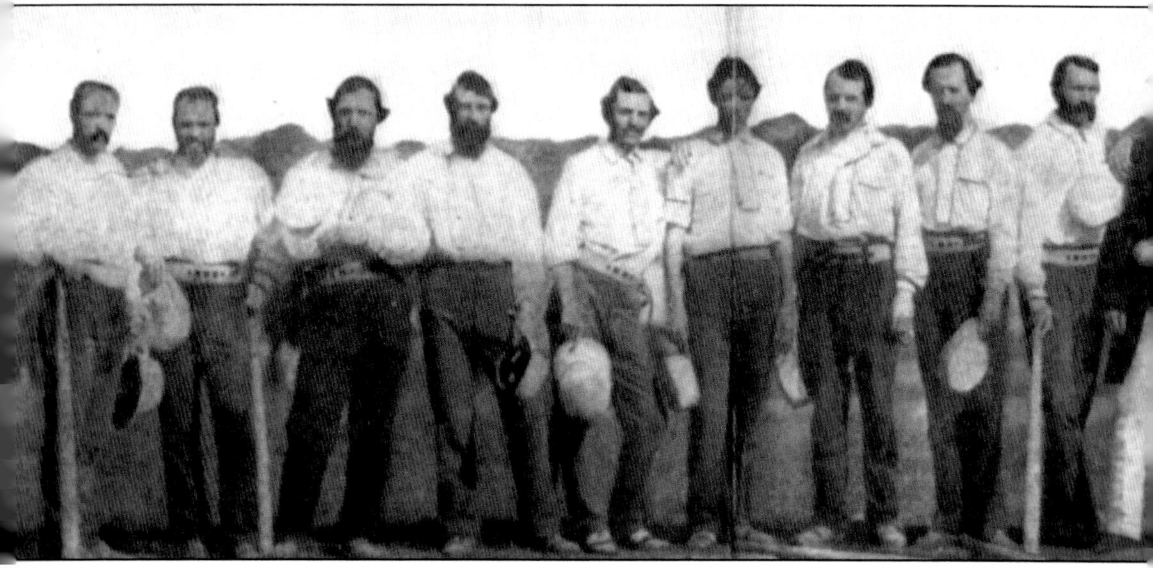

GOTHAM CLUB

The Gotham Base Ball Club, of New York, was organized early in 1852, with Mr. Tuche as its first President. Among its veteran players were Mssrs. Winslow, Vail, Murphy, and Davis. At the time of the organization of the Gotham, their only competitor was the famous Knickerbockers, and the years between 1852 and 1853 will be remembered for the interesting contests between them. Soon, however, the Eagle and Empire Clubs entered the lists, and base ball games became more popular and general. The Gotham Club, from the day of its formation to the present, has occupied an influential position in base ball circles, and has numbered upon its roll many of our most respected citizens. The Gothams, also, for a period, displayed the champion colors. We will here remark that the rules of the National Association do not recognize either the title of "champion," or "championship games;" these titles being the pet terms of the press and the public, applied to clubs for continuous and remarkable success. Without further remark we will give the record of all games which Mr. Charles H. Beadle, the present Secretary of the Club, has been able to obtain for us.

July 5, 1853.—Gotham and Knickerbocker, at Hoboken; Gotham, twelve runs; Knickerbocker, twenty-one runs. Umpires, Hone and Brown. Referee, Curry, of the Knickerbocker Club.

October 14.—Gotham and Knickerbocker, on the grounds of the former, at the Red House, Harlem. Gotham, fourteen runs; Knickerbocker, twenty-one runs. Umpires, Van Cott and Brown. Referee, Moncrief, of the Knickerbocker Club.

June 30, 1854.—Gotham and Knickerbocker, Red House grounds. Sixteen innings were played, occupying three hours, before the requisite twenty-one aces were made. Gotham, 21; Knickerbocker, 16. Umpires, Brown and Hone. Referee, W. S. Tucker, of the Gotham Club.

September 20.—Gotham and Knickerbocker, at Hoboken. Gotham, thirteen runs; Knickerbocker, twenty-four runs. Referee, William Cotheal, of the Eagle Club.

Gotham and Knickerbocker, at the Red House grounds. This game was played late in the season of 1854, the score standing 12 to 12, when twelve innings had been played, occupying two hours. Darkness obliged the game to be suspended.

June 1, 1855.—Gotham and Knickerbocker, at the Red House grounds. Eleven innings were played in two and a half hours, the score standing twenty-one to twelve in favor of the

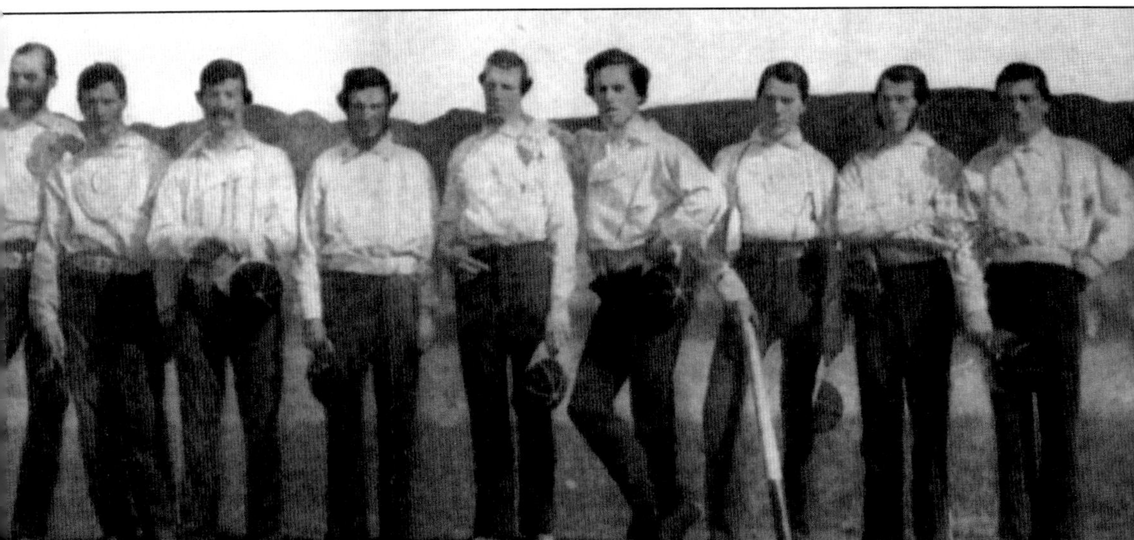

Gothams. Referee, Armfield, of the Eagle Club.

June 22.—Gotham and Eagle, at Hoboken. Eagle, three runs; Gotham, twenty-one runs.

September 5.—Gotham and Empire, at Hoboken. Gotham twenty-five; Empire, four.

September 13.—Gotham and Knickerbocker, at Hoboken. Five innings were played in one and a half hours, the Knickerbockers winning by a score of 22 to 7. Referee, Armfield, of the Eagle Club.

October 1.—Gotham and Eagle, at Hoboken. Won by the Gotham by a score of 22 to 11.

September 5, 1856.—Gotham and Knickerbocker, at the Red House. Seven innings. The Gothams victorious by a score of 21-7. Referee, A. J. Bixby, of the Eagle Club.

September 26.—Gotham and Eagle, at Hoboken. Tie game, 18 to 18. Five innings. Umpire, J.W. Mott, of the Eagle Club.

October 17.—Gotham and Eagle, at the Red House. Score: Eagle, 6 Gotham, 2. Three innings. G. Van Cott, Umpire.

October 28.—Gotham and Eagle, at Hoboken. Eagle, four runs; Gotham, twenty-three runs. Five innings. Umpire, J. W. Mott.

July 10, 1857.—Gotham and Eagle. Won by the Gotham, by a score of 43 to 20.

September 8.—Gotham and Eagle, at Hoboken. Eagle, fifteen runs; Gotham, nine runs.

October 19.—Gotham and Eagle, at Hoboken. Won by the Gotham, by a score of 25 to 19.

August, 31,1858.—Gothams and Eckford, at Greenpoint, Long Island. Eckford, 23; Gotham, 17. Umpire, Foster, of the Baltic Club.

September 14.—Gotham and Excelsior, at Hoboken. Excelsior, 24; Gotham, 13.

September 27.—Gotham and Putnam, at Wheat Hill, Williamsburgh. Gotham, 28; Putnam, 20.

October 19.—Gotham and Eckford, at Hoboken. Seven innings. Gotham, 23; Eckford, 6. Umpire, Thomas Leary, of the Empire Club.

October 25.—Gotham and Atlantic, at Bedford, Long Island. Gotham, 17; Atlantic, 31. Umpire, T.S. Dakin, of the Putnam Club.

October 27.—Gotham and Empire, at Hoboken. Four innings. Gotham, 14; Empire, 23. Darkness prevented the game from being finished.

July 29, 1859.—Gotham and Eagle, at Hoboken. Gotham, 36; Eagle, 22.

August 12.—Gotham and Eckford, at Brooklyn, Gotham, 10; Eckford, 17. Gotham and Eckford, at Hoboken. Gotham 23; Eckford, 6. Home-and-home game. Gotham and Eckford. Gotham, 27. Eckford, 38.

September 7.—Gotham and Newark, at Newark, New Jersey. Gotham, 21; Newark, 13. Umpire, gelston, of the Eagle Club.

September 15.—Gotham and Mutual, at Hoboken. Gotham, 37; Mutual, 25. Umpire, Gelston, of the Eagle.

September 29.—Gotham and Excelsior, at Brooklyn. Gotham, 12; Excelsiors, 37. Umpire, Gelston, of the Eagle Club.

June 26, 1860.—Gotham and Newark, at Newark. Gotham, 26; Newark, 15. Umpire, Rowland, of Jefferson Club.

July 10.—Gotham and Eagle, at Hoboken. Gotham, 18; Eagle 18. Tie game. Empire, Rowland, of Jefferson Club.

July 17.—Gotham and Mutual, at Hoboken. Gotham, 25; Mutual, 25. Tie game. Umpire, Williams, of the Eagle Club.

July 23.—Gotham and Baltic. Gotham, 35; Baltic, 16. Umpire, Tilton, of the Malta Club.

July 24.—Gotham and Jefferson, at Hoboken. Gotham, 13, Jefferson, 13. Tie game. Umpire, Beard, of Mutual Club.

August 22.—Gotham and Independent, at Brooklyn. Gotham, 12; Independent, 18. Umpire, Whitney, of Katy-Did Club.

August 24.—Gotham and Enterprise, at Hoboken. Gotham, 56; Enterprise, 15. Umpire, Beard, of Mutual Club.

August 29.—Gotham and Enterprise, at Brooklyn. Gotham 21; Enterprise, 15. Umpire, Pearce, of Atlantic Club.

September 4.—Gotham and Mutual, at Hoboken. Gotham, 18; Mutual, 18. Tie game. Umpire, Ticknor, of Atlantic Club.

September 11.—Gotham and Eagle, at Hoboken. Gotham, 25; Eagle, 11. Umpire, R.H. Thorn, of Empire Club.

September 17.—Gotham and Independent, of Brooklyn, at Hoboken. Gotham, 19; Independent, 13. Umpire, Beard, of Mutual Club.

September 27.—Gotham and Mutual, at Hoboken. Gotham, 19; Mutual, 12. Umpire, Benson, of Empire Club.

October 8.—Gotham and Jefferson, at Hoboken. Gotham, 22; Jefferson, 3. Umpire, Anson B. Taylor, of Mutual Club.

August 7, 1861.—Gotham and Mutual, at Hoboken. Gotham, 22; Mutual, 25. Umpire, Martin O'Brien, of Atlantic Club.

August 20.—Gotham and Enterprise, of Brooklyn, at Hoboken. Gotham 14; Enterprise, 13. Umpire, R.H. Thorn, of Empire Club.

October 15.—Gotham and Eagle, at Hoboken. Gotham, 15; Eagle, 30. Umpire, Thomas Culyer, of Empire Club.

July 29, 1862.—Gotham and Eagle, at Hoboken. Gotham, 14; Mutual, 9. Umpire, M. O'Brien, of Atlantic Club.

August 7.—Gotham and Charter Oak, of Brooklyn. Gotham, 17; Charter Oak, 13. Umpire, Wm. Mc Mahon, of Mutual; Club.

August 14.—Gotham and Mutual, at Hoboken. Gotham, 15; Mutual, 14.

August —. Gotham and Eureka, of Newark, New Jersey, at Hoboken. Gotham, 13; Eureka, 18.

September 4.—Gotham and Harlem, at Mount Morris Square, Gotham, 15; Harlem, 29. Umpire, Dr. Bell, of Henry Eckford Club.

September —. Gotham and Eagle, at Hoboken. Gotham, 17; Eagle, 16.

October 14.—Gotham and Harlem, at Hoboken. Gotham, 19; Harlem, 10. Umpire, B. Harris, of Mutual Club.

October 20.—Gotham and Harlem, at Hoboken. Gotham, 24; Harlem, 17 Home-and-home game. Umpire, Wm. McMahon, of Mutual Club.

June 10, 1863.—Gotham and Star, of Brooklyn, at Brooklyn. Gotham, 16; Star 41.

June 23.—Gotham and Eagle, at Hoboken. Gotham, 19; Eagle, 15. Umpire, A.B. Taylor, of Mutual Club.

July 1.—Gotham and Empire, at Hoboken. Gotham, 16; Empire, 14. Umpire, J. Seaver Page, of Active Club.

July—.Gotham and Mutual, at Hoboken, Gotham, 15; Mutual, 21.

September 11.—Gotham and Star, of Brooklyn, at Hoboken. Gotham, 19; Star, 22. Umpire, Snow, of Henry Eckford Club.

July 1, 1864.—Gotham and Eagle, at Hoboken. Gotham, 22; Eagle, 16. Umpire, Miller, of Empire Club.

July 8.—Gotham and Newark, at Hoboken. Gotham, 25; Newark, 12. Umpire, Samuel Yates, of Eagle Club.

July 26.—Gotham and Enterprise, at Hoboken. Gotham, 22; Empire, 13. Umpire, B. Harris, of Mutual Club.

July—. Gotham and Newark, at Newark, New Jersey. Gotham, 10; Newark, 44. Umpire, Brientnall, of Eureka Club.

August—. Gotham and Mutual, at Hoboken. Gotham, 7; Mutual, 23.

August 23.—Gotham and Atlantic, at Hoboken. Gotham, 9; Atlantic, 14. Umpire, B. Harris, of Mutual Club.

August 30.—Gotham and Newark, of Newark, New Jersey at Williamsburgh. Gotham, 14;

Newark, 18. Home-and-home game. Umpire, Wilson, of Resolute Club.

September 19.—Gotham and Atlantic, at Brooklyn. Gotham, 12; Atlantic, 38. Umpire, Westervelt, of Empire Club.

October 2.—Gotham and Mutual, at Hoboken. Gotham, 10; Mutual, 12. Umpire, Westervelt, of Empire Club.

October 11.—Gotham, 12; Empire, 12. Tie game. Umpire, Snow, of Active Club.

May 9, 1865.—Gotham and Eagle, at Hoboken, Gotham, 19; Eagle, 15.

June 6.—Gotham and Enterprise, of Brooklyn, at Hoboken. Gotham, 19; Enterprise, 18. Umpire, Colonel Fitzgerald, of Philadelphia. This match was a very exciting game. On the ninth inning the Gothams tied the Enterprise, and thirteen innings had to be played before the game was decided. On the thirteenth inning the Enterprise Club made one run, and the Gothams made two runs, the Gothams winning by one run.

June 16.—Gotham and Athletic, of Philadelphia, at Hoboken. Gotham, 20; Athletic, 28. Umpire, Chapman, of Atlantic Club.

July 11.—Gotham and Mutual, at Hoboken. Gotham, 4; Mutual, 27. Umpire, Samuel Yates, of Eagle Club.

July 14.—Gotham and Atlantic, at Hoboken. Gotham, 21; Atlantic, 38. Umpire, Wm. McMahon, of Mutual Club.

July 18.—Gotham and Eagle, at Hoboken. Gotham, 38; Eagle, 16. Umpire, Westervelt, of Empire Club.

August 1.—Gotham and Hudson River, of Newburgh, New York. Gotham, 34: Hudson River, 5. Umpire, Little, of Nassau Club, of Princeton, New Jersey.

August 8.—Gotham and Empire, at Hoboken. Gotham, 6; Empire, 29. Umpire, W. McMahon, of Mutual Club.

August 11.—Gotham and Hudson River Club, of Newburgh, at Hoboken. Gotham, 29; Hudson River, 26. Umpire, Hugh Burns, of Mutual Club.

August 15.—Gotham and Olympic, of Paterson, New Jersey, at Hoboken. Gotham, 77; Olympic, 18., Umpire, Vanderwerken, of Active Club.

August 22.—Gotham and Mutual, at Hoboken. Gotham, 12; Mutual, 17. Umpire, Jewett, of Empire Club.

September 5.—Gotham and Eckford, at Hoboken. Gotham, 9; Eckford, 18. Umpire, Burns, of Mutual Club.

September 29.—Gotham and Active, at Hoboken. Gotham, 9; Active, 25. Umpire, Martin, of Empire Club.

October 1.—Gotham and Olympic, of Paterson, New Jersey, at Paterson. Gotham, 26; Olympic, 20.

October 4.—Gotham and Empire, at Hoboken. Gotham, 22; Empire, 23. Umpire, Theo. Bomeisler, of Eureka Club.

During the winter of '65 and '66 the Gotham Club played three games on the ice with the Atlantic Club. The first game was played on the Capitoline Pond, at Bedford, Long Island, and resulted in favor of the Atlantics. The second game was played on the Sylvan Lake, Hoboken, and resulted in the success of the Gothams. The third game was played on the Washington Pond, Brooklyn, and resulted in favor of the Atlantics.

June 26, 1866.—Gotham and Eagle, at Hoboken. Gotham, 29: Eagle, 12. Umpire, Thorn, of the Mutual Club.

July 6.—Gotham and National, of Washington, at Hoboken, 34 to 22 in favor of Gotham. After this game the Gotham Club entertained the National Club handsomely.

July 10.—Gotham and Eclectic, at Hoboken. Won by the Gotham, whose score was 20 to the Eclectic's 12. Time of game, two hours thirty minutes.

July 17.—Gothams and Union, of Morrisania, on the grounds of the latter. Union, 52;

Gotham, 25. Time of game, three hours forty minutes. Umpire, Bogart, of the Mutual Club.

July 31.—Gotham and Olympic, of Paterson, New Jersey, at Hoboken. 21 to 10, in favor of Gotham. In July, five of the Gotham first nine resigned from the club, joining other organizations; which left them in a poor plight to engage in matches for the remainder of the season.

August 17.—Gotham and Liberty, at New Brunswick, New Jersey. Won by the latter, by a score of 41 to 29. Time of game, four hours. Umpire, Wilson, of the Empire Club.

August 31.—Gotham and Liberty of New Brunswick, at Hoboken., 23 to 24, in favor of Liberty. In the ninth inning the Gotham had tied the Liberty, and had a man on the third base, when the rain obliged the Umpire to call the game.

September 25.—Gotham and Jefferson, at Hoboken. 20 to 21, in favor of Jefferson.

OFFICERS OF THE GOTHAM CLUB, FROM 1856

1856.—President, William H. Van Cott; Vice-President, Reuben H. Cudlip; Secretary, Charles S. Riblet; Treasurer, Gabriel Van Cott.

1857.—President, Wm. H. Van Cott; Vice-President, Joseph E. Ebling; Secretary, Charles S. Riblet; Treasurer, Seaman Lichtenstein.

1858.—President, Wm. H. Van Cott; Vice-president, Henry B. Venn; Secretary, Charles, S. Riblet; Treasurer, Seamen Lichtenstein.

1859.—President, Wm. H. Van Cott; Vice-President, Henry B. Venn; Secretary, J.A.P. Hopkins; Treasurer, Seamen Lichtenstein.

1860.—President, Gabriel Van Cott; Vice-President, J.A.P. Hopkins; Secretary, Andrew J. Dupignac; Treasurer, James Forsyth.

1861.—President, J.A.P. Hopkins; Vice-President, James B. Mingay; Secretary, A. J. Dupignac; Treasurer, James Forsyth.

1862.—President, J.A.P. Hopkins; Vice-President, James B. Mingay; Secretary, N.W. Redmond; Treasurer, James Forsyth.

1863.—President, James B. Mingay; Vice-President, Leonard G. Cohen; Secretary, Peter Roe; Treasurer, James Forsyth.

1864.—President, James B. Mingay; Vice-President, Cornelius Stokem; Secretary, Charles H. Beadle; Treasurer, Leonard G. Cohen.

1865.—President, Peter Roe; Vice-President, Albert Squires; Secretary, Charles H. Beadle; Treasurer, Leonard G. Cohen.

1866.—President, Thomas Hendry; Vice-President, M.B. Sweet; Secretary, Charles, H. Beadle; Treasurer, Leonard G. Cohen.

The location of the Gotham grounds and club-room is at the Elysian Fields, Hoboken. They practice on Tuesday and Friday of each week during the base-ball season.

The uniform consists of a blue merino cap, with a white star in the center; white flannel shirt, with red cord binding; blue flannel pants, red belt, and white buckskin shoes. Number of active members, forty; honorary members, forty.

EAGLE CLUB

The Eagle Base Ball Club, of New York, was organized in the Spring of 1854. Among its founders the following gentlemen will be remembered and recognized by many of the auld lang syne base ball fraternity: Messrs. John W. Mott, Walter Bensel, William C. Connor, the present popular County Clerk; Gelston and Grigletti, now of the Eagle Base Ball Club of San Francisco; W. W. Armfield, A.J. Bixby, and the veterans Phil. Cozans and Samuel Yates. The Eagles rank as the third base ball club of the country in their institution; and it is no eulogy to say of them that, in all the attributes of a solid, respectable, and honorable organization, they are second to none. With these brief comments, we will refer the reader to the following summary of the Eagle's, principal games.

June 22, 1854.—Eagle and Gotham, at Hoboken. Won by the Gothams, by a score of 21 to 3 runs.

November 10.—Eagle and Knickerbocker, at Hoboken. This game was played barring six of the Knickerbocker's first nine. Eagles, 21 runs; Knickerbockers, 4 runs. Umpires, John W. Mott and A.H. Drummond. Referee, W.H. Van Cott, of the Gotham Club.

November 17.—Eagle and Knickerbocker. Won by the Eagles: score, 22 to 21 runs. Referee, T.G. Van Cott, of the Gotham Club; 5 innings. Umpires, John W. Mott and A. H. Drummond.

June 5, 1855.—Eagle and Knickerbocker. Eagle score, 14 runs; Knickerbocker score, 27 runs.

June 22.—Eagle and Gotham. Won by the Gothams, by a score of 21 to 3 runs.

September 20.—Eagle and Knickerbocker. Won by the latter, by a score of 21 to 10 runs; 6 innings.

October 1.—Eagle and Gotham. Won by latter, by a score of 22 to 11.

October 15.—Eagle and Empire. Eagle score, 21 runs: Empire score, 15 runs.

September 10, 1856.—Eagle and Empire. Eagle score, 10 runs; Empire score, 21 runs.

September 26.—Eagle and Gotham. Tie game; 18 to 18 runs; 5 innings.

October 9.—Eagle and Knickerbocker. Won by the Eagles by a score of 21 to 10 runs. J.W. Mott, Umpire.

October 17.—Eagle and Gotham, at the Red House, Harlem. 3 innings played; score 6 to 2, in favor of the Eagles.

October —.—Eagle and Gotham; score 23 to 4, in favor of the Gothams. Five innings.

June 8, 1857.—Eagle and Knickerbocker; score, 25 to 16, in favor of the Eagles.

June 16.—Eagles and Eckford. The latter defeated by a score of 35 to 20 runs.

July 10.—Eagle and Gotham. The latter won by a score of 43 to 20 runs. R.H. Thorne, Referee.

July 21.—Eagle and Empire. Eagle score, 39 runs; Empire score, 7 runs.

September 8.—Eagle and Gotham. Score, 15 to 9, in favor of the Eagles.

September 15.—Eagle and Knickerbocker. Score, 18 to 17, in favor of the Knickerbockers.

September 22.—Eagle and Eckford. Won by the Eagles, by a score of 23 to 22 runs.

September 30.—Eagle and Empire. Score, 23 to 21, in favor of the Empire.

October 9.—Eagle and Gotham. Victory for latter by a score of 25 to 19 runs.

June 24, 1858.—Eagle and Excelsior. Score, 32 to 13, in favor of the Excelsiors. Umpire, Sheridan, of Gotham Club.

July 29.—Eagle and Knickerbocker. Eagle won by a score of 45 to 18 runs. Umpire, J.J. Grum, of Eckford Club.

August 20.—Eagle and Empire. Score, 39 to 15, in favor of the Empire.

August 29.—Eagle and St. Nicholas. Eagle score, 33 runs; St. Nicholas, 18 runs.

September 28.—Eagle and Excelsior. The latter won by a score of 36 to 25 runs.

June 24, 1859.—Eagle and Putnam. Won by the Putnam. Eagle's score, 8 runs; Putnam's score, 24 runs.

August 9.—Eagle and St. Nicholas. Score, 30 to 37, in favor of the Eagles.

August 19.—Eagle's first nine, 12 runs; Gothams' first nine, 11runs.
August 26.—Eagle, 26 runs; Hoboken, 25 runs. J.A.P. Hopkins, Umpire.
September 2.—Eagle, 24 runs; Pastime, 19 runs. Umpire, C. Sniffin, Atlantic Club.
September 8.—Eagle, 20 runs; Excelsior, 24 runs. Umpire, Thorn, of Empire Club.
September 23.—Eagle, 23 runs; Empire, 8 runs. J.V.W. Rowland, Jefferson Club, Umpire.
October 4.—Eagle, 25 runs; Gotham, 21 runs. Samuel Patchen, of Star Club, Umpire.
June 12, 1860.—Eagle, 26 runs; Union (Morrisania), 15 runs. A. Liscomb, Harlem Club, Umpire.
July 2.—Eagle, 18 runs; Adriatic (of Newark, N.J.), 15 runs. H. Smith, Newark Club, Umpire.
July 6.—Eagle, 24 runs; Mutual, 10 runs. R.H. Thorn, Adriatic Club, Umpire.
July 10.—Eagle, 18 runs; Gotham, 18 runs; tie game. S. Van Winkle, Gotham Club, Umpire.
July 10.—Eagle, 16; Charter Oak, 25. Umpire, A.J. Burns, of Putnam Club.
July 14.—Eagle, 14 runs; Empire, 33 runs. Peter O'Brien, Atlantic Club, Umpire.
September 7.—Eagle, 9; Harlem, 17. Umpire, Rowland, of Jefferson Club.
September 11.—Eagle, 11; Gotham, 25. Umpire, R.H. Thorne.
July 23, 1861.—Eagle, 32; Eckford, 23. Umpire, Thomas Culyer, of the Empire Club.
September 3.—Eagle, 7; Mutual, 18. Umpire, Martin O'Brien, of the Atlantic Club.
September 23.—Eagle and Empire Clubs, 9; Gotham and Mutual Clubs, 19; eight innings. Umpire, John J. Grum, of the Eckford Club.
September 24.—Eagle, 18; Jefferson, 22. Umpire, Wm. McMahon, of the Mutual Club.
October 15.—Eagle, 30; Gotham, 15. Umpire, Wm. Culyer, of the Empire Club.
May 13, 1862.—Eagle, 15; Gotham, 17. Umpire, W.F. Eagan.
July 29.—Eagle, 5; Eckford, 18. Umpire, Chas. Smith, of the Atlantic Club.
September 9.—Eagle, 15; Gotham, 17. Umpire, Anson B. Taylor, of the Mutual Club.
August 26.—Eagle, 50; Alpine, 24. Umpire, J. Stevens, of the Mutual Club.
September 26.—Eagle, 15; Henry Eckford, 33. Umpire, Westervelt, of Empire Club.
June 23, 1863.—Eagle, 15; Gotham, 19. Umpire, A.B. Taylor, of Mutual Club.
July 1.—Eagle, 5; Resolute, of Brooklyn, 27. Umpire, Spence, of Eckford Club.
August 25.—Eagle, 12; Mutual, 25. Umpire, Spence, of Eckford Club.
October 17.—Eagle, 6; Excelsior, of Brooklyn, 5. Umpire, J. Seaver Page, of Active Club.
June 1, 1864.—Eagle "Muffins," 57; Atlantic "Muffins," 44. Umpire, James Cameron, of Empire Club.
July 21.—Eagle, 10; Empire, 19. Umpire, J.C. Forsyth, of Gotham Club.
July 14.—Eagle, 8; Mutual, 39. Umpire, J. Benson, of Empire Club.
July 20.—Eagle, 12; Atlantic, 45. Umpire, J. Forsyth, of Gotham Club.
July 27.—Eagle, 18; Active, 20. Umpire, J. Westervelt, of Empire Club.
August 20.—Eagle "Muffins," 58; Empire "Muffins," 30. Umpire, T Coffin.
September 12.—Eagle, 34; Resolute, of Brooklyn, 23. Umpire, Simon Burns, of Mutual Club.

The first match played by the Eagle Club in 1865 was that with the Star Club, of Brooklyn, in May, and their last was that with the New York Cricket Club, in November. The following is the summary of the first nine matches played by the Eagle with clubs belonging to the National Association:

May 30.—Eagle vs. Star, at Hoboken; score, 31 to 40 (won by the Star); nine innings; time of game, 3:30; best batting score by Collins; best fly-catching by Slote.
June 13.—Eagle vs. Athletic, at Hoboken; score 14, to 24; nine innings; time of game 2:25.
June 20.—Eagle vs. Newark, at Newark; score, 32 to 43; nine innings; time of game, 3.25.
July 14.—Eagle vs. Eckford, at Brooklyn; score, 7 to 38; nine innings.
July 18.—Eagle vs. Gotham, at Hoboken; score, 16 to 38; nine innings.
August 28.—Eagle vs. Atlantic, at Bedford; score, 10 to 48; nine innings.
September 13.—Eagle vs. Empire, at Hoboken; score, 6 to 37; seven innings; time of game,

2.30.

September 15.—Eagle vs. Active, at Hoboken; score, 9 to 54; nine innings; time of game, 2.20.

October 7.—Eagle vs. Hudson River, at Newburgh; score, 10 to 45; nine innings; time of game, 2.30.

October 30.—Eagle vs. Mutual, at Hoboken,; score, 7 to 13; nine innings; time of game, 1.40.

November 14.—Eagle vs. New York Cricket Club, at Hoboken; score, 34 to 16; nine innings.

The Eagle Club, in the above matches, scored a total of 176 runs against 396; the number of innings played being 97, gives an average of one run, with 79 over, to an inning, and 16 runs to a match. The highest score made in a match was 32, and the lowest 6; the highest score made in an inning being 9. Of blank scores, in single innings, they scored a total of 26 against 15 made by their adversaries. Of fly-catches made in six of the games, they made 53 against 57 by their opponents. As no fielding score was published of nine of their games, we are unable to give any statistics of foul balls, or of who took the lead in fly-catches. The shortest full game played occupied but an hour and forty minutes—the shortest of the season, we believe. Shafer led the score at the bat the most times; Collins and Chapin being next. Among those who took part in three games and over are Messrs. Willis, W. Shafer, Pennington, Thompson, Howe, and Coursen. Of these, Willis, Howe, Coursen, and Thompson, all average two runs and over to a match.

June 26, 1866.—Eagle, 12; Gotham, 29. Umpire, Thorne, of Mutual Club.

July 19.—Eagle, 24; Olympic, of Paterson, N.J., 28; played at Paterson. Umpire, J.E. Hartley, Jefferson Club.

July 24.—Eagle, 33; Eckford, 38; Hoboken. Umpire, Jewett, Mutual Club. Time, three hours.

July 26.—Eagle second nine, 17; Eckford second nine, 60; Williamsburgh Union. Umpire, Mills, Atlantic.

August 3.—Eagle "Muffins." 50; Atlantic "Muffins,"35; at Hoboken. Umpire, Henry Chadwick, of National Club.

August 8.— Eagle, 19; Empire, 45: at Morrisania. Umpire, Thorne, of Empire Club.

September 8.—Eagle, 10; Active, 29. Umpire, Demarest, of National Club, Jersey City.

September 17.—Eagle, 20; Waterbury Club, of Connecticut, 31; at Hoboken. Umpire, Connell, of Enterprise Club.

September 19.—Eagle, 15; National, 30; played at Jersey City. Umpire, Houghtalin, of Active Club.

September 28.—Eagle, 23; Olympic, of Paterson, N.J., 18; at Hoboken. Umpire, J. Russell, of Empire Club.

October 19.—Eagle, 20; Empire, 25. Umpire, Martin, of Mutual club.

October 19.—Eagle, 29; National, of Jersey City, 13; at Hoboken. Umpire, Thorne, of Mutual Club.

The delegates from the Eagle Club to the first convention of the National Association held in 1857, consisted of Messrs. John W. Mott, W.W. Armfield, and A. J. Bixby. The clubroom and grounds are at the Elysian Fields, Hoboken. Practice days, Tuesdays and Fridays. The uniform of the club consists of dark blue flannel pants, check shirt, and blue cap with white visor. Officers of the Eagle Club for 1866: President, N.B. Shaffer; Vice-President, Fenton C. McElroy; Secretary, Martin A. Kelly; Treasurer, James G. Powers.

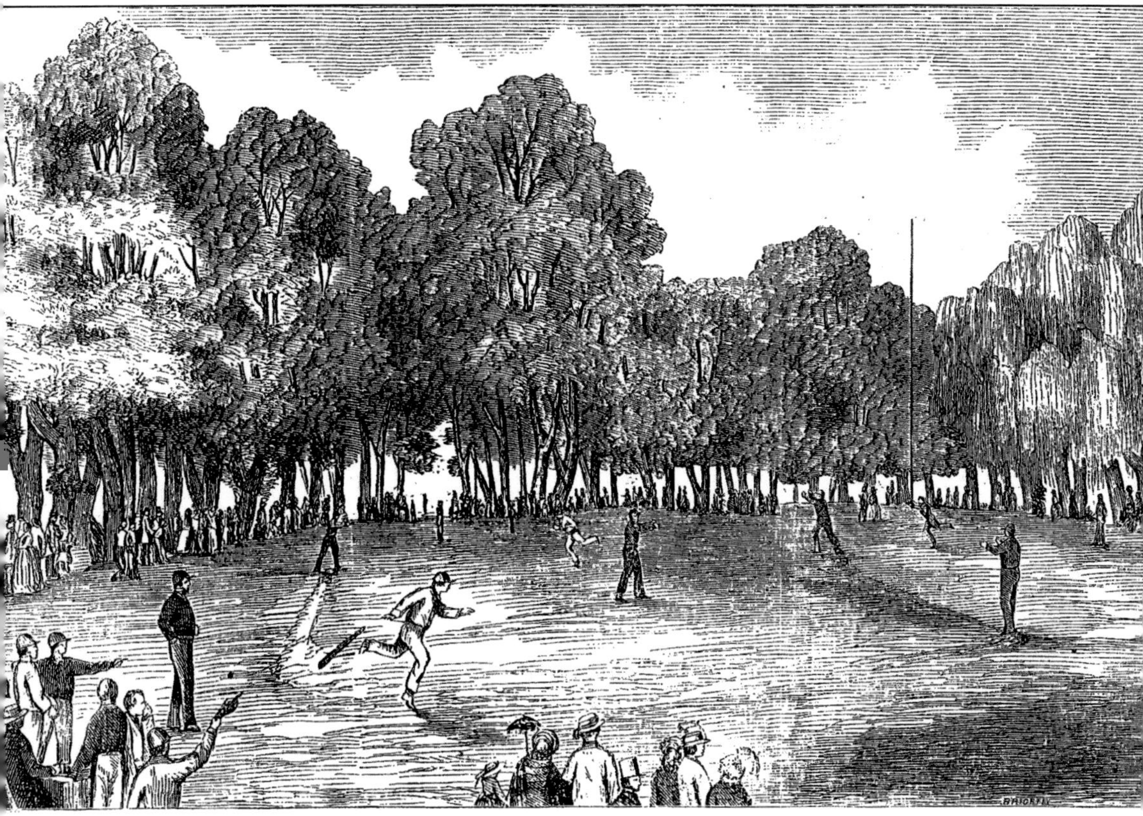

(DRAWN AND ENGRAVED EXPRESSLY FOR "PORTER'S SPIRIT OF THE TIMES.")

BASE BALL IN AMERICA.

E EAGLES AND GOTHAMS PLAYING THEIR GREAT MATCH AT THE ELYSIAN FIELDS, ON TUESDAY, SEPTEMBER 8T

PORTER'S SPIRIT OF THE TIMES, *EAGLES VS. GOTHAMS*, 1857. *This woodcut shows the Elysian Fields the in all its green grandeur. The game was pastoral and a grand happening for the clubs involved. Base Ball clubs had dozen of members. The Gothams were the second strongly developed team after the Knickerbockers. Some of the earliest Gotham players—Davis, Vail, and Winslow, Sr.—have roots dating back to the earliest development of the game. (Source:* Vintage Ballist.*)*

EMPIRE CLUB

The Empire Base Ball Club, of New York, was organized October 23, 1854, with only thirteen members. The club did not engage in any games their first season, as it was late when they organized, and they played but two matches during 1855, which are recorded in their summary. The Empire's crack players, in its earlier days, consisted of R. H. Thorn, pitcher; James Mullen, catcher; Thomas Leary, first base; Thomas Miller, second base; Scott, third base; while R.L. Haydock, H.H.R. Smith, Monson Hoyt, G.M. Tice, Isaac Gough, with C.W. Grant, Moore, Merwin, Myers, and Newkirk, made the old Empires hard to vanquish on the base ball field. Among the earliest officers of the Empire Club were the following: President, Thomas G.

Voorhis; Vice-President, Walter Scott; Secretary, Thomas Chalmers, Jr.; Treasurer, William G. Odell; Vigilance Committee, James Cameron and R.L. Haydock. It will be seen that some of these gentlemen still continue their active membership with the club. Messrs. John J.

Bloomfield, John Kennard, Wm. Culyer, Joseph Russell, etc., have all bestowed a generous share of their time and influence towards keeping the time-honored 1854 colors of the Empire Club flying unsullied, and with credit, over their headquarters.

September 5, 1855.—Empire and Gotham. Won by the Gotham by a score of 25 to 4.
October 15.—Empire and Eagle, at Hoboken. Won by Eagle; score, 21 to 15.
May 22, 1856,—Empire and Knickerbocker, at Hoboken. Tie game; score, 21 to 21; eight innings.
September 25.—Empire and Knickerbocker, at Hoboken. Score, 21 to 12, in favor of the Knickerbockers; seven innings. Referee, Gelston, of the Eagle Club.
June 24, 1857.—Empire and Knickerbocker. Won by the latter; score, 37 to 23; nine innings. Referees, M. E. Gelston, of Eagle Club.
July 21.—Empire and Eagle, at Hoboken. Eagle, 39; Empire, 17. J. W. Mott, Umpire.
August 20.— Empire and Eagle, at Hoboken. Empire's score, 39; Eagle's score, 15 runs.
September 10.—Empire and Knickerbocker. Won by the Empires by a score of 28 to 17.
September 30.— Empire and Eagle, at Hoboken. Won by the Empires score, 23 to 21. Mott and Cameron, Umpires.
July 17, 1858.—Empire and St. Nicholas, at Hoboken. Empire's score, 30; St. Nicholas score, 13. Umpire, Dr. Jones, of the Excelsior Club.
July 21.—Empire and Empire of, Newark,, N. J. Won by Empire, of New York; score, 27 to 7.
August 11.—Empire and Knickerbocker. Won by the latter by a score of 60 to 33.
September 3.— Empire and Gotham, at Hoboken. Empire, 22 runs; Gotham, 11 runs. Umpire, W. Gelston, of Eagle Club.
September 15.— Empire and St. Nicholas, at Hoboken. Score, 24 to 3, in favor of the Empire. Umpire, Van Cott, of the Gotham.
September 22.— Empire and Knickerbocker. Tie game—21 to 21.
October 18.— Empire and Mutual, at Hoboken. Won by the Empire, by a score of 37 to 22; seven innings.
October 18.—Empire and Mutual, at Hoboken; seven innings. Won by Empire; score, 37 to 22.
August 26, 1859.—Empire and Eckford; the latter winning. Score 21 to 8. Umpire, Clark, of the St. Nicholas.
August 29.—Empire and Mutual, at Hoboken. Empire's score, 27; Mutual's score, 23. Umpire, Rowland, of the Jefferson.
September 14.—Empire and Mutual, at Hoboken. Excelsior won by a score of 25 to 20. Umpire, Morrow, of the Knickerbockers.
September 23.— Empire and Eagle, at Hoboken. Empire, 8 runs; Eagle, 23 runs.
October 6.—Empire and Pastime, in the Excelsior grounds, South Brooklyn. Score, 20 to 13, in favor of Empire. Umpire, S. Patchen, of the Star Club.
October 14.— Empire and Union, on the Red House ground. Score, Empire, 26; Union, 8 runs. Umpire, T.G. Van Cott, of the Gotham Club.
August 8, 1860.—Empire and Eckford, ay Hoboken. Won by the Eckford, by a score of 21 to 13. Umpire, A. Pearsall, of the Excelsior Club.
August 13.— Empire and Mutual, at Hoboken. Won by the Empires, by a score of 17 to 7 in a game of eight innings. Umpire, Peter O'Brien, of the Atlantic Club.
August 14.—Empire and Henry Eckford, at Hoboken. Score, 28 to 11. Umpire, T.S. Dakin.
August 22, 1861.—Empire and Mutual. Score, 16 to 22. Umpire, Griswold, of the Gotham Club.
September 1.—Empire and Excelsior, at Hoboken. Won by the Excelsior by a score of 23 to 7.
September 2.—Empire and Jefferson. Won by the latter by as score of 25 to 15.
September 22.— Empire and Hamilton, of Jersey City, at Hoboken. Seven innings. Empire,

15 runs; Hamilton 14.
September 29.— Empire and Excelsior, at South Brooklyn. Won by the Excelsior by a score of 23 to 7 runs. Umpire, A. J. Bixby, of the Eagle Club.
October 4.—Empire and Eckford, at Manor House grounds. Won by Eckfords, by a score of 26 to 10. Umpire, C. Sniffin, of the Atlantic Club.
August 13.-1862.—Empire and Alpine, at Hoboken. Won by the Empire. Score, 39 to 21 runs.
June 24, 1863.—Empire and Henry Eckford, upon the grounds of the latter. Won by the Henry Eckford.
July 1.—Empire and Gotham. Score, 16 to 14, in favor of the latter.
July 21.— Empire and Eagle. Score, 19 to 10, in favor of the Empire.
July 29.—Empire and Henry Eckford, at Hoboken. Score: Empire, 21 runs; Henry Eckford, 16 runs.
August 6.—Empire and Mutual, at Hoboken. Score: Mutual, 21 runs; Empire, 16 runs.
August 18.— Empire and Star, at Carroll Park, South Brooklyn. Score: Star, 28 runs: Empire, 9 runs.
July 26, 1864.—Empire and Gotham, at Hoboken. Score, 13 to 22. Umpire, Harris, of Mutual Club.
October 11.— Gotham and Empire, at Hoboken. Tie game. Umpire, Snow, of Active Club.

The Empire Club played in twenty-two first-nine matches during 1864, of which they won seven and lost thirteen, two being tie games, they being defeated by the Eureka twice, Atlantic twice, Active twice, Mutual twice, Gotham, Union, and Hudson River twice. The games they won were with the Active, Eagle, Enterprise, twice; Knickerbocker and Eckford, of Albany, and Manhattan Cricket Club, and were successful in there second game with the Henry Eckford. The total number of runs obtained in these games was three hundred and ninety-one, against three hundred and ninety-eight by their opponents, yielding an average of two runs to an inning, with five over, or seventeen to a match. Their highest score in a single inning was thirteen, and in a match forty-five; their lowest in a game being three.

The Empire Club played sixteen first-nine matches during 1865, of which fifteen were with the clubs belonging to the National Association. Of these latter they won seven and lost eight. The following is the summary of their games with clubs of the Association:

June 17.—Empire and Mystic, at Sixty-third street grounds. Score, 42 to 5; won by the Empire; nine innings; time of game, 2 hours 30 minutes.
June 21.—Empire and Atlantic, at Hoboken; score, 10 to 21; nine innings; time, 2.10.
June 28.—Empire and Mutual, at Hoboken; score, 5 to 12; nine innings; time, 1.35.
July 8.—Empire and Resolute, at Brooklyn; score, 29 to 26 nine innings; time 3.15.
July 20.—Empire and Mutual, at Hoboken; score, 15 to 26; nine innings; time, 2.50.
July 27.—Empire and Atlantic, at Bedford; score, 3 to 65; nine innings; time, 3 hours.
August 2.—Empire and Eckford, at Brooklyn; score, 37 to 48; seven innings; time, 3.10.
August 8.—Empire and Gotham, at Hoboken; score, 29 to 6; nine innings; time, 2.05.
August 16.—Empire and Enterprise, at Bedford; score, 37 to 33; nine innings; time, 3 hours.
August 23.—Empire and Athletic, at Philadelphia; score, 28 to 40; nine innings; time, 3.40.
August 26.—Empire and Keystone, at Philadelphia; score, 15 to 45; six innings; time, 2.30.
September 13.—Empire and Eagle at Hoboken; score, 37 to 6; seven innings; time, 2.30.
September 27.—Empire and Mystic, at Hoboken: score, 50 to 16; eight innings; time, 2.50.
October 11.—Empire and Active, at Hoboken; score, 15 to 24; eight innings; time, 2.30.

The total score made by the Empire Club in the above matches was three hundred and seventy-four against three hundred and eight-eight by their adversaries; and the number of innings played was one hundred and twenty-six, giving an average of two runs to inning, with one hundred and twenty-two over, and twenty-four to a match, with fourteen over. In the innings played they scored thirty blanks against thirty -three by their opponents. Their highest score in a match was fifty, and the lowest three; their highest score in an innings being seventeen. They scored double figures in single innings in four matches, their opponents doing the same in five. Their shortest game occupied one hour and thirty-five minutes. They scored the large number of one hundred and eighty-three fly-catches, against one hundred and twenty-four by their adversaries, thus excelling every other club in this respect, their average being over twelve to a match. In nine of the above games they put out their adversaries on foul balls eighty-eight times, they being similarly put out only fifty-three times; thus showing effective pitching and good out-fielding.

June 28, 1866.—Athletic (of Philadelphia), and Empire , at Hoboken. Won by the Athletic, by a score of 64 to 10; time of game, 3 hours 20 minutes. Umpire, Connell, of the Gotham Club.
August 1.—Empire and Eckford, at Hoboken. Won by the Eckford, by a score of 53 to 23.
August 8.—Empire and Eagle, at Hoboken; time of game, 2 hours 40 minutes. Won by the Empire, by a score of 45 to 19. Umpire, R.H. Thorn, of the Mutual Club.
August 15.—Empire and Active, at Hoboken. Won by the Active, by a score of 28 to 9; time of game, 2 hours 45 minutes. Umpire, Jewett, of the Mutual Club.
August 20.—Empire and Eureka, at Newark, N.J. Empire's score, 11 runs; Eureka's 15 runs. Time of game, 2 hours 30 minutes. Umpire, Glover, of the Eclectic Club.
September 4.—Empire and Eckford, on Union grounds, Brooklyn. Won by the Eckford, by a score of 32 to 19.
September 10.— Empire and Jefferson, at Hoboken., Won by Empire, by a score of 31 to 21; 8 innings. Time, 2 hours 30 minutes. Umpire, Evans, of the Mutual; Club.

The Empire play-ground and club-room is at Elysian Fields, Hoboken. The number at present seventy-four, active and honorary. The officers for 1866 are: President, Thomas S. Voorhis; Vice-President, Samuel E, Horsford; Secretary, James Ward; Treasure, Edward Benson. Uniform: white shirts trimmed with red; light grey pants; white caps; red belt.

The following delegates from the Empire Club to the first Convention of the Base Ball Players in 1857: Messrs. R.H. Thorn, Walter Scotte, and Thomas Leavy.

BASE BALL.

EAGLE *vs.* EMPIRE.—The conquering game between the above clubs was played on Wednesday, Sept. 10, at Elysian Fields, and was decided in favor of the latter. Unfortunately for the Eagles, two of their men, on whom they relied for some splendid play, were invalids, and unable to play. Had Messrs. Place and Gilman been in the field, we feel confident the result would have shown at least a better list of runs for the Eagles. By the following it will be seen that on the fourth, even innings the game stood eight, and but one unhappy change in position was made, which resulted unfortunately to the defeated:

EAGLE'S.

	Innings.					*Runs.*
Armsfield,.......	1			1		1
Houseman......						11
Williams	2					11
Bixby...........	3		1	2		
Vanderbilt......		1	2	3		
Gelston.........					1	11
Brinkerhoff......		2			2	1
Baker..........					3	11
Jordan..........		3	3			
					Total,	10 runs.

EMPIRE.

	Innings.					*Runs.*
Thom......	1				2	111
Hoyt.......			1	1	3	11
Levy.......						1111
Smith......	2					111
Miller......						111
Scott.......	3		2	3		1
Goff........		1			1	11
Tice........		2				11
Wandle....		3	3	2		1
					Total, 21	runs.

EMPIRES AND EAGLES BOX. *The Eagles were one of the earliest developed teams that actually spawned a team on the West Coast. Gelston of the Eagle Club was an honorary member of the San Francisco Eagle Base Ball club. By 1866, Gelston and Grigletti were active among the San Francisco Eagle membership. It is believed that the team was started in 1859. By the time Peverelly had written his book in 1866, there were a good dozen teams established in and around San Francisco. This primitive box shows outs and runs. The 1, 2, 3 numbers in the columns under innings denotes the players making outs in the inning. The blanks mean the runners were on base, but doesn't assume that they scored. This box is the only one of this kind that I have found. (Source:* Vintage Ballist.*)*

ACTIVE CLUB

The Active Base Ball Club, of New York, was organized in October, 1856, and remained a Junior club until 1863, when it was admitted at the annual meeting of the National Association, December 9. From the period of its formation, the Active Club has filled an honorable and influential space in the advancement and progress of our national game. A body of young men of admitted first-class playing abilities, they occupy a social position second to none in the Association— a fact of which they may well feel proud. Many of the Active's junior contests attracted a great deal of interest; among them our readers will probably remember their exciting game with the Young America, Waverly, and Onalaska, of New York, and the National, of Brooklyn. One of their first games was with the celebrated Invincible Club, which was deemed something far ahead of any other junior club. The Actives, however, soon settled all their pretensions by a sweeping victory over them by a score of 31 to 1. In any allusion to the Active Club the name J. Seaver Page should be gratefully indited, as he has performed yeoman service in assisting the Club to win its present popularity and name. Mr. Page was President of the Club for nine years. The following is a summary of their games since they have been a senior club:

June 11, 1864.—Active and Empire, at Hoboken.. Empire, 29 runs; Active, 16 runs; time, 1 hour 35 minutes.

July 4.—Active and Eureka, of Newark, N.J. Active, 29 runs; Eureka, 27 runs; time, 3 hours.

July 13.—Active and Empire, return game , at Hoboken. Active, 37 runs; Empire, 16 runs.

July 27.—Active and Eagle, at Hoboken. Active, 20 runs; Eagle, 18 runs; time, 2.15

August 26.—Active and Mutual, at Hoboken. Active, 3 runs; Mutual, 22 runs; time, 2.15.

September 14.—Active and Eureka, at Hoboken; return game. Eureka, 11 runs; Active, 10 runs; time, 2.45.

September 21.—Active and Mutual, at Hoboken. Active, 8 runs; Mutual, 14 runs; time, 1.45.

October 5.—Active and Empire, at Hoboken. Active, 9 runs; Empire, 3 runs; time, 2.45.

October 27.—Active and Rose Hill Club, at Fordham. Active, 32 runs; Rose Hill Club, 16 runs.

June 13, 1865.—Active and Newark, at Newark, N. J. Active, 12 runs; Newark, 11 runs.

June 24.—Active and Resolute, Union ball ground, Brooklyn. Active, 37 runs; Resolute, 26 runs; eight innings.

July 4.—Active and Union , at Morrisania. Active , 16 runs; Union, 25 runs.

July 8.—Active and Empire, at Hoboken. Active, 15 runs; Empire, 21 runs.

July 29.—Active and Enterprise, of Brooklyn, at Hoboken. Active, 27 runs; Enterprise, 12 runs.

August 8.—The Active Club visited Philadelphia for the purpose of playing some friendly games with the clubs of that city. On the ninth of August they played with the Olympic Club, and won, by a score of 34 to 12.

August 10.—Active and Athletic, in Philadelphia. Won by th Active, by a score of 28 to 13.

August 11.—Active and Camden, on the ground of the latter. Active, 17 runs; Camden, 22 runs.

August 19.—Active and Union, of Morrisania, at Hoboken. Return game. Active, 22 runs; Union, 12 runs.

August 23.—Active and Atlantic, of Brooklyn, at Hoboken. Active, 19 runs; Atlantic, 24 runs.

August 30.—Active and Mutual, at Hoboken. Active, 21 runs; Mutual, 22 runs; eleven innings.

September 2.—Active and Enterprise, on Capitoline ground. Active, 28 runs; Enterprise, 18 runs.

September 15.—Active and Eagle, at Hoboken. Active, 54 runs; Eagle, 9 runs; eight innings.

September 21.— Active and Mutual, at Hoboken. Active, 20 runs; Mutual, 26 runs.

September 23.—Active and Union, on St, George Cricket ground, Hoboken. Active, 32 runs; Union 10 runs. Home-and-home game.

September 29.—Active and Gotham, at Hoboken. Active, 23 runs; Gotham, 9 runs; seven innings.

October 7.—Active and Empire, at Hoboken. Active, 24 runs; Empire, 15 runs; eight innings.

October 20.—Active and Eureka, on Capitoline ground. Active, 3 runs; Eureka, 6 runs. Home-and-home game.

November 16.—Active and Alert, at Seaton Hall, South Orange, N.J. Active, 22 runs; Alert, 10 runs.

June 2, 1866.—Active and Harvard, of Harvard College; at Hoboken. Active, 24 runs; Harvard, 15 runs.

June 9.—Active and Union, at Morrisania. Active, 13 runs; Union,. 56 runs.

June 16.—Active and Una, at Hoboken. Active, 23 runs; Una, 23 runs.

June 30.—Active and Enterprise, at Hoboken. Active, 31 runs; Enterprise, 26 runs.

July 4.—Active and Enterprise, on Capitoline Ground. Active, 29 runs; Enterprise, 26 runs; ten innings; tie game on the ninth.

July 12.—Active and Mutual, at Hoboken. Active, 16 runs; Mutual, 23 runs.

July 21.—Active and Star, at Carroll Park, Brooklyn. Active, 32 runs; Star, 33 runs; six innings.

August 15.—Active and Empire, at Hoboken. Active, 28 runs; Empire, 9 runs.

August 18.—Active and Una, at Mount Vernon. Return game. Active, 43 runs; Una, 22 runs; seven innings.

August 22.—Active and Eckford, at Hoboken. Active, 19 runs; Eckford, 16 runs; eight innings.

September 8.—Active and Eagle, at Hoboken. Active, 29 runs; Eagle, 10 runs; eight innings.

September 12.—Active and Eureka, at Hoboken. Active, 9 runs; Eureka, 24 runs.

October 3.—Active and Irvington, of Irvington, N.J. At the Sussex County Fair, held at Newton, N.J., for a silver ball. Won by the Active, by a score of 19 to 10.

October 6.—Active and Star, of Brooklyn, at Hoboken. Active, 17 runs; Star, 10 run; seven innings.

October 17.—Active and Eureka, of Newark, N. J., at Hoboken. Active, 11 runs; Eurekas, 44 runs; six innings.

The Active club-room and ground is at the Elysian Fields, Hoboken, N.J. They are now in an extremely flourishing condition, numbering 150 members, active and honorary. The uniform is white cap, white and blue shirt, and blue pants. The officers for 1866 are: President, Charles. D. Walker; Vice-President, W.J. Kelley; Recording Secretary, Cornelius T. Williamson; Corresponding Secretary, E. Hallock; Treasurer, Edgar Tilton; Delegates to National Association, Messrs. J. Seaver Page and H.A. Rogers.

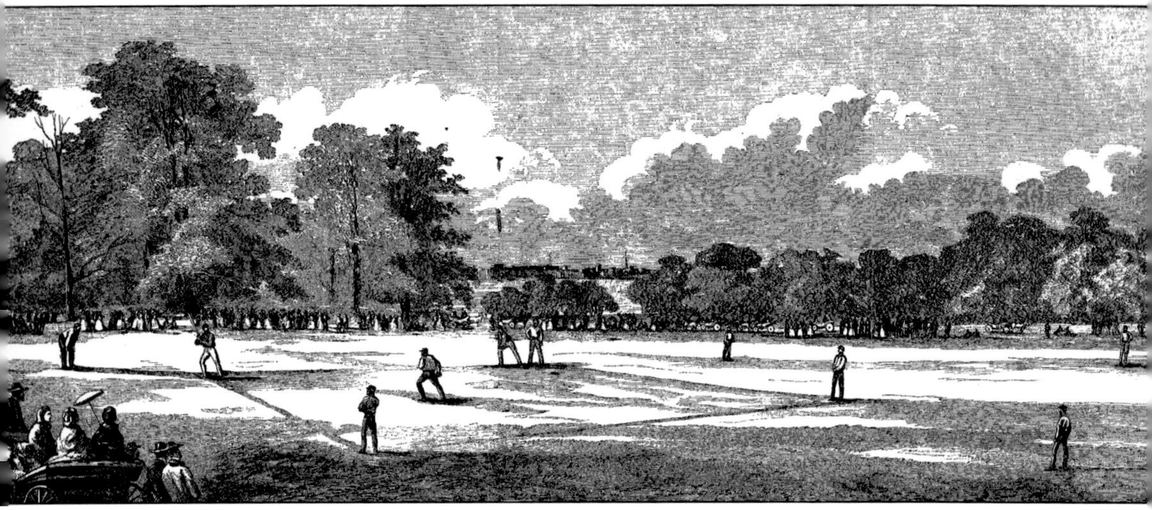

HARPER'S WEEKLY PRINT OF THE ELYSIAN FIELDS, PANORAMIC VIEW, 1859. *The game shown here is at the Elysian Fields. Notice the position of the infielders. The short stop or rover is playing a shallow left field, not inside the base line as usually depicted in diagrams in the base ball guides of the era. The second base man plays on the bag and the right fielder plays a shallow right, a defensive strategy that helps fill the void of the second baseman playing at the bag. More may be learned from matching up images with rule books of the era. Many nuances of the old game do not show up in rule books, like shifts in the infield. (Source:* Vintage Ballist.*)*

MUTUAL CLUB

* In preparing this record of the Mutual Club, we have been assisted greatly by an old and valued friend, Mr. James McConnell.

The Mutual Base Ball Club, of New York, was organized June 24, 1857, but they did not engage in many games during their first season. They were, how ever, successful in most of their earlier contests. The first officers of the Club were: President, John Carland; Vice-President, Edward J. Shandley; Secretary, James J. Kelso; Treasurer, David Lennox.

July 29.—Mutual and Monument, at Hoboken; 70 to 13, in favor of Mutual.
August 10.—Mutual and St, Nicholas, at Hoboken 31 to 24, won by the Mutual.
August 13.—Mutual and Monument; won by Mutual, by 67 to 17.
August 26.—Mutual and Independent; 56 to 12, in favor of Mutual.
August 23.—Mutual and Baltic: won by Mutual by 48 to 21.
August 30.—Mutual and Hoboken, at Hoboken; 29 to 25, in favor of Mutual.
September 10.—Mutual and Baltic; won by Mutual, 47 to 26.
September 22.—Mutual and St,. Nicholas; 51 to 21, in favor of Mutual.
September 26.—Mutual and Hoboken, at Hoboken; won by Mutual, by 31 to 19.
September 30, 1858.—Mutual and Empire, at Hoboken; 18 to 17, in favor of Mutual.
October 6.—Mutual and Independent; 54 to 13, in favor of Mutual.

OFFICERS FOR 1858: President, John Carland; Vice-President, Edward J. Shandley; Secretary, Lawrence Clancy; Treasurer, David Lennox.

August 4, 1859.—Mutual and Hoboken; ten innings; won by Mutual, by 19 to 15.
August 6.—Mutual and Jefferson; won by the Mutual; score 33 to 17.
August 18.—Mutual and Empire; score, 17 to 13, in favor of Empire.
September 15.—Mutual and Gotham , at Hoboken; score, 37 to 25, in favor of Gotham.
September 19.—Mutual and Atlantic, at Hoboken; score, 39 to 20, in favor of Mutual.
September 26.—Mutual and Hoboken; won by Mutual, by 31 to 19.
October 14.—Mutual and Atlantic, at Bedford; score, 15 to 5, in favor of Atlantic.

OFFICERS FOR 1859: President, Lawrence Bogart; Vice -President, James McConnell; Secretary, Thomas W. Bovell; Treasurer, Warren Davids.

July 6, 1860.—Mutual and Eagle; score, 10 to 18, in favor of Eagle.
July 30.—Mutual and Atlantic; won by the latter, by 34 to 15.
July 17.—Mutual and Gotham; 25 to 25; tie game.
August 3.—Mutual and Henry Eckford; score, 15 to 11, in favor of Mutual.
August 13.— Mutual and Empire; score, 7 to 13; eight innings; in favor of Empire.
August 20.— Mutual and Atlantic; score 14 to 26, in favor of Atlantic.
Sept.4.—Mutal and Gotham, return game; a second tie, 18 to 18.
Sept.13.—Mutual and Henry Eckford; 12 to 16, in favor of the latter.
Sept,. 24.—Mutual and Jefferson; score, 17 to 18, in favor of the Jefferson.
Sept. 27.—Mutual and Gotham; 12 to 19; won by the Gotham.
Oct. 15.—Mutual and Henry Eckford; 24 to 19; won by Henry Eckford.

OFFICERS FOR 1860: President, Lawrence Bogart; Vice-President, James McConnell; Secretary, Warren Davids; Treasurer, A B. Taylor.

July 12, 1861.—Mutual and Alpine; score, 36 to 12, in favor of Mutual.
July 22.—Mutual and Alpine; score 37 to 15, in favor of Mutual.

August 7.—Mutual and Gotham; score, 25 to 22, in favor of Mutual.
August 22.—Mutual and Empire; won by the Mutual, by 23 to 16.
August 27.—Mutual and Jefferson; 32 to 12, in favor of Mutual.
Sept. 3.—Mutual and Eagle; 18 to 7; won by Mutual.
Spt.25.—Mutual and Enterprise; 33 to 21; won by Mutual.
Oct. 3.—Mutual and Atlantic, at Hoboken; 23 to 18, in favor of Mutual.
Oct. 16.—Mutual and Atlantic; 27 to 52, in favor of Atlantic.

OFFICERS FOR 1861: President, Anson B. Taylor; Vice-President, John Wildey; Secretary, Thomas W. Bovell; Treasurer, Warren Davids.

July 19, 1862.—Mutual and Gotham; 52 to 14; won by Mutual.
Jul 27.—Mutual and Gotham; score, 14 to 9, in favor of Gotham.
July 28.—Mutual and Jefferson; 58 to 25, in favor of Mutual.
August 4.—Mutual and Eckford; 24 to 28; won by Eckford.
August 14.—Mutual and Gotham; 14 to 15; won by Gotham.
August 21.—Mutual and Eureka, at Newark, N.J.; 14 to 13; ten innings; won by Mutual.
August 26.—Mutual and Adriatic, at Philadelphia; 33 to 5; won by Mutual.
August 27.—Mutual and Olympic, at Philadelphia; 10 to 7; won by Mutual.
August 28.—Mutual and Athletic, at Philadelphia; 10 to 17, in favor of Athletic.
Spt. 8.—Mutual and Harlem, at Harlem; 47 to 16; won by Mutual.
Spt.22.—Mutual and Atlantic, at 65 street and 3d avenue; 15 to 10; won by Mutual
Sept. 24.—Mutual and Eckford; 14 to 28, in favor of Eckford.
Oct. 7.—Mutual and Harlem, at Hoboken; Mutual won, by 24 to 13.

OFFICERS FOR 1862: President, Anson B. Taylor; Vice-President; Lawrence H. Bogart; Secretary, William L. Green; Treasurer, Warren Davids.

June 16, 1863.—Mutual and Atlantic; 17 to 11; won by Mutual.
July 13.—Mutual and Gotham; 31 to 15; won by Mutual.
July 20.—Mutual and Empire; 24 to 12; won by Mutual.
July 22.—Mutual and Eckford, at Brooklyn; 9 to 10; won by Eckford.
July 28.—Mutual and Gotham; 19 to 5; won by Mutual.
August 3.—Mutual and Atlantic, at Bedford; 27 to 26; won by Mutual.
August 6.—Mutual and Empire; 21 to 16; won by Mutual.
August 11.—Mutual and Eureka, at Hoboken; 13 to 7; won by Mutual.
August 24.—Mutual and Eagle; 25 to 12; won by Mutual.
Spt. 4—Mutual and Star; 32 to 19; won by Mutual.
Spt. 10.—Mutual and Atlantic; 11 to 15; won by Atlantic.
Sept. 17.-Mutual and Star, at Hoboken; 23 to 12; won by Mutual.
Sept. 24.—Mutual and Atlantic; Atlantic 42 to 18; won by Mutual.
Oct. 6.—Mutual and Eckford; 10 to 18 ; won by Eckford.

OFFICERS FOR 1863; President, Anson B. Taylor; Vice-President, Edwin Brown; Secretary, James McConnell; Treasurer, Phineas Smith.

June 20, 1864.—Mutual and Newark; 19 to 18; won by Mutual.
June 27.—Mutual and Atlantic; 26 to 16; won by Mutual.
July 14.—Mutual and Eagle; 39 to 8, won by Mutual.
August 12.—Mutual and Gotham; 23 to 7; won by Mutual.
August 26.—Mutual and Active; 22 to 3, won by Mutual.
Sept.24.—Mutual and Active; 48 to 8; won by Mutual.
Oct. 3.—Mutual and Gotham,; 12 to 10; won by Mutual.

Oct. 10.—Mutual and Eagle; 23 to 19; won by Mutual.

OFFICERS FOR 1864: President, Anson B. Taylor; Vice-President, Edwin Brown; Secretary, William H., Dongan; Treasurer, Henry T. Clark.

June 28, 1865.—Mutual and Empire; 12 to 5; won by Mutual.
July 11.—Mutual and Gotham; 27 to 4; won by Mutual.
July 20.—Mutual and Empire; 26 to 15; won by Mutual.
August 4.—Mutual and Active; 22 to 21; won by Mutual.
August 22.—Mutual and Gotham; 18 to 12; won by Mutual.
August 25.—Mutual and Eckford; 19 to 10; won by Mutual.
October 3.—Mutual and Gotham; 12 to 10; won by Mutual.
October 30.—Mutual and Eagle; 18 to 7; won by Mutual.

OFFICERS FOR 1865.—President, John Wildey; Vice-President, James O'Neill; Secretary, William H. Dongan; Treasurer, Henry T. Clark.

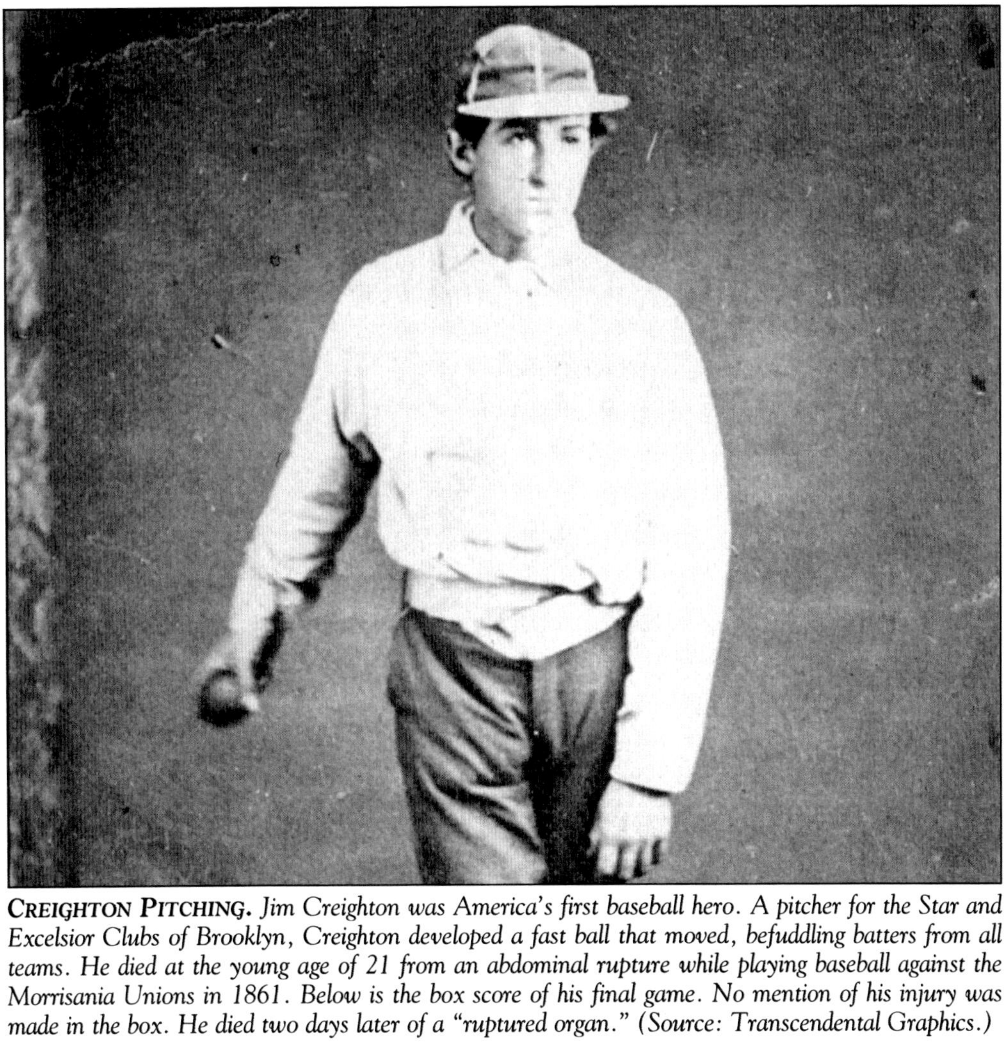

CREIGHTON PITCHING. *Jim Creighton was America's first baseball hero. A pitcher for the Star and Excelsior Clubs of Brooklyn, Creighton developed a fast ball that moved, befuddling batters from all teams. He died at the young age of 21 from an abdominal rupture while playing baseball against the Morrisania Unions in 1861. Below is the box score of his final game. No mention of his injury was made in the box. He died two days later of a "ruptured organ." (Source: Transcendental Graphics.)*

June 20, 1866.—Mutual and Union, at Morrisania; 25 to 23, in favor of Mutual.
June 28.—Mutual and Eureka; 24 to 13; won by Mutual.
July 12.—Mutual and Active, 23 to 16; won by Mutual.
August 9.—Mutual and Union, of Lansingburgh; 15 to 13; won by Union.
August 14.—Mutual and Excelsior; 32 to 13; won by Mutual.
August 21.—Mutual and Star; 45 to 16, in favor of Mutual.
August 25.—Mutual and Harlem; 34 to 20; won by Mutual.
August 28.—Mutual and Union, at Lansingburgh; 32 to 18, in favor of Union.
Spt.6.—Mutal and Harlem, at Hoboken; 40 to 1; won by Mutual.
Spt. 13.—Mutual and Atlantic; 15 to 17; won by Atlantic.
October 11.—Mutual and Eckford; 18 to 10; won by Mutual.
October 18.—Mutual and Atlantic 34 to 24; won by Atlantic.
October 22.—Mutual and Excelsior, at Hoboken. 23 to 6, in favor of Mutual.

OFFICERS FOR 1866: President, John Wildey; Vice-President, Robert Lindsay; Secretary, William H. Dongan; Treasurer, Warren Davids.

The Mutual Club ranks as the most popular and strongest club in the City of New York. For a long period they have taken the lead of all the New York clubs, and have only yielded trophies to the Atlantics of all the Association clubs they have played for the last four or five years. Their nine this season included Jewett, Martin—the most effective medium pitcher in the United States—Goldie, Hatfield, Waterman, R. Hunt, Zeller, Paterson, and Reed. Among their trophies during 1866 were those from the Excelsior, Union, Eureka, Eckford, Star, Active, Empire, Eagle and Gotham Clubs, of Brooklyn, New York, Newark, etc. The largest assemblages gathered at any contest at Hoboken, during each season, have been those present at the Mutual matches.

JEFFERSON CLUB

The Jefferson Base Ball Club, of New York, was organized on the 2d of August, 1858, with the following officers: President, George Starr; Vice-President, Charles Hedden; Secretary, William Rankin; Treasure, John Devoe. On Monday, October 4, 1858, they played their first game, their opponents being the Manhattan Base Ball Club. The game was played on the grounds of the Manhattan at Hamilton Square. Five innings only were played, the result being a decided victory for the Jefferson, by a score of 26 to 16 runs. The following players composed the Jefferson's nine: Van Kleek, catcher; McKever, pitcher; Bradford, second base; Springsteen, third base; Davis, first base; Paul, left field; Brewster, centre field; Simpson, short stop; Scorer, Benjamin F. Okie; Umpire, Samuel Yates, of the Eagle Club. On Friday, October 15, the return game was played on the Jefferson ground, at Hoboken, the result being in favor of Manhattan, by a score of 32 to 11, in a game of seven innings. Umpire, John Goldie, of the Metropolitan Club.

June 15, 1859.—Jefferson and Hoboken, at Hoboken; 8 innings. Score, 49 to 15, in favor of the Hoboken Club. Umpire, Samuel Yates.

August 8.— Jefferson and Monument at Hoboken. Won by the Jefferson, by a score of 31 to 20. Scorers, Abraham Devoe and Isaac L. Lent. Umpire, M.A. Curtis, of Gotham Club.

August 11.— Jefferson and Lexington, at Hoboken. Jefferson, 10 runs; Lexington, 27 runs. Scorers, Devoe and Myers. Umpire, William R. Harrison, of Hoboken Club.

August 16.—Jefferson and Yorkville, on the ground of the latter at Eighty-first street and Second avenue. Yorkville, 37 runs; Jefferson, 28 runs. Scorers, Devoe and Lynch, Umpire, Holden, of Baltic Club.

September 20.—Jefferson and Monument, on the ground of the latter. Game suspended after two innings had been played, in consequence of the rain. Score, 6 to 4, in favor of the Monument.

September 27.— Jefferson and Ashland, at Hoboken; 7 innings. Won by the Jefferson,, by a score of 29 to 11. Umpire, H. Josephs, of the St., Nicholas Club.

October 4.—Jefferson and Monument, at Yorkville. Jefferson, 36, Monument 8, 8 innings. Scorers, Devoe and Downing. Umpire, J. Ross Postley, of the Metropolitan Club.

June 28,1860.—Jefferson and Lexington, at Hoboken, 7 innings. Won by Jefferson. Score, 30 to 21. Umpire, M.A. Curtis, of Gotham Club.

July 24.—Jefferson and Gotham, at Hoboken, 9 innings. Score, 13 to 13, tie game. Umpire, J. Beard, of the Mutual Club.

August 16.—Jefferson and Champion, at Hoboken. Score, Jefferson, 12 runs; Champion, 14 runs.

October 8.—Jefferson and Gotham, return game, at Hoboken, 6 innings. Score, 22 to 3, in favor of the Gotham. Umpire, A B. Taylor, of the Mutual Club.

October 15.—Jefferson and Alpine, at Hoboken. 6 innings. Score, 30 to 11. Umpire, James McConnell, of the Mutual Club.

During the season of 1861, The Jefferson won games from the Henry Eckford, September 16; from the Empire, September 20; from the Eagle, September 21, and one from the Alpine Club. They were defeated by the Mutuals, August 19, at Hoboken, by a score of 32 to 12.

September 2.—Jefferson and Henry Eckford, at Hoboken. Henry Eckford won by a score of 31 to 27.

July 3, 1862.—Jefferson and Union (of Morrisania). Score, 42 to 15 runs, in favor of the Jefferson.

July 17.—Jefferson and Alpine, at Hoboken. Score, 45 to 10 runs, in favor of the Jefferson.

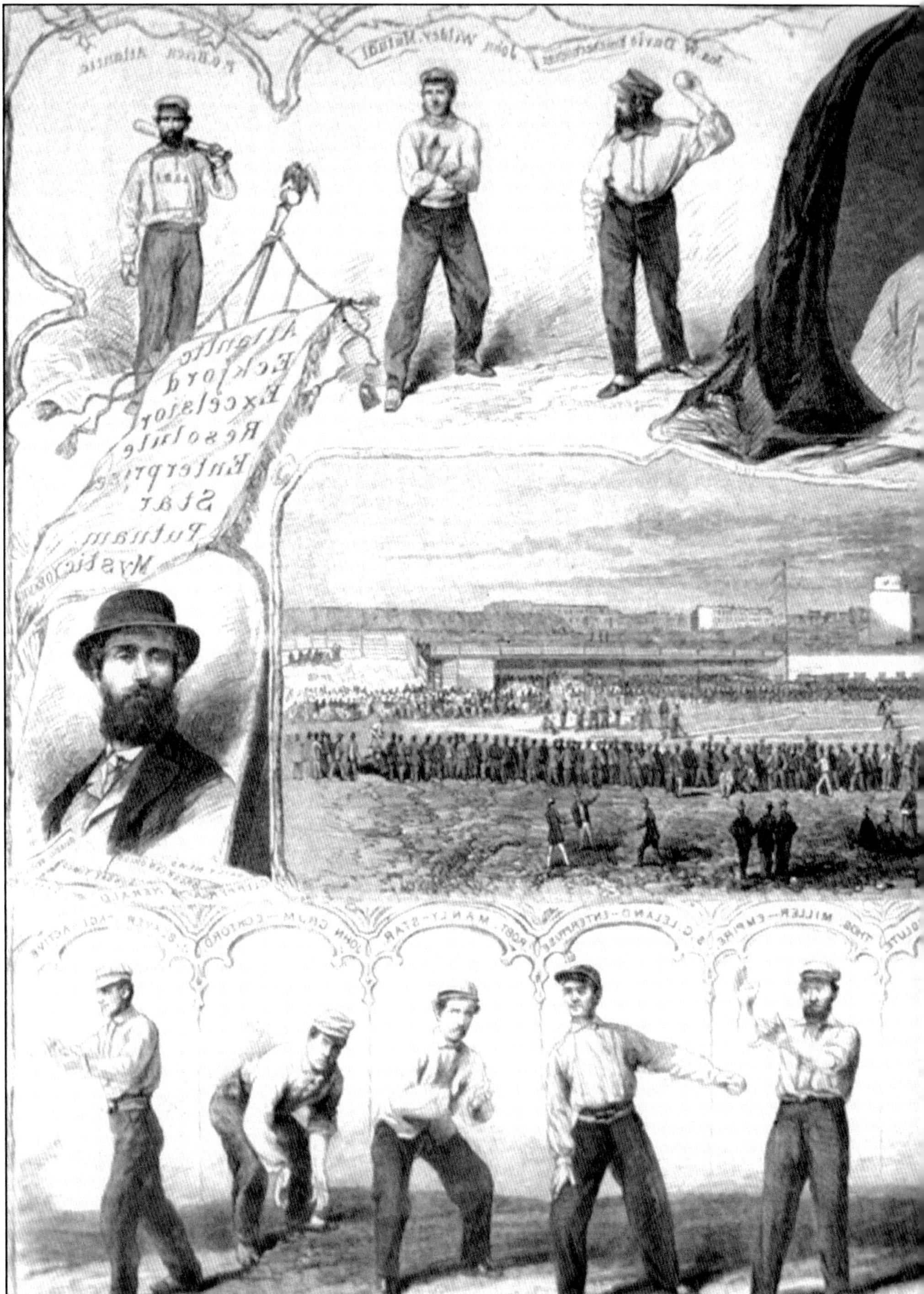

CREIGHTON PLUS STARS, LESLIE PRINT. *These two pages are graced by a Frank Leslies Pictorial Newspaper print, featuring baseball stars from all the teams in and around New York City just after the season of 1865. That is Jim Creighton, once again, under the shroud in the print's central point. The ballpark in the middle of the print appears to be the Excelsior Grounds or Union Grounds in South*

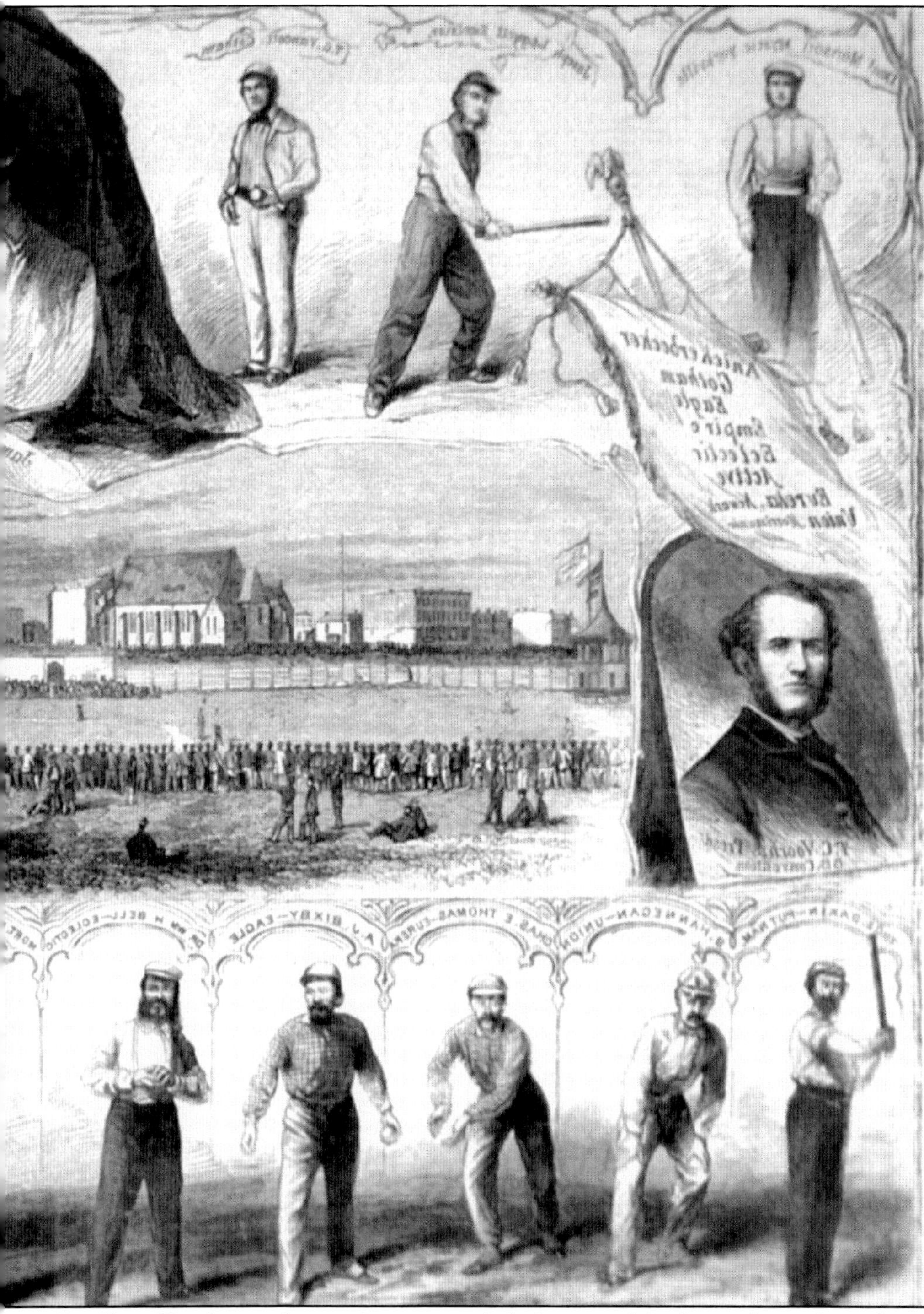

Brooklyn. The players adorning the picture include the stars of the days and a good sampling of the uniforms of the era (1865). Take a good, close look at the subtle difference in styles of hats and shirts. (Source: Transcendental Graphics.)

Soon after this a large number of the Jefferson Club enlisted in the Union Army, and the organization was virtually suspended until the autumn of 1865, when the club was reorganized, but too late to participate in any games until 1866, of which we append the summary:

Reorganized August 12, 1865, with the following officers: President, Leonard Springsteen; Vice-Present, Charles Paul; Secretary, Charles Merritt; Treasurer, William M. Richardson; Director, Henry L. Davis, P. Murray, M.J. Foly; Directors to Convention, Leonard Springsteen, William M. Richardson.

OFFICERS FOR 1866.—President, Henry L. Davis; Vice-President, Charles McDade; Secretary, Charles F. Merritt; Treasurer, William M. Richardson; Directors, Henry L. Davis, P. Murray, Peter Lynch.

August 16, 1866.—Jefferson and Social, at Harlem. Victory for the Jefferson, 44 to 27.
August 30.—Jefferson and Social, return game, at Hoboken. Won by the Jefferson, 46 to 25.
September 10.—Jefferson and Empire, at Hoboken. Defeat for the Jefferson, 21 to 31.
September 25.—Jefferson and Gotham, Won by the Jefferson, 21 to 20.

Number of members, fifty; grounds, Elysian Fields, Hoboken; practice-days, Mondays and Thursdays. Uniform: white cap, white flannel shirt, dark blue pants, regular made ball-shoes. First nine, Murray, pitcher; Paul, catcher; Davis, first base; E. Hedden, second base; Delany, third base; McGorman, short stop; Braisted, left-fielder; Lent, centre-fielder; Hegeman, right-fielder.

SOCIAL CLUB

The Social Base Ball Club, of New York, was organized September 8, 1859, with the following board of officers: President, M.T. Durgin; Vice-President, Nathaniel Buckley; Secretary, Benjamin Neilson; Treasurer, W.H. Withey.

OFFICER FOR 1860.—President, Geo. W. Holmes; Vice-President, Peter Doyle; Secretary, Benjamin Neilson; Treasurer, W. H. Withey.

OFFICERS FOR 1861.—President, Mr. Chichester; Vice-President, Benjamin Neilson; Secretary, M. Everiss; Treasurer, Wm. H. Withey.

Location of ground, 1859, 1860.—Red House, Harlem. 1861, Brooklyn, E.D. number of members, 38.

Social and Waverly, at Greenpoint, L.I., October, 12 1859. Won by Social. Score, 49 to 18.
Social and Baltic, June 17, 1860. 21 to 25. Red House.
Social and Henry Eckford, July 24, 1860. 14 to 38. Greenpoint.
Social and Malta, July 31, 1860. 30 to 35. Red House.
Social and Independent, October 3, 1860. 33 to 3. Red House.

The Social Club was organized October 18, 1865, with the following officers; President, Ignatius Flynn; Vice-President, R. J. Byrnes; Recording Secretary, P. Devitt; Corresponding Secretary, John J. Foster; Treasurer, D. C. Layman.

The Socials played the following games during 1866:

July 28.— Social and Americus, at Newark, N.J. Score, 21 to 28.
August 16.—Social and Jefferson, at Hoboken. Score, 27 to 44.
August 24.— Social and Eclectic, at Hoboken. Social won. Score, 27 to 23.
August 30.—Social and Jefferson, at Hoboken. Score, 25 to 46.
September 5.— Social and Americus, at Hoboken. Score, 20 to 28.
October 24.— Social and Eclectic, at Hoboken, return game. Social, 14; Eclectic, 16; seven innings.

Location of play-ground and club-room, at the Elysian Fields, Hoboken. Number of members, active and honorary, seventy. Uniform: blue flannel pants, white shirt trimmed with blue, and white cap.

ECLECTIC CLUB

The Eclectic Base Ball Club, of New York, was organized November 17, 1864, and was represented in the Convention of December 14, 1864, by Dr. W.H. Bell and M.H. Wright.

Their play-days are Tuesday and Friday afternoons, at the Elysian Fields, Hoboken, N.J. The uniform of the Club consists of dark blue flannel pants; white flannel shirts, with blue trimmings; red belt, and white cap (with blue star). Number of members in the club, 76 , of which 40 are active members. The officers for 1866 are as follows, viz.: President, Doctor William H. Bell; Vice-President, Samuel M. Barr; Secretary, M. Engle; Treasurer, Col. William H. Lynch; Scorer, Alfred H. M. Wright; Delegates, Dr. W.H. Bell and M.T. Humphrey; Directors, M. H. Wright, W. Bell, and M.T. Humphrey; Directors, M. H. Wright, W. Bell, and M .T. Humphrey. The club, since its organization, has played 23 matches—of which they have won 9, lost 13, and one game was a tie. Thirty-five different men have played, the club never playing the same nine twice. The following are the results:

September 20, 1865.— Eclectic and Americus, at Newark, N.J. Eclectic, 45; Americus, 6.

October 4.—Eclectic and Mystic, at Red House, N.Y. Eclectic, 23; Mystic, 25.

October 12.—Eclectic and Americus, return game, at Hoboken, N.J. Eclectic, 18; Americus, 11; eight innings.

October 17.—Eclectic and Mystic, return game, at Hoboken, N.J. Eclectic, 35; Mystic, 21; six innings.

October 20.—Eclectic and Knickerbocker, at Hoboken, N. J. Eclectic, 31; Knickerbocker, 31; seven innings.

June 5, 1866.—Eclectic and Americus, at Hoboken, N.J. Eclectic, 40; Americus, 11.

June 20.—Eclectic and Irvington, at Irvington, N.J. Eclectic, 18; Irvington, 57.

July 4.—Eclectic and Hudson River, of Newburgh, at Matteawan, N.Y. Eclectic, 14; Hudson River, 26.

July 10.— Eclectic and Gotham, at Hoboken. Eclectic, 12; Gotham, 20.

July 25.—Eclectic and Una, of Mt. Vernon, at Hoboken. Eclectic, 25; Una, 23; seven innings.

August 15.—Eclectic and Harlem, at Harlem. Eclectic, 19; Harlem, 21.

August 20.—Eclectic and Olympic, of Paterson, at Paterson. Eclectic, 9; Olympic, 21.

August 24.—Eclectic and Social, at Hoboken. Eclectic, 23; Social, 27; eight innings.

September 4.—Eclectic and Enterprise, at Hoboken. Eclectic, 12; Enterprise, 24.

September 19.—Eclectic and Americus, return game, at Newark. Eclectic, 20; Americus , 28; eight innings.

October 3.—Eclectic and Una, of Mt. Vernon, return game, at Mount Vernon. Eclectic, 8; Una, 37; six innings.

October 11.—Eclectic and Mohawk, at South Brooklyn. Eclectic, 25; Mohawk, 27; six innings.

October 20.—Eclectic and Enterprise, return game, at Capitoline grounds, Brooklyn. Eclectic, 18; Enterprise, 31; six innings.

October 24.— Eclectic and Social, return game, at Hoboken. Eclectic, 16; Social, 14; seven innings.

October 26.—Eclectic and Una, of Mt. Vernon, home-and-home, at Morrisania. Eclectic, 29; Una, 21; five innings.

November 2.—Eclectic and Mohawk, return game, at Hoboken. Eclectic, 24; Mohawk, 22; seven innings.

November 13.—Eclectic and Mohawk, home-and-home game, at Capitoline grounds, Brooklyn. Eclectic, 24; Mohawk, 56; seven innings.

November 17.—Eclectic and Americus, home-and-home game, at Hoboken. Eclectic, 25;

Americus, 17; seven innings.

The Eclectic Club was originated by Dr. Bell, its worthy President, who was formerly connected with the Eckford and Henry Eckford Clubs. Dr. Bell has always taken an enthusiastic part in promoting the prospects of our national game in this vicinity, and is deservedly popular with the base ball fraternity of the country.

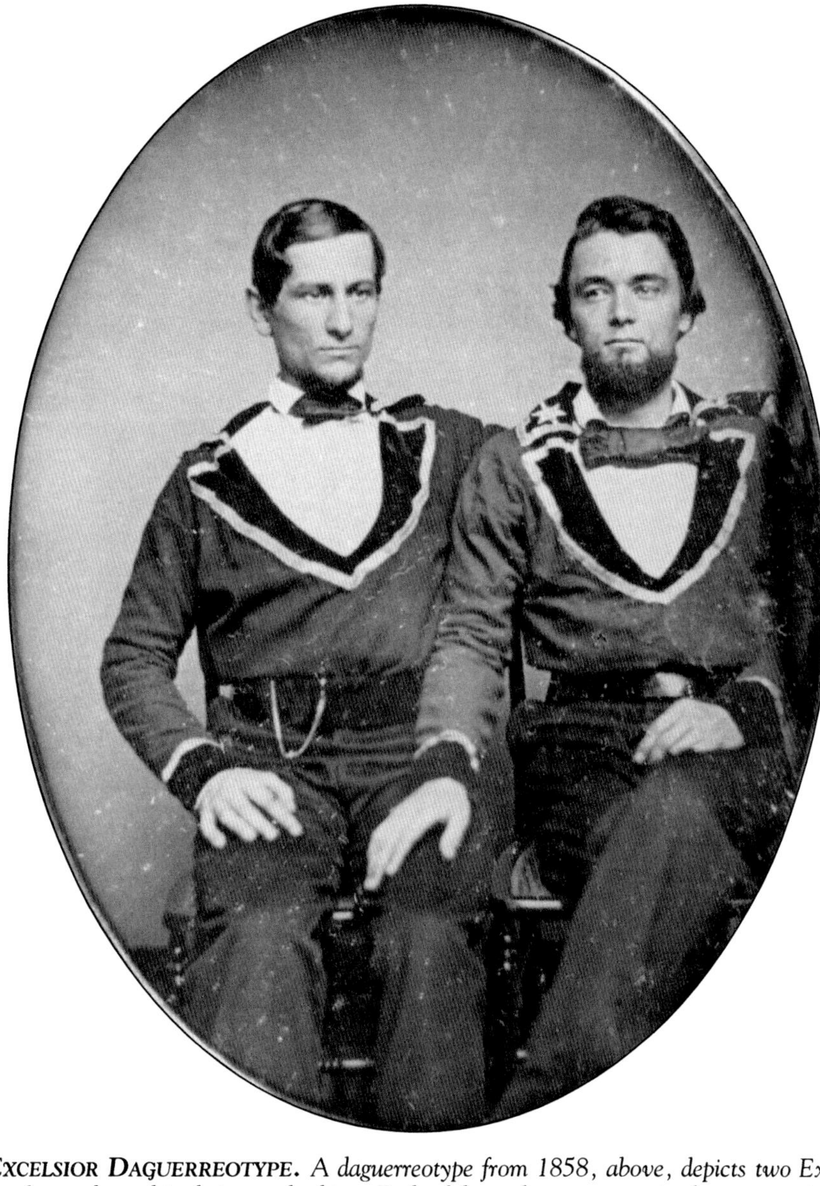

1858 EXCELSIOR DAGUERREOTYPE. *A daguerreotype from 1858, above, depicts two Excelsior of Brooklyn players dressed in their parade shirts. Both of these players appear in the panoramic photo on Pages 20 and 21, A.T. Pearsall (left) with Holder at his side. They would discard these shirts on the field of play for greater mobility. (Source: Transcendental Graphics.)*

SPARTA CLUB

The Sparta Base Ball Club, of New York, was organized in 1864. The officers are: John J. Worden, President; William Bogert, Vice-President; James A. Harriott, Recording Secretary; James Hart, Corresponding Secretary; C. Loucks, Treasurer. Playing-ground, head of Erie street, Jersey City; practice-days, Mondays and Thursdays. Uniform: white cap, blue binding; white shirt, blue binding, "S" on breast in old English; white belt, with name Sparta on it. The Club is composed of forty-four active members, and one honorary member. The Club has confined itself principally to recreation games, but in 1866 they engaged in the annexed games:

August 16.—Sparta and Olympic. Score in favor of Olympic, by 23 to 14.

Early in September they played with the Neptune Club at Shrewsbury, N.J. Five innings; tie game; score, 15 to 15.

September 21.—Return game with the Neptune, at Jersey City; score, 20 to 8, in favor of the Sparta.

On the 5th of October, the home-and-home game between the Neptune and Sparta was played at Hoboken; won by the Sparta, by 47 to 29.

M.M. VAN DYKE CLUB

The M. M. Van Dyke Base Ball Club, of New York, was organized August 6, 1865, with Wm. M. Brinley, President; James Grady, Vice-President; John Davis, Secretary, and Sidney. B. Van Dyke, Treasurer; James Grady and Wm. Bates, Delegates to the Convention. The Club entered the Convention, December, 1865. The officers for the year 1866 are : Wm. M. Brinley, President: James Grady, Vice-President; John H. Ackerman, Recording Secretary; Sidney B. Van Dyke, Corresponding Secretary; Wm. Bates and James Grady, Delegates to the Convention.

August 1, 1866.—Fulton Market and M.M. Van Dyke, on Satellite Cricket ground, Brooklyn; score, in favor of Fulton Market, by 43 to 30.

August 15, 1866.—M.M. Van Dyke and Constellation, on Union grounds; Van Dyke won the game, by a score of 71 to 23.

Sept. 1, 1866.—M.M. Van Dyke and Fulton Market, on Union grounds. The Fulton Market victors, by a score of 37 to 35.

Sept. 5, 1866.—M.M. Van Dyke and Oriental, on the Oriental grounds, at Greenpoint; the Van Dyke winning by a score of 36 to 27.

Sept. 18, 1866.—M.M. Van Dyke and Oriental, on Union ground; score, M.M. Van Dyke, 28; Oriental, 23.

M.M. Van Dyke and Olympic, at Paterson, N.J.; Olympics victors, by a score of 58 to 43.

Oct..17, 1866.—M. M. Van Dyke and Constellation, on Union grounds; score, in favor of the Van Dyke, 43 to 38.

Oct. 19, 1866.—M.M. Van Dyke and Eckford, on Union grounds; the Eckfords winning, by a score of 59 to 12.

Practice ground, Union Base Ball ground, Brooklyn, E.D. Uniform: white flannel shirt, gray flannel pants, and white cap. The M.M. Van Dyke Club numbers sixty active members, and about fifty honorary members.

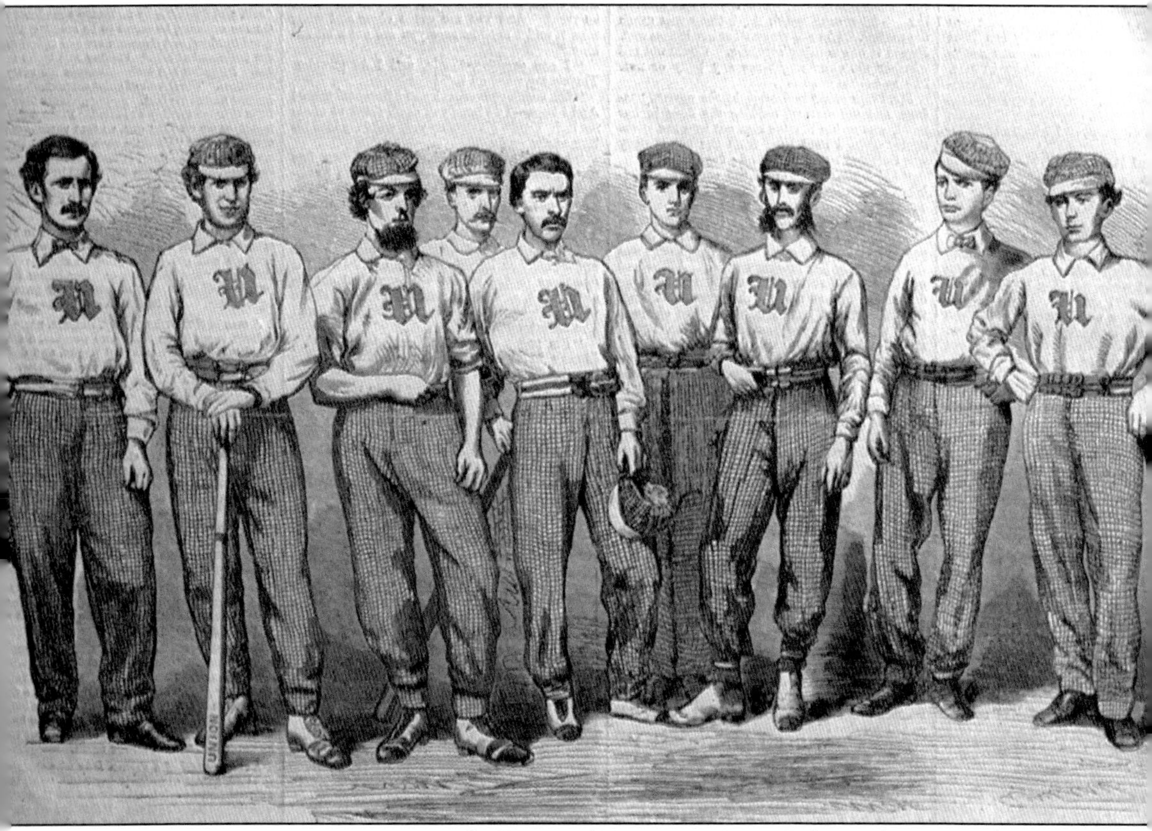

UNIONS OF MORRISANIA. *In 1866, the Unions of Morrisania, New York, in what is now the Bronx, took the championship of America after defeating the top clubs from around the Northeast in best two-of-three championship contests. Their image comes from a* Harper's Weekly *newspaper woodcut. The Morrisania's record for the 1866 season was 25-3, their only losses coming to the powerful teams of the New York Mutuals, Philadelphia Athletics, and Brooklyn Excelsiors. George Wright played in nine games for the Unions that season. George Smith, Al Martin, and Dan Ketchum were the leading ballists on this club. (Source: Transcendental Graphics.)*

UNION CLUB

The Union Base Ball Club, of Morrisania, Westchester county, N.Y., was organized July 17, 1855, with President, Thomas E. Sutton. The club has had but four presidents, including the present incumbent, Mr. Albro. Mr. David Milliken followed Mr. Sutton; Mr. William Herring was President in 1865. Subjoined will be found a summary of the Union's games since their organization:

October 25, 1855.—Union and Young America. Won by the Union, by a score of 25 to 8.
July 31, 1856.—Union and Baltic. Won by the Union, by a score of 23 to 17.
August 27.—Union and Baltic. Score, 15 to 12, in favor of the Union Club.
September 17.—Union and Eckford. The latter won by a score of 22 to 8.
September 25.—Union and Baltic. Won by the Union, by a score of 25 to 11.
October 15.—Union and Eckford. The Union lost by a score of 6 to 22.
August 3, 1857.—Union and Harlem. Won by the Union, whose score was 22 to 21.
September 8.—Union and Harlem. The score was 25 to 14, in favor of the Harlem Club.
September 16.—Union and Excelsior. Won by the Union, by a score of 30 to 8.
September 25.—Union and Adriatic.—The latter was defeated by a score of 28 to 11.
September 28.—Union and Excelsior.—The Excelsior won by a score of 41 to 23.
July 22, 1858.—Union and Excelsior.—The Union lost the game; score, 30 to 18, in favor of the Excelsior.
August 5.—Union and Adriatic. Won by the Union, whose score was 33 to 16.
September 27, 1859.—Union and Atlantic. Won by the Atlantic, by a score of 39 to 5.
October 5.—Union and Excelsior. The Union victors by a score of 19 to 15.
October 7.—Union and Putnam. Result in favor of the Union; score, 23 to 22.
October 14.—Union and Empire. Won by the latter, by a score of 26 to 8.
October 25.—Union and Excelsior. The Union defeated; score, 13 to 3.
May 23, 1860.—Union and Eckford.—The latter won by a score of 22 to 19.
June 8.—Union and Atlantic.—Union score, 4 runs; Atlantic score, 15 runs.
June 26.—Unions and Eagle. The latter won by a score of 26 to 15.
July 17.—Union and Putnam.. Union score, 12 runs. Putnam score, 18 runs.
August.—Unions and Adriatic. Won by the Union, by a score of 17 to 8.
September 7.—Unions and Excelsior.—Union score, 4 runs; Excelsior score, 4 runs.
September 15.—Union and Putnam. Score, 12 runs for the Putnam, to 6 runs for the Union.
September 19.—Unions and Eckford. Won by the latter, by a score of 41 to 5.
October 12.—Unions and Independent. Result, a victory for the Union Club, by a score of 20 to 9.
October 27.—Union and Constellation. The latter score 4 runs to the Union's 36 runs.
August 24, 1861.—Union and Constellation. Union score, 21 runs; Constellation score, 7 runs.
October 1.—Union and Henry Eckford. Score, 25 to 10, in favor of the Union.
October 15.—Union and Henry Eckford. Won by the latter by a score of 32 to 19.
October 29, 1861.—Union and Eagle. Union score, 33 runs; Eagle score, 18 runs.
July 10, 1862.—Eagle and Henry Eckford; score, 26 to 10, in favor of the Union.
July 18, 1862.—Union and Harlem; Union won by a score of 23 to 13.
July 26, 1862.—Union and Excelsior; score, 12 to 4, in favor of the Union Club.
August 2, 1862.—Union and Newark. The Newark Club lost by a score of 11 to 12.

The Union Club played more games with Association clubs than any other club during 1865. They obtained creditable victories over such strong Clubs as the Eckford, Active, Star, Keystone, Camden, and Olympic; and also Newark, Hudson River, Mystic, and Pioneer Clubs. Their worst defeats were sustained at the hands of the Atlantic, Athletic, Eureka, and

Excelsior Clubs; the Actives also won two balls from them.

June 14, 1865.—Unions and Athletic, at Morrisania; score, 21 to 31; 9 innings; time, 3.25.
June 21.—Unions and Eckford, at Morrisania; score, 27 to 18; 9 innings; time, 3.15.
June 30.—Unions and Pioneer, at Newark; score, 18 to 13; 9 innings; time, 2.30.
July 4.—Union and Active, at Morrisania; score, 25 to 16; 9 innings; time, 2.25.
July 8.—Union and Eureka, at Newark; score, 5 to 30; 9 innings, time, 2.25.
July 15.—Union and Excelsior, at Morrisania; score, 14 to 43; 9 innings; time, 2.35.
July 24.—Union and Atlantic, at Morrisania; score, 5 to 15; 9 innings; time, 3 hours.
July 28.—Union and Newark, at Newark; score, 30 to 8; 9 innings; time, 3 hours.
August 2.—Union and Camden, at Philadelphia. Camden, 5 runs; Union, 31 runs.
August 3.—Union and Athletic, at Philadelphia; score, 13 to 26; 9 innings; time, 3.10.
August 5.—Union and Keystone, at Philadelphia; score, 24 to 7; 5 innings; time, 1.05.
August 10.—Unions and Eckford, at Brooklyn; score, 34 to 22; 9 innings; time, 3 hours.
August 19.—Union and Active, at Hoboken; score, 12 to 22; time, 2.20.
September 1.—Union and Newark, at Morrisania; score, 18 to 17; 9 innings; time, 2.10.
September 7.—Union and Eureka, at Morrisania; score, 10 to 30; 9 innings; time, 2.30.
September 13.—Union and Mystic, at Morrisania; score, 54 to 9; 9 innings; time, 3 hours.
September 15.—Unions and Excelsior, at Bedford; score, 34 to 35; 9 innings; time, 2.35.
September 23.—Unions and Active, on the St. George's Cricket grounds, at Hoboken; score, 10 to 32; 9 innings.
September 25.—Union and Star, at Morrisania; score, 37 to 12; 6 innings; time, 2.30.
October 5.—Union and Atlantic, at Bedford; score, 30 to 58; 8 innings; time, 3.15.
October 11.—Union and Mystic, at Red House grounds; score, 55 to 19; 9 innings.
October 14.—Union and Star, at South Brooklyn; score, 57 to 21; 8 innings; time, 2.30.
November 10.—Union and Hudson River, at Newburgh; score, 21 to 13; 9 innings; time, 2.10.
Union and Pioneer, of Newark, N. J., return game; won by the Union by a score of 31 to 9.
May 24, 1866.—Unions and Surprise, at Morrisania; won by the Union by a score of 31 to 9.
June 6.—Union and Eckford, at Union grounds, Brooklyn; score, 15 to 11; in favor of the Union.
June 9.—Unions and Active, at Morrisania; won by the Union by a score of 56 to 13.
June 12.—Union and Eureka, at Morrisania; Union, 28 runs; Eureka, 26 runs.
June 16.—Union and Enterprise, at Morrisania; score, 42 to 16, in favor of the Union.
June 20.—Unions and Mutual, at Morrisania. Mutual won by a score of 25 to 23.
June 26.—Union and Athletic of Philadelphia, at Morrisania; Union score, 20 runs; Athletic score 33 runs.
July 4.—Union and National of Washington, D.C., at Morrisania; score, 22 to 8, in favor of Union; time, 2.20. Umpire, T.S. Dakin, of the Excelsior Club.
July 17.—Unions and Gotham, at Morrisania; won by the Union by a score of 52 to 25.
July 19.—Unions and Excelsior, at Morrisania; score, 20 to 15, in favor of the Union; time, 2.40.
July 24.—Union and Uncas, at William's Park, Norwich, Connecticut; Uncas score 1 run; Union score, 51 runs.
July 25.—Union and Chester, at Norwich, Connecticut; won by the Union by a score of 45 to 25.
July 25.—Unions and Chester, at Norwich, Connecticut; second nines. Won by Union; score, 43 to 22.
July 26.—Union and Charter Oak, at Hartford, Conn.; Union score, 32 runs; Chester Oak score, 20 runs.
August 16.—Union and National of Albany, N.Y., at Morrisania. Union score, 53 runs; National score, 18 runs; time, 2.45.
August 22.—Union and Surprise, at West Farms. Union won by a score of 46 to 9; 8 innings.

September 18.—Union and Eureka, at Newark, N.J.; Union score, 25 runs; Eureka score, 23 runs; time, 2.40.

October 5.—Union and Picked Nine, on the St. George Cricket-ground, Hoboken. Union, 15 runs; Picked Nine, 22 runs; time of game, 2.30.

October 6.—Union and Enterprise of Brooklyn, on the grounds of the latter; score, 43 to 6, in favor of the Union; 8 innings; time, 2.15.

October 18.—Unions and Eckford, at Morrisania; won by the Union; score, 20 to 9; 5 innings.

October 27.—Union and Athletic of Philadelphia, on the grounds of the latter; won by the Union by a score of 42 to 29; 8 innings; time, 3.35. Umpire, C. Anspach, of the Olympic Club.

October 20.—Union and Hudson River of Newburgh, at Morrisania. Union score, 43 runs; Hudson River score, 4 runs; time, 2.05.

October 22.—Union and Oriental, at Greenpoint, L.I.; score, 24 to 5, in favor of the Union; 8 innings.

November 3.—Union and Excelsior, on Union ball grounds, Brooklyn; Excelsior score, 14 runs; Union score, 43 runs; time, 2.45.

November 7.—Union and Excelsior, on Union ball grounds, Brooklyn; Excelsior score, 14 runs; Union score, 43 runs; time, 2.45.

The Union Club's ground and club-room is at Melrose Station, Morrisania. They now number about one hundred active, and twenty-five honorary members. Their uniform is blue cap and pants, trimmed with red; white shirt, trimmed with blue; tri-colored web belt. The officers of the Club for 1866 are: President, George A. Albro; Vice-President, W.F. Hudson: Secretary, Charles N. Swift; Game-keeper, William Anner.

EXCELSIOR CLUB.*

* For this full and complete history of the Excelsior Club we are indebted to Van Brunt Wyckoff, Esq., a gentleman who has been connected with that crack organization for many years.

The Excelsior Base Ball Club, of Brooklyn, was organized December 8, 1854.

While witnessing a game played November 10 or 17, 1854, between the Knickerbockers and Eagles, it occurred to John H. Suydam and several others, to "get up" a Base Ball Club, and accordingly on Thanksgiving Day in November of that year they met for practice, but under no especial organization. They styled themselves the "J.Y.B.B.B.C's" (Jolly Young Bachelors' Base Ball Club). Soon after, Committees on Constitution and By-Laws, and on Grounds, were formed; and December 8, 1854, a formal meeting was held at Florence's Hotel, New York, when the report of the Committee on Constitution and By-Laws was read and adopted, and the name of "Excelsior" was proposed by Charles C. Suydam, and adopted; and those present, nineteen in number, proceeded to the election of officers, with the following result: Jeremiah Nelson Tappan, President; Elisha Bacon, Vice-President; Frederick G. Eldridge, Secretary; Jonathan O. Bartholomew, Treasurer; John H. Suydam, George T. Dalton, Robert J. Hubbard, Directors.

Officers elected April 17, 1855: Jeremiah O. Bartholomew, President; Peter Van Schaack, Vice-President; J. Le Baron Willard, Secretary; P. Remsen Chadwick, Treasurer.

Officers elected April 5, 1856: James W. Andrews, president; John J. McLaren, Vice-President; Charles W. Thomas, Secretary; P. Remsen Chadwick, treasurer.

Officers elected April 1, 1857: P. Remsen Chadwick, President; Frederick S. Well, Vice-President; G. Henry Howell, Secretary; Henry M. Congdon, Treasurer. October 6, 1857. The Wayne Base Ball Club consolidated with the Excelsior Base Ball Club.

The following officers were elected November 12, 1857: Joseph Bainbridge Jones, President; Joseph Bowne Leggett, Vice-President; G. Henry Howell, Secretary, to January 5, 1858; James B. Bach, Secretary, from January 5, 1858; Richard Oliver, Treasurer, to April 6, 1858; William H. Young, Treasurer from April 6, 1858; Joseph Bainbridge Jones, * M.D., Joseph B. Leggett, and James B. Bach, Delegates to Convention, March 10, March 24, March 31, and April 7, 1858, when the "National Association of Base Ball Players" was organized.

Officers elected January 14, 1859.—Joseph Bainbridge Jones, M.D., President; Joseph B. Leggett, Vice-President; Gilbert Lawrence Haight, Secretary, to May 24, 1859; Wm. B. Kendall, Secretary, from May 24, 1859; Charles P. Gulick, Treasurer.

Officers elected January 3, 1860.—Joseph B. Jones, M.D., President; J. Bowne Leggett, Vice-President; Wm. B. Kendall, Secretary; Charles P. Gulick, Treasurer.

Officers elected December 12, 1860.—Joseph B. Jones, M.D., President; Joseph Ketchum, Jr., Vice-President; Charles L. Whiting, Secretary; Charles P. Gulick, Treasurer.

Officers elected January 17,1862.—Joseph B. Jones, M.D., President; Gilbert Lawrence Haight, Vice-President; William H. Holt, Secretary; Richard Oliver, Treasurer.

Officers elected March 12, 1863.—Joseph B. Jones M.D., President, to Sept.9, 1863; Joseph B. Leggett, President, from Sept. 9, 1863; Charles P. Gulick, Vice-President; Wm. H. Holt, Secretary; Charles J. Holt, Assistant Secretary; Van Brunt Wyckoff, Treasurer.

Officers elected March 10, 1864.—Joseph B. Leggett, President; Richard K. Cooke, Vice-President; Charles J. Holt, Secretary; Wm. H. Holt, Assistant Secretary: Van Brunt Wyckoff.

Officers elected March 9, 1865.—Richard K. Cooke, President Charles P. Gulick, Vice-President; Charles J. Holt, Secretary, to May 11, when, by the Constitution, he became Recording Secretary; William H.. Holt, Assistant Secretary, to May 11, when he became Financial Secretary; Van Brunt Wyckoff, Treasurer.

OFFICERS ELECTED March 8, 1866.—Joseph B. Jones, M.D., President; Richard

Oliver, Vice-President; Chas. J. Holt, Recording Secretary; William H. Holt, Financial Secretary; William W. Kelly, Treasurer.

* The title "National Association of Base Ball Players' was inserted in the Report of the Committee at the suggestion of Joseph B. Jones, M.D., President of The Excelsior Club.

EXCELSIOR AND PUTNAM GAMES

Oct. 8, 1856.—Played on Excelsior's ground, corner of Smith and Degraw streets. Excelsior, 16 runs; Putnam, 15 runs; six innings. Umpires, Wm. P. Dean, of Excelsior Club; Samuel Godwin, of Putnam Club. Referee, George A. Brown, of Knickerbocker Club.

October 25, 1856.—Played on Putnam's ground, between Lee and Bedford avenues, Ross and Hewes streets, E.D. (Wheat Hill.) Excelsior, 15 runs; Putnam, 21 runs. Referee, J. Drummond, of Knickerbocker Club.

July 14, 1857.—Excelsior's ground. Excelsior, 20 runs; Putnam, 37 runs; eight innings. Referee, Charles E. Place, of Eagle Club.

June 10, 1858.—Excelsior's ground. Excelsior, 18 runs; Putnam, 31 runs; nine innings. Umpire, James W. Davis, of Knickerbocker Club.

October 16,1858.—Putnam's ground. Excelsior, 15 runs; Putnam, 19 runs; 9 innings. Umpire, Norman M. Welling, of Knickerbocker Club.

October 22, 1859.—Excelsior's ground. Excelsior, 19 runs; Putnam, 17 runs; six innings. Umpire, Marvin E. Gelston, of Eagle Club.

August 4, 1860.—Putnam's ground. Excelsior, 23 runs; Putnam, 7 runs; nine innings. Umpire, Peter O'Brien, of Atlantic Club.

EXCELSIOR AND UNION GAMES.

September 16, 1857.—Union's ground, at Morrisania. Excelsior, 8 runs; Union, 30 runs; seven innings. Referee, Charles E. Place, of Eagle Club.

November 6, 1857.—Excelsior's ground. Excelsior, 41 runs; Union, 23 runs; eight innings. Referee, Thomas S. Dakin, of Putnam Club.

July 22, 1858.—Home-and-home game. Played on the Monumental's ground, at the Red House, Harlem. Excelsior, 30 runs; Union, 18 runs; nine innings. Umpire, E. McKinstry, of Putnam Club.

October 5, 1859.—Union's ground, at Morrisania. Excelsior, 15 runs; Union, 19 runs; nine innings. Umpire, Wm. H. Van Cott, of Gotham Club.

October 25, 1859.—Excelsior's ground. Excelsior, 13 runs; Union 3 runs; nine innings. Umpire, Thomas S. Dakin, Putnam Club; time of game, 2.05.

September 7, 1860.—Home-and-home game. Played on the Union's ground, at Morrisania. Excelsiors, 7 runs; Unions, 4 runs; nine innings. Umpire, John Van Horn, of Baltic Club; time of game, 2.23.

July 26, 1862.—Unions' ground, at Morrisania. Excelsior, 4 runs; Union, 12 runs; six innings. Umpire, Louis F. Wadsworth, of Gotham Club.

October 14, 1862.—Excelsior's ground, "foot of Court street," South Brooklyn. Excelsior, 13 runs; Union, 9 runs; six innings. This was the last game in which James Creighton played. He died Oct. 18, 1862, in the 22d year of his age.

August 15, 1863.—Home-and-home game, Excelsior's ground. Excelsiors, 9 runs; Unions, 20 runs; nine innings. Umpire, Richard J. Pearce, of Atlantic Club.

October 1, 1864.—Excelsior's ground. Excelsiors, 8 runs; Unions, 6 runs; nine innings. Umpire, David A. Sutton, of Enterprise; time of game, 1.30.

October 8, 1864.—On the Union's ground, at Morrisania. Excelsior, 33 runs; Union, 26; seven innings. Umpire, F. Stevens, of Harlem Club.

July 15, 1865.—At Morrisania. Excelsiors, 43 runs; Unions, 14 runs; nine innings. Umpire, Thomas S. Dakin, of Excelsior Club; time, 2.35.

September 15,1865.—Played on the Capitoline ground, at Bedford. Excelsiors, 35 runs; Unions, 34 runs; nine innings. Umpire, William Dick, of Enterprise Club; time of game, 3.20.

EXCELSIOR AND EAGLE GAMES

June 24, 1858.—Excelsior's ground. Excelsiors, 32 runs; Eagles, 13 runs; nine innings. Umpire, P. Sheridan, of Gotham Club.

September 28,1858.—Eagle's ground, at Hoboken. Excelsiors, 36 runs; Eagles, 25 runs; eight innings. Umpire, William H. Van Cott, of Gotham Club.

September 8, 1859.—Gotham's ground, Hoboken. Excelsior, 24 runs; Eagle, 20 runs; ten innings; tie on the ninth. Umpire, R.H. Thorn, of Empire Club.

October , 1863.—Gotham's ground, Hoboken. Excelsior, 5 runs; Eagle, 6 runs; nine innings. Umpire, J. Seaver Page, of Active Club; time of game, 1.55.

October 11, 1864.—Excelsior's ground. Excelsiors, 32 runs; Eagles, 22 runs; nine innings. Umpire, John Chapman, of Atlantic Club; time of game, 2.40.

Excelsior and Harlem.— August 5, 1858. Played on Harlem's ground, Mount Morris, One Hundred and Twenty-third street and Fifth avenue. Excelsior, 17 runs; Harlem, 17 runs; nine innings. Umpire, S. Clarke, of St. Nicholas Club.

EXCELSIOR AND KNICKERBOCKER GAMES.

July 8, 1858.—Excelsior's ground. Excelsiors, 31 runs; Knickerbockers, 13 runs; nine innings. Umpire, Samuel Yates, of Eagle Club.

August 20.—Gotham's ground, Hoboken. Excelsiors, 15 runs; Knickerbockers, 14 runs; nine innings. Umpire, William H. Van Cott, of Gotham Club.

June 30, 1859.—Knickerbocker's ground, Hoboken. Excelsiors, 26 runs; Knickerbockers, 22 runs; nine innings. Umpire, A. J. Bixby, of Eagle Club; time of game, 1.27.

August 2, 1859.—Excelsior's ground. Excelsiors, 20 runs; Knickerbockers, 5 runs; nine innings. Umpire, Peter O'Brien, of Atlantic Club; time of game, 1.50.

August 25, 1860.—Excelsior's ground. Excelsiors, 32 runs; Knickerbockers, 9 runs; nine innings. Umpire, C. A. Burtis, of Gotham Club.

A series of friendly games played between the "old friends" of the Clubs in the years 1863, 1864, and 1865, as follows:

September 3, 1863.—On Knick's ground, at Hoboken. Excelsior, 20 runs; Knickerbocker, 23 runs; nine innings.

September 22, 1863.—Excelsiors ground. Excelsior, 45 runs; Knickerbocker, 56 runs; eight innings.

October 12, 1863.—Knickerbocker's ground, at Hoboken. Excelsiors, 43 runs; Knickerbocker, 27 runs; nine innings.

July 21, 1864.—Excelsior's ground. Excelsiors, 85 runs; Knickerbockers, 39 runs; eight innings.

Sept.22, 1864.—Knickerbocker's ground, at Hoboken; Excelsiors, 48; Knickerbockers, 53; 9 innings.

July 6, 1865.—Knickerbocker's ground, at Hoboken; Excelsiors, 28; Knickerbockers, 20; 9 innings.

July 25, 1865.—Excelsior's ground, at Bedford, L.I.; Excelsiors, 60; Knickerbocker, 45; 9 innings.

Sept.21, 1865.—Knickerbocker's ground, at Hoboken; Excelsiors, 17; Knickerbockers, 22; 9 innings.

Two muffin games have taken place between the Excelsiors and Knickerbockers, which with the foregoing, constitute all the games played between these two clubs.

August 22, 1859.—Excelsior's ground; Excelsiors, 41; Knickerbockers, 37; 7 innings.
Sept. 12, 1859.—Knickerbocker's ground, at Hoboken; Excelsiors, 56; Knickerbocker's 47; 6 innings.

EXCELSIOR AND ATLANTIC

Nov. 9, 1858.—Excelsior's ground, between Smith, Hoyt, Carroll and President streets, near Carroll Park, South Brooklyn; Excelsiors, 10; Atlantics, 22; 9 innings; Umpire, Thomas S. Dakin, of Putnam Club.
Nov. 16, 1858.—Atlantic's ground, at Bedford; Excelsiors, 6; Atlantics, 27; 6 innings; Umpire, J. McCosker, of Gotham Club.
July 19,1860.—Excelsior's ground; Excelsior's, 23; Atlantics, 4; 9 innings; Umpire, William Barre, of Pastime Club.
August 9, 1860.—Atlantic's ground; Excelsiors, 14; Atlantics, 15; 9 innings; Umpire, William Barre, of Pastime Club.
August 23, 1860.—Putnam's ground, on Broadway; Excelsiors, 8; Atlantics, 6; 5 innings were played, when the game was *drawn*; Umpire, R.H. Thorn, of Empire Club.

EXCELSIOR AND GOTHAM.

Sept. 14, 1858.—Played on Gotham's ground, at Elysian Fields, Hoboken; Excelsiors, 24; Gothams, 13; 9 innings; Umpire, Thomas S. Dakin, of Putnam Club.
Sept. 29, 1859.—Played on Excelsior's ground, foot of Court street, S.B.; Excelsiors, 37; Gothams, 12; 9 innings; Umpire, M. E. Gelston, of Eagle Club.

EXCELSIOR AND PASTIME.

Sept. 23, 1858.—Played on Pastime's ground, at Bedford, L.I.; Excelsiors, 43; Pastimes, 14; 9 innings; Umpire, Thomas S. Dakin, of Putnam Club.
October 8, 1858.—Played on Excelsior's ground; Excelsiors, 27; Pastimes, 11; 9 innings; Umpire, Thomas S. Dakin, of Putnam Club.
August 18, 1859.—Pastime's ground at Bedford; Excelsiors, 20; Pastimes, 12; 9 innings; Umpire, Caleb Sniffen, of Atlantic Club.

EXCELSIOR SECOND NINE AND ESCULAPIAN FIRST NINE.

October 21, 1858.—Played on Excelsior's ground; Excelsiors, 38; Esculapians, 15; 9 innings; Umpire, G. Holt, of Pastime Club.
Nov. 1, 1858.—Played on Esculapian's ground; Excelsiors, 52, 12 Esculapians, 12; 8 innings; Umpire, G. Holt, of Pastime Club.
Excelsior and Charter Oak of Brooklyn.—May 12, 1859.—Charter Oak's ground, between Smith, Hoyt, Sackett, and Degraw streets, South Brooklyn. Excelsiors, 17 runs; Charter Oaks, 18 runs; nine innings. Umpire, Peter O'Brien, of Atlantic Club.
June 9, 1859.—Excelsior's ground. Excelsior's, 62 runs; Charter Oaks, 13 runs; nine innings. Umpire, A. J. Bixby, of Eagle Club.
June 21, 1860.—Excelsior's ground. Excelsiors, 36 runs; Charter Oaks, nine runs; nine innings. Umpire, Andrew J. Bixby, of Eagle Club.
Excelsior and Charter Oak Games.— June 26, 1862.—Excelsiors, 20 runs; Charter Oaks, 19 runs; seven innings. Umpire, Peter O'Brien, of Atlantic Club.
Excelsior and Neosho, of New Utrecht, L.I.— June 18, 1859. Played on Neosho's ground, at

the head of United States avenue, near Fort Hamilton, L.I. Excelsiors, 46 runs; Neoshos, 11 runs; nine innings. Umpire, Peter O'Brien, of Atlantic Club.

Excelsior and Baltic.— July 28, 1859. Played on Baltic's ground, corner of Eighty-first street and Second avenue. Excelsiors, 30 runs; Baltic, 19 runs; nine innings. Umpire, S. Pinckney, of Union Club.

August 11, 1859.—Excelsior's ground. Excelsiors, 41 runs; Baltics, 16 runs; nine innings. Umpire, Caleb Sniffen, of Atlantic Club.

Excelsior and Star.— September 3, 1859. Star's ground, near Carroll park. Excelsiors, 12 runs; Stars, 17 runs; nine innings. Umpire, Peter O'Brien.

June 28, 1860.—Excelsior's ground. Excelsiors, 16 runs; Stars, 5 runs. Umpire, Andrew J. Bixby, of Eagle Club.

October 4, 1862.—Game made up in consequence of absence of Charter Oaks. Played on Excelsior's ground. Excelsiors, 5 runs; Stars, 5 runs; six innings played, when overtaken by darkness.

Excelsior and Empire Games.— September 14, 1859.—Gotham's ground at Hoboken; Excelsiors, 25 runs; Empires, 20 runs; nine innings; umpire, Henry Morrow, of Knickerbocker Club.

September 1, 1860.—Empire's ground, Hoboken; Excelsiors, 23 runs; Empires, 7 runs; nine innings; Umpire, Samuel W. Patchen, of Charter Oak Club.

September 29, 1860.—At Elysian Fields, Hoboken; Excelsiors, 23 runs; Empires, 7 runs, nine innings; Umpire, Andrew J. Bixby, of Eagle Club.

Excelsior and Independent.— September 15, 1860.—Excelsior ground; Excelsiors, 46 runs; Independents, 14 runs; nine innings.

Excelsior and St. George's Cricket Club.— November 5, 1860. St. George's Cricket ground,

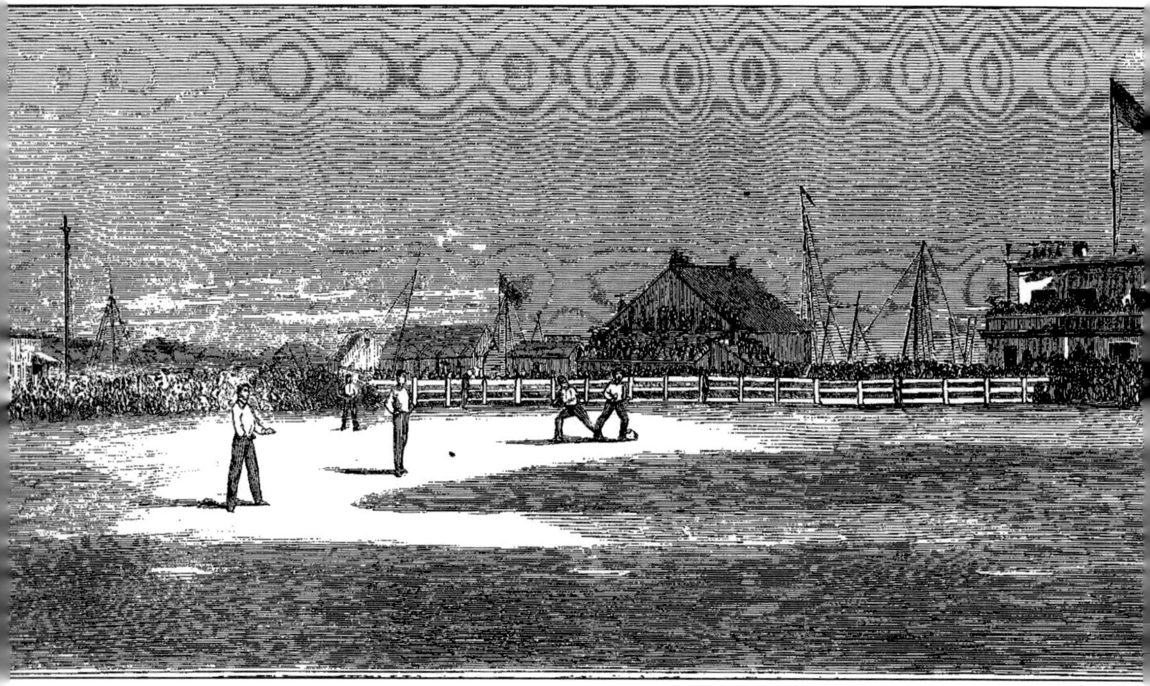

1860 CHAMPIONSHIP AT EXCELSIOR GROUNDS EXCELSIOR VS. ATLANTIC. *This stunning* New York Illustrated News *panoramic shows the beauty and the simplicity of the one the first baseball grounds, the Excelsior Grounds in South Brooklyn. At this time (1860), the game was developing into a spectator sport. The grounds resemble a circus atmosphere with tents and flags adorning a simple*

Hoboken; Excelsiors, 25 runs; St. George's Cricket Club, 0 runs; nine innings.

Tour to Buffalo.—Saturday, June 20, 1860, the Excelsior Nine and others left for Albany. They were received by a delegation from the Champion Club of Albany, and registered at Stanwix Hall.

July 2, 1860.—Excelsior and Champion, of Albany. Excelsiors, 24 runs; Champions, 6 runs; nine innings.

After the game the Champions entertained their guests at the Merchant's Hotel.

July 3, 1860.—Excelsior and Victory, of Troy. The Excelsiors were received by Dr. Hegeman, Robert Green, and others. Played on Victory's ground at Wier's Course, Troy. Excelsiors, 13 runs; Victories, 7 runs; nine innings. After the game the Excelsiors were well entertained at the "Troy House."

July 5, 1860.—Excelsior and Niagara, of Buffalo.—The Excelsiors were met by a delegation of the Niagara at the depot, and taken to the Mansion House. Excelsior, 50 runs; Niagara, 19 runs; 9 innings. Umpire, Frank P. Whiting, of Excelsior Club. The Excelsiors were escorted to Bloomfield's Hotel, where a splendid supper was provided. The Niagaras also went with them to Canada, to the Clifton House, where they were hospitably treated; and throughout, the attention shown the Excelsiors by their friends could not have been exceeded, and is remembered with the utmost pleasure.

July 7, 1860.—Excelsior and Flour City, of Rochester. The Excelsiors were received by a delegation of the Flour City at the depot, and were conducted to the Osborne House. Excelsior, 21 runs; Flour City, 1 run; 9 innings.

July 9, 1860.—Excelsior and Live Oak, of Rochester. Excelsior, 27 runs; Live Oak, 9; 9 innings.

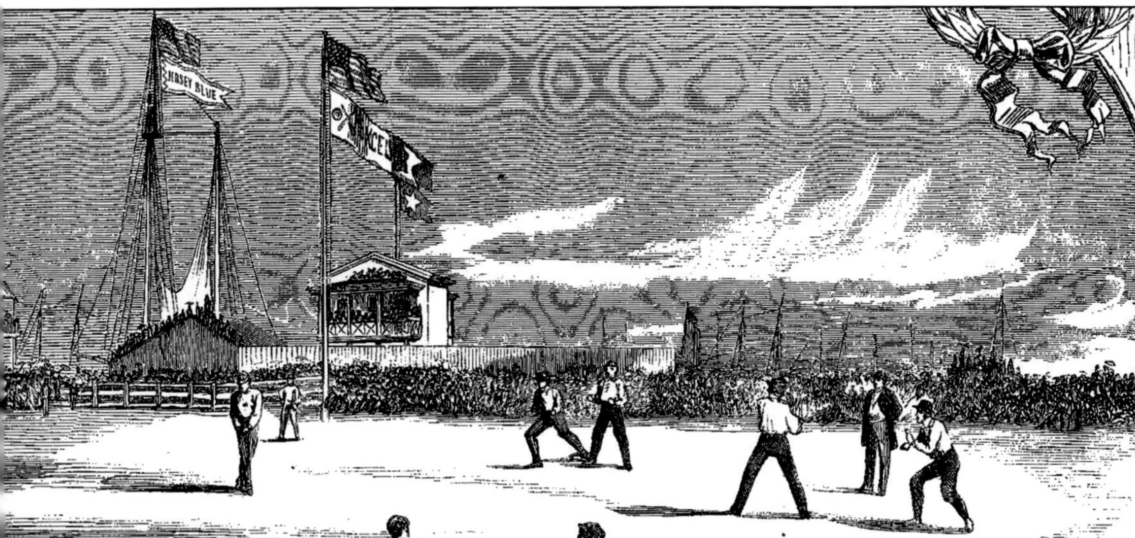

grandstand. People crowded the streets around the grounds and sat on rooftops. It appears from the single letter on the jersey of the pitcher that it is the Excelsiors(E) in the field. The Atlantic had a ABBC adorn the shirt. If indeed this is the Excelsiors in the field, then that would likely be Jim Creighton on the mound for the Excelsiors. (Source: Vintage Ballist.*)*

July 11, 1860.—Excelsior and Hudson River, of Newburgh. The Excelsiors were received by Mr. Miller and associates, and conducted to the Orange Hotel. Excelsior, 59 runs; Hudson River, 14 runs; 9 innings.

July 22, 1860.—Excelsior of Brooklyn, and Excelsior of Baltimore. Excelsior of Brooklyn, 51 runs; Excelsior of Baltimore, 6 runs; 9 innings. The Excelsiors were entertained with true Southern hospitality. A magnificent dinner at Guy's, after the game, was partaken of, at which flowers in profusion decorated the tables' toasts and songs abounded. From 4 A.M. of Saturday, until 5 P.M. of Sunday, the Excelsiors of Brooklyn were occupied in one entire round of pleasure.

Played at Camac Woods, Philadelphia. Excelsior, 15 runs; All Philadelphia, 4 runs; 9 innings.

Excursion to Baltimore, Md., Friday, September 21, 1860.—The Excelsior Nine and others, left for Baltimore, where they arrived at about four o'clock on Saturday morning, and were received by George Beam and associates, and taken to Guy's Monument House.

Visit to Boston, July 9, 1862.—The Excelsior nine and others left for Boston; received by a delegation of the Bowdoin Club, and conducted to the Tremont House.

July 10, 1862.—Excelsiors and Bowdoin of Boston, played on "Boston Common." Excelsiors, 41 runs; Bowdoins, 15 runs; nine innings. After the game the Excelsiors were furnished a very splendid entertainment at the "Parker House," Mayor Wightman and other distinguished guests being present.

July 11, 1862.—Excelsior and Lowell and Tri-Mountain, played on "Boston Common." Excelsiors, 39 runs; Lowell and Tri-Mountain, 13 runs; nine innings. Umpire, John A. Lowell, of Bowdoin Club. The Excelsiors were treated by the Bostonians in a very cordial manner.

Excelsior and Athletic, of Philadelphia.— June 15, 1863.—Excelsior, 17 runs; Athletic, 18 runs; ten innings.

August 3, 1863.—Excelsior and Hudson River, of Newburgh. Excelsior, 16 runs; Hudson River, 13 runs; 9 innings.

September 10, 1863.—Excelsior and Newark, N.J., on the Newark's ground, at Newark, N.J. Excelsiors, 17 runs; Newarks, 10 runs; nine innings.

September 16, 1863.—Excelsior and Henry Eckford, played on Henry Eckford's ground. Excelsiors, 26 runs; Henry Eckfords, 21 runs; nine innings.

September 23, 1863.—Excelsior ground. Excelsiors, 19 runs; Newarks, 17 runs; nine innings.

September 30, 1863.—Excelsior's ground. Excelsiors, 15 runs; Henry Eckfords, 8 runs; nine innings.

October 20, 1863.—Excelsior and Nassau of Princeton, N.J. Excelsior's grounds. Excelsiors, 11 runs; Nassau, of Princeton, 12 runs; nine innings.

July 16, 1864.—Excelsior and Enterprise. Capitoline ground, at Bedford. Excelsiors, 25 runs; Enterprise, 19 runs; nine innings.

August 10, 1864.—Played on the Newark's ground, at Newark, N.J. Excelsiors, 24 runs; Newarks, 20 runs; nine innings.

August 13, 1864.— Excelsior's ground. Excelsior, 33 runs; Enterprise, 6 runs; nine innings.

Excelsior and Mutual.— August 17, 1864.—Mutual's ground, at Hoboken. Excelsior, 10 runs; Mutual, 21 runs; five innings.

Sept. 10, 1864.—Excelsiors ground. Excelsiors, 19 runs; Newarks, 35 runs; nine innings. Umpire, Peter O'Brien, of Atlantic Club.

Excelsior and St. George Cricket and Picked Nine from New York.— September 23, 1864.— Played on St. George's cricket ground, at Hoboken. Excelsior, 28 runs; St. George's Cricket and New York Base Ball Club, 15 runs; nine innings.

September 26, 1864.—Excelsior ground. Excelsior, 22 runs; Mutual, 33; nine innings.

Excelsior and Lowell, of Boston.—Played on Capitoline ground, at Bedford. Excelsior, 39 runs; October 19, 1864.—Played on Mutual's ground, at Hoboken. Excelsior's 27 runs; Newarks, 5 runs; nine innings.

Excelsior and Pioneer, of Newark, N.J..—May 20, 1865.—Pioneer's ground. Excelsior, 14 runs;

Pioneer, 32 runs; nine innings.

September 26, 1865.—Capitoline ground, at Bedford. Excelsior, 46 runs; Enterprise, 21 runs; five innings.

Visit of Excelsior Club to Washington, Baltimore, and Philadelphia.—The Excelsiors left for Washington, on Saturday P.M., October 7, 1865, and arrived at Washington on Sunday A.M., where they were received by a delegation of the National Club, who conducted them in carriages to Willard's Hotel.

October 9, 1865.—Played on the President's (National's) ground, at Washington. Excelsior, 30 runs; National, 36; nine innings. After the game, the Excelsiors were sumptuously entertained by the Nationals at the National Hotel. On the following morning they left for Baltimore.

October 10, 1865.—Played on the Pastime's ground, near Druid Park, on Madison avenue. Excelsior, 51 runs; Pastime, 22 runs; six innings. Umpire, Van Brunt Wyckoff, of Excelsior Club. The Excelsiors were received by a delegation of the Pastime Club, who escorted them in carriages to the Maltby House, where an excellent dinner was provided for them. It is worthy of remark that no money could be expended by the Excelsiors while in Baltimore. They left Baltimore in the 9.30 train for Philadelphia, quartering at the Girard House.

October 11, 1865.—Played on Athletic ground. Excelsior, 11 runs; Athletic, 45 runs; nine innings.

November 11, 1865.—Capitoline ground, at Bedford. Excelsior, 43 runs; Enterprise, 16 runs; 9 innings. After the game, the members of both clubs proceeded to the St. James Hotel, where, at eight P.M., a large party sat down to an elegant supper.

[One of the most remarkable games was played September 13, 1864, on the Excelsior ground, foot of Court street, South Brooklyn, between five members of Excelsior Club, and four members of other clubs on each side, in the remarkably short time of fifty-eight minutes; George H. E. Fletcher's side, 13 runs; Thomas S. Dakin's side, 6 runs; nine innings. This game is considered the shortest on record.]

Excelsior and Harvard, of Cambridge College Mass.— June 1, 1866. Capitoline ground; Excelsiors, 46 runs; Harvards, 28 runs; nine innings.

Excelsior and Star.— June 19, 1866. Capitoline ground, excelsiors, 27 runs; Stars, 20 runs; nine innings.

Excelsior and National, of Washington.— July 5, 1866. Capitoline ground; Excelsiors, 46 ruins; Nationals, 33 runs; nine innings.

Excelsior and Union.— July 19, 1866. At Morrisania, Excelsiors, 15 runs; Union, 20 runs; nine innings.

Excelsior and Contest.— July 24, 1866.—Capitoline ground. Excelsior, 34 runs; Contest, 5 runs; nine innings.

July 28, 1866.—Excelsior and Active. Active's ground, at Hoboken. Excelsiors, 7 runs; Actives, 9 runs; five innings. Time of game, 1.25.

August 7, 1866.—Excelsior and Peconic. Capitoline ground. Excelsior, 32 runs; Peconic, 4 runs; nine innings. Time of game 2.30.

August 14, 1866.—Excelsior and Mutual. Capitoline ground. Excelsiors, 13 runs; Mutuals, 32 runs; nine innings. Umpire, Charles Wilson, of Empire Club; time of game 1.50.

August 17, 1866.—Excelsior and National of Albany. Capitoline ground. Excelsior, 48 runs; National, 29 runs; nine innings.

August 24, 1866.—Excelsior and Independent. Capitoline ground. Excelsior, 30 runs; Independent, 11 runs; eight innings. Time of game, 2.05.

August 28, 1866.—Excelsior and Eureka, of Newark, N. J. Eureka's ground, at Newark, N. J. Eureka's ground, at Newark, N. J. Excelsior, 24 runs; Eureka, 12 runs; nine innings. Time of game, 2 hours.

September 4, 1866.—Excelsior and Star. Capitoline ground. Excelsior, 32 runs; Star, 9 runs; nine innings. Time of game, 2 hours.

September 14, 1866.—Excelsior and Enterprise. Capitoline ground. Excelsior, 16 runs; Enterprise, 18 runs; nine innings. Time of game, 1.50.

Tour to Washington, etc. September 15 to 22.—On Saturday afternoon, September 15, 1866, between forty and fifty Excelsiors left for Washington. Near Baltimore they were met by a Committee of the National Club, and on their arrival at Washington a large delegation received them at the depot, and took them in carriages and stages to Willard's Hotel (on the morning of September 16), where choice rooms were provided for them. After breakfast, the entire party entered carriages and were taken by their guests to the Little Falls of the Potomac, and thence in the packet Minnesota to the Great Falls, where they were sumptiously feasted at the Pavilion Hotel.

On Monday, September 17th, they were conveyed in carriages to the steamer Wawset for an excursion to Mount Vernon, the Lower Potomac, Indian Head, and Fort Washington. A select and fashionable assemblage of ladies accompanied them; also the Marine Band, led by Prof. Scala; a dirge was played by the band at the tomb of Washington, and at Fort Washington the commandant received them with military honors. Early in the evening they returned, and next they proceeded to Stagg's fine rooms, which were inaugurated on this occasion, and an elegant entertainment was provided for them.

September 18, 1866.—Excelsior and National, of Washington, On the "President's Grounds." Excelsior, 33 runs; National, 28 runs; nine innings.

On Wednesday, September 19th, the Excelsiors were given in charge of the Union Club of Washington.

Excelsior and Union, of Washington. September 19, 1866. Excelsior, 40 runs; Union, 23 runs; eight innings. In the evening the Unions entertained the Excelsiors hospitably at the National Hotel.

Thursday morning, September 20, 1866, the Excelsiors left for Baltimore. On their arrival the Excelsiors were met at the depot by a committee of the Pastimes. After partaking of a lunch at a well provided table, they were escorted to the ball ground.

Excelsior and Pastime, of Baltimore.— September 20, 1866. Excelsior, 28 runs; Pastime, 19 runs; nine innings. After the game the Excelsiors were taken to the Howard House. In the evening they were hospitably entertained at Chambaing's. On Friday morning the Excelsiors left for Philadelphia. Here they were met by a delegation of the Keystone Club. After a dinner at the Continental, the party left for the scene of action.

Excelsior and Keystone of Philadelphia, September 21, 1866. Excelsiors, 18; Keystones, 18; 8 innings.

In the evening the Keystones took the Excelsiors to Carncross & Dixie's Minstrel Hall, and paid them courteous attention. On Saturday the Excelsiors became the guests of the Olympics.

Sept. 22, 1866.— Played on the Olympic's ground; Excelsiors, 41; Olympic, 16; 9 innings. The treatment of the Excelsiors by the Olympics was most courteous, their reception of them laying the foundation of a permanent friendship.The Excelsiors left Philadelphia on the "Owl train," on Saturday night, Sept. 22, 1866, and arrived at home the following morning.

October 2, 1866.—Capitoline ground; Excelsior, 30 runs; Union, 29 runs; nine innings.

October 22, 1866.—Excelsior and Mutual. Played on the Mutual's ground at Hoboken; Excelsiors, 6; Mutuals, 23; 9 innings; time of game, 1 hour and 50 minutes.

Nov. 3, 1866.—Excelsior and Union. Union base ball ground, Brooklyn, E.D. Excelsior, 14; Union, 43; 9 innings. Umpire, Mills, of Atlantic Club; time of game 2 hours and 45 minutes.

Uniform.—Blue pants with white cord; white shirts trimmed with blue, and the letter "E" in German text over the chest; white cap, trimmed with blue cord at the bottom and blue braid at the top, white vizor; belt, white enamelled leather with the word Excelsior in old English.

Number of members, November 24, 1866.—Active members, three hundred and fifty; life members, sixteen; honorary members, four. Total, three hundred and seventy.

Of the original members, two remain connected with the club, as honorary members, viz. John H. Suydam, the father of the club, and Peter Van Schaack. Of those who were members (active) at the time of consolidation with the Wayne Base Ball Club, eleven exist, six of whom were Excelsiors and five were Waynes.

ATLANTIC CLUB.

The Atlantic Base Ball Club, of Brooklyn, was organized August 14, 1855, and from the day of its entrance upon the base ball field it has occupied and filled a front rank position as a crack playing club. Unlike many of its kindred associations, who place a strong nine in the field for one summer, and perhaps a weak body of players for the ensuing season, the Atlantics have always and at all times had a nine from whom any rival club might almost despair of winning any lasting laurels. It is this extraordinary and unvarying success which has gained for them the title of "Champion;" and although this name is in every sense, for obvious reasons, ignored by the National Association, it is certain that the Atlantic Club will continue to be so styled by the press and the public, until some other organization prove themselves their superiors by defeating them in a home-and-home match. The Atlantic Club has maintained its preeminence for a long series of years, never losing it but for a season or two, when the Eckford Club bravely carried off the honors from them. The Atlantics, however, were not long in regaining their lost laurels from those who had so fairly vanquished them; and from that period to the present, the "whip" has waved from the Atlantic flagstaff.

The first officers of the club were: President, Thomas S. Powers; Vice-President, Caleb Sniffen; Secretary, Joshua H. Ackerman; Treasurer, T.S. Powers. Games played in 1855: October 21, Atlantic and Harmony, at Brooklyn. Won by the Atlantic by 24 to 22 runs. Umpire, Thomas Leavy, of the Empire Club. November 5.—Atlantic and Harmony, at Brooklyn. Won by the Atlantic by a score of 27 to 10 runs.

OFFICERS FOR 1856.—President, Caleb Sniffen; Vice-President, Stephen A. Mann; Secretary, Joshua H. Ackerman; Treasurer, Peter O'Brien.

September 18, 1856.—Atlantic and Baltic, at New York. Atlantic, 21; Baltic, 19 runs.
September 27.—Atlantic and Columbia, at Brooklyn. Atlantic, 34; Columbia, 7.
October 4.—Atlantic and Columbia, at Brooklyn. Atlantic, 23; Columbia, 4.
October 7.—Atlantic and Baltic, at Brooklyn. Atlantic, 27; Baltic, 7.

During the year (1856), three games were played with the Empire Club, of New York. At that time the rule was twenty-one runs. The two first games were drawn games, and a third game was played to decide who was the victor. The game was played at the Red House, Harlem, the Empires winning; but as we have a very imperfect record, we cannot give the particulars.

OFFICERS FOR 1857.—President, Thomas Tassie; Vice-President, William F. Babcock; Secretary, John H. Ireland; Treasurer, Peter O'Brien.

August 21.—Atlantic and Continental, on Atlantic ground. Atlantic, 37; Continental, 21.
September 3.—Atlantic and Gotham, on Atlantic ground. Atlantic 41; Gotham, 11.
September 15.—Atlantic and Eckford, on Eckford ground. Atlantic, 26; Eckford, 17.
September 24, 1857.—Atlantic and Putnam, on Atlantic ground. Atlantic, 19; Putnam, 3.
October 1.—Atlantic and Continental, on Continental ground. Atlantic, 34; Continental, 34; tie game.
October 6.—Atlantic and Continental, on Continental ground. Atlantic, 26; Continental, 13.

October 20.—Atlantic and Putnam, on Putnam ground., Atlantic, 37; Putnam, 15.
October 22.—Atlantic and Eckford, on Atlantic ground. Atlantic, 29; Eckford, 11.

OFFICERS FOR 1858.— President, Thomas Tassie; Vice-President , Folkert R. Boerum; Secretary, John H. Ireland; Treasurer, Peter O'Brien,

June 17, 1858.—Atlantic and Putnam, on Putnam ground. Atlantic, 17; Putnam, 13. Thomas Van Cott, Gotham Club, Umpire.
September 12.—Atlantic and Liberty, of New Brunswick, N. J., on Liberty ground. Atlantic, 24; Liberty, 8.
October 11.—Atlantic and Liberty, of New Brunswick, N.J., on Atlantic ground. Atlantic, 61; Liberty, 14.
October 18.—Atlantic and Putnam, on Atlantic ground. Atlantic, 18; Putnam, 7. John J. Grum, Eckford Club, Umpire.
——- ——- Atlantic and Gotham, on Gotham ground. Atlantic, 19; Gotham, 24.
October 25.—Atlantic and Gotham, on Atlantic ground. Atlantic, 31; Gotham ,17. Thomas S. Dakin, Putnam Club, Umpire.
November 9.—Atlantic and Excelsior, on Excelsior ground. Atlantic, 22; Excelsior, 10. Umpire, Thomas S. Dakin, Putnam Club.
November 16, 1858.—Atlantic and Excelsior, on Atlantic ground. Atlantic, 27; Excelsior, 6. Umpire, John McCosker, Gotham Club.

OFFICERS FOR 1859.—President, Samuel V. Millard; Vice-President, Folkert R. Boerum; Secretary, John B. Oliver; Treasurer, John G. Price.

June 23, 1859.—Atlantic and Pastime, on Pastime ground. Atlantic, 29; Pastime, 15. Umpire, F. S. Massey, Osceola Club.
July 8.—Atlantic and Eckford, on Eckford ground. Atlantic, 25; Eckford, 15. Umpire, C. De Post, Knickerbocker Club.
August 15.—Atlantic and Pastime, on Atlantic ground. Atlantic, 22; Pastime, 13. Umpire, A. H. Mills, Eckford Club.
August 20.—Atlantic vs. Baltic, on Baltic's ground. Atlantic, 48; Baltic, 10. Umpire, J. J. Grum, Eckford Club.
September 8.—Atlantic vs. Eckford, on Atlantic's ground. Atlantic, 16; Eckford, 22. Umpire, A. Liscomb, Harlem Club.
September 15.—Atlantic vs. Baltic, on Atlantic's ground. Atlantic, 55; Baltic, 11. Umpire, H. Manolt, Eckford Club.
September 19.— Atlantic vs. Mutual, on Mutuals' ground. Atlantic, 39; Mutual, 20. Umpire, W. Fisher, Baltic Club.
September 27.—Atlantic vs. Union (of Morrisania), on Union's ground. Atlantic, 39; Union, 5. Umpire, M. E. Gelston, Eagle Club.
October 5.—Atlantic vs. Harlem, at Harlem. Atlantic, 24; Harlem, 11. Umpire, J. J. Grum, Eckford Club.
October 12.—Atlantic vs. Eckford, on Eckford's ground. Atlantic, 22; Eckford, 12. Umpire, A. Liscomb, Harlem Club.
October 14.—Atlantic vs. Mutual, on Atlantics' ground. Atlantic, 15; Mutual, 5. Umpire, M. E. Gelston, Eagle Club.
October 19.—Atlantic vs. Star, on Star ground. Atlantic, 15; Star, 12. Umpire, M. E. Gelston, Eagle Club.
Second Annual Ball, held at Musical Hall, December 12, 1859.

OFFICERS FOR 1860.—President, Thomas Tassie; Vice-President, Folkert R. Boerum; Secretary, F. K. Boughton; Treasurer, John G. Price.

May 25.—Return game; Atlantic vs. Star, on Atlantic's ground. Atlantic, 30; Star, 11. Umpire, T.S. Dakin, Putnam Club.

June 8.—Return game; Atlantic vs. Union (of Morrisania), on Atlantic's ground. Atlantic, 15; Union, 4. Umpire, E. Russell, Excelsior Club.

June 29.—Atlantic vs. Putnam, on Putnam's ground. Atlantic, 14; Putnam, 11. Umpire, Joseph Miller, Empire Club.Return game not played, on account of the disbandment of the Putnams.

July 16.—Atlantic vs. Enterprise, on Enterprise ground. Atlantic, 38; Enterprise, 20. Umpire, John J. Grum, Eckford Club.

July 19.—Atlantic vs. Excelsior, on Excelsior's ground. Atlantic, 4; Excelsior, 23. Umpire, William Barre, Pastime Club.

July 30.—Atlantic vs. Mutual, on Mutual's ground. Atlantic, 34; Mutual, 15. Umpire, William Barre, Pastime Club.

August 9.—Atlantic vs. Excelsior, on Atlantics' ground. Atlantic, 15; Excelsior, 14. Umpire, William Barre, Pastime Club.

August 16.—Atlantic vs. Enterprise, on Atlantic's ground. Atlantic, 16; Enterprise, 14. Umpire, F. A. Biggs, Pastime Club.

September 3.—Return game; Atlantic vs. Harlem, on Atlantic's ground. Atlantic, 28; Harlem, 8. Umpire, G. Flanley, Excelsior Club.

September 20.—Atlantic vs. Mutual, on Atlantic's ground. Atlantic, 26; Mutual, 14. Umpire, John J. Grum, Eckford Club.

The home-and home game played on the Putnam ground, was brought to a close by the Excelsior nine withdrawing from the field. The Umpire decided it no game. Umpire, R. H. Thorn, Empire Club.

October 8.—Atlantic and Liberty (of New Brunswick), on Atlantic's ground. Atlantic, 15; Liberty, 10. Umpire, S. F. Davenport, Hamilton Club.

October 15.—Atlantic vs. Eckford, on Eckford's ground. Atlantic, 17; Eckford, 15. Umpire, Edward Brown, Putnam Club.

October 22.—Atlantic vs. Eckford, on Atlantic's ground. Atlantic, 15; Eckford, 20. Umpire, Asa Brainard, Excelsior Club.

October 29.—Home-and-home; Atlantic vs. Eckford, on Putnam's ground. Atlantic, 20; Eckford, 11. Umpire, Asa Brainard, Excelsior Club.

The Atlantic's Third Annual Ball was held at Montague Hall, January 30, 1861.

OFFICERS FOR 1861.—President, George P, Phelps; Vice-President, John Brown; Secretary, F. K. Boughton; Treasurer, A G. Babcock.

February 4.—Atlantic vs. Charter Oak, played on the Washington Skating Pond, with skates, for a sliver ball. Atlantics, 36; Charter Oak, 27. Umpire, R. E. Ellembrock, Live Oak Club (of Rochester).

August 5.—Atlantic vs. Newark, on Newark ground. Atlantic, 21; Newark, 11. Umpire, Asa Brainard, Excelsior Club.

August 16.—Atlantic vs. Exercise, on Exercise ground. Atlantic, 32; Exercise, 17. Umpire, S. F. Davenport, Hamilton Club.

August 25.—Atlantic vs. Newark, on Atlantic's ground. Atlantic, 36; Newark, 18. Umpire, J. J. Grum, Eckford Club.

September 14.—Atlantic vs. Exercise, on Atlantic's ground. Atlantic, 36; Exercise, 14. Umpire, S. F. Davenport.

October 3.—Atlantic vs. Mutual, at Hoboken. Atlantic, 18; Mutual, 23. Umpire, A T. Pearsall, Excelsior Club.

October 16.—Atlantic vs. Mutual, on Atlantic's ground. Atlantic, 52; Mutual, 27. Umpire,

A. J. Bixby, Eagle Club.
October 28.—Atlantic vs. Liberty (of New Brunswick), on Liberty's ground. Atlantic, 11; Liberty, 31. Umpire, E. C. Stockton.

OFFICERS FOR 1862.—President, F. K. Boughton; Vice-President, Thomas R. Mercein; Secretary, S. A. Smith, Jr.; Treasurer, Alex G. Babcock.

GAMES PLAYED IN 1862.— August 11.—For silver ball, best two out of three games. Atlantic and Eckford, on Eckford ground. Atlantic, 14; Eckford, 20. Umpire, A. B. Taylor, Mutual Club.
August 18.—Atlantic and Eckford, on Eckford ground. Atlantic, 39; Eckford, 5. Umpire, A. T. Pearsall, Excelsior Club.
September 16.—Atlantic and Harlem, on Harlem's ground. Atlantic, 27; Harlem, 12. Umpire, A. B. Taylor, Mutual Club.
September 18.—Atlantic and Eckford, on Eckford ground. Atlantic, 3; Eckford, 8. Umpire, E. Brown, Mutual Club.
September 22.—Home-and-home. Atlantic and Mutual, at Sixty-third street, N. Y. Atlantic, 10; Mutual, 15. Umpire, A. Liscomb, Harlem Club.

OFFICERS FOR 1863.—President, Frederick K. Boughton; Vice-President, William V. Babcock; Secretary, S. Alpheus Smith, Jr.; Treasurer, Henry J. Adair.

June 18, 1863.—Atlantic and Athletic, of Philadelphia, at Brooklyn. Atlantic, 21; Athletic, 13. Umpire, R W. Skatts, Star Club.
August 3.—Atlantic and Mutual, on Atlantic ground. Atlantic, 26; Mutual, 27. Umpire, John J. Grum, Eckford Club.
August 6.—Atlantic and Henry Eckford, at Sixty-third street, N.Y. Atlantic, 14; Henry Eckford, 10. Umpire, A. Liscomb, Harlem Club.
August 13.—Atlantic and Henry Eckford, on Atlantic ground. Atlantic, 30; Henry Eckford, 13. Umpire, George Flanley, Excelsior Club.
August 31.—Atlantic and Eureka, at Newark. Atlantic, 16; Eureka, 15. Umpire, William Culyer, Empire Club.
September 2.—Atlantic and Eckford, on Atlantic ground. Atlantic, 10; Eckford, 31. Umpire, J. Forsyth, Gotham Club.
September 8.—Atlantic and Eckford, on Eckford ground. Atlantic, 11; Eckford, 21. Umpire, A. B. Taylor, Mutual Club.
September 10.—Atlantic and Mutual, on Mutual ground. Atlantic, 15; Mutual, 11. Umpire, W. F. Hudson, Henry Eckford Club.
September 24.—Home-and-home. Atlantic and Mutual, at Hoboken. Atlantic, 42; Mutual, 18. Umpire, E. Pennington, Eureka Club.
October 22.—Atlantic and Nassau, of Princeton, N.J., on Atlantic ground. Atlantic, 18; Nassau, 13. Umpire, George A. Chappell, Excelsior Club.
October 26.—Atlantic Nine and 18 Cricketers; the Atlantic to put out six for an innings, the Cricketers to put out three for an inning. Atlantic, 23; Cricketers, 8. Umpire, P. O'Brien, Atlantic Club.

OFFICERS FOR 1864.—President, William V. Babcock; Vice-President, W.H. Lockwood; Secretary, James Mowlem; Treasurer, Henry J. Adair. Fourth annual ball was held at Gothic Hall, February 18, 1864.

June—.—Atlantic and Combination Nine (prize game), on Atlantic ground. Atlantic, 45; Combination Nine, 11. Umpire, C. Bomeisler, Olympic Club, of Philadelphia.

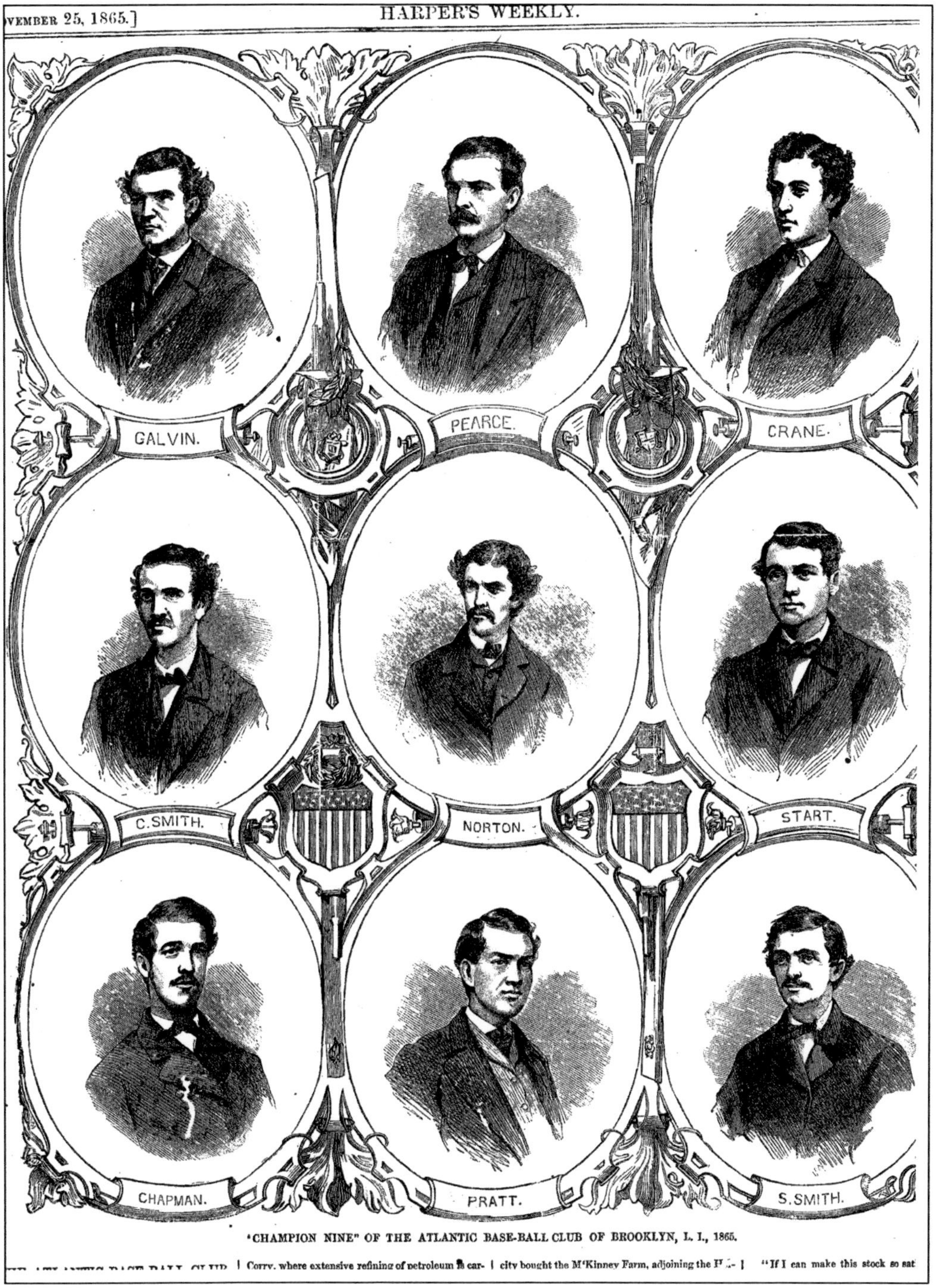

HARPER'S WEEKLY WOODCUT, BROOKLYN ATLANTICS OF 1865. *The Champion Nine of 1865 included such early stars as Dicky Pearce, Fred Crane, and Joe Start. The Atlantics of 1865 went 18–0. Start and Crane led the team in runs scored. Peter O'Brien was also on this team, but did not appear in this woodcut. (Source:* Vintage Ballist.*)*

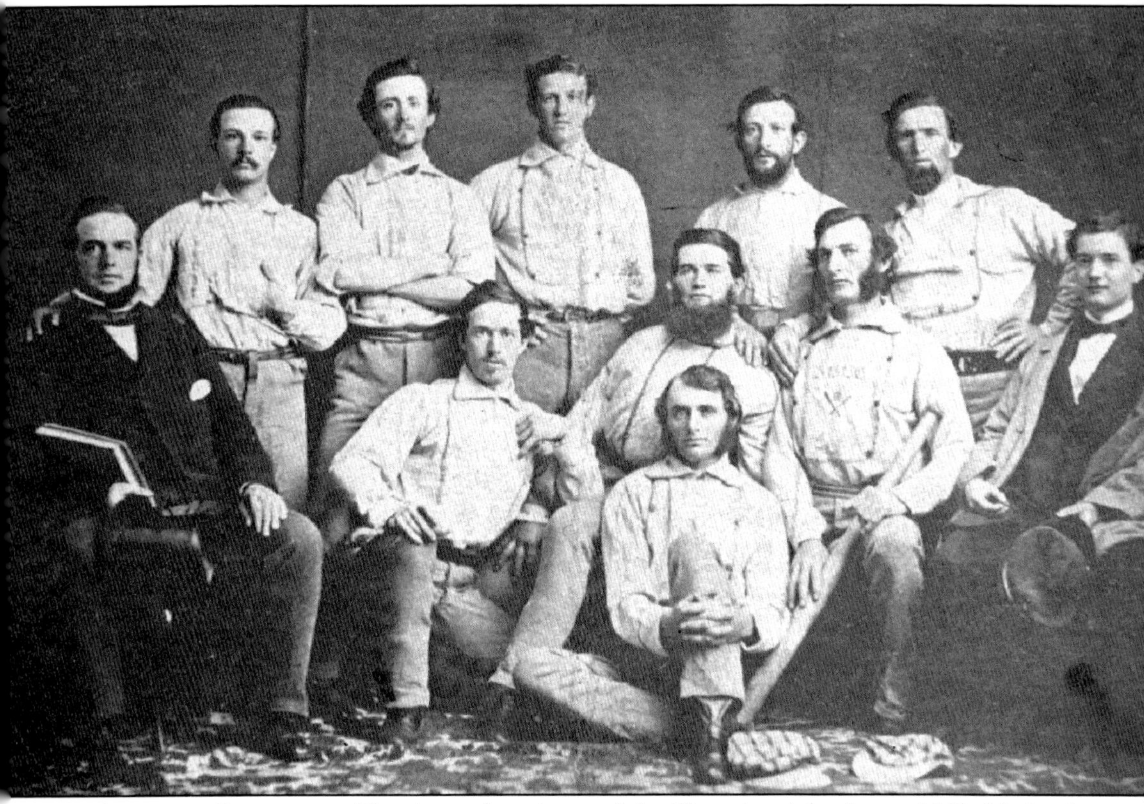

Atlantic Champions. *Here is another picture of the Champion Atlantics, c. 1862. Notice the uniforms, bibbed front, and checkered hats on the floor in front of them. The Atlantics faded out of "major" league ball when the National Association was transformed into a professional association in 1871. The Atlantics decided to remain amateurs and compete for the amateur championship. Amateur teams of the 1870s drew as well or better than their professional counterparts in and around New York City. (Source: Transcendental Graphics.)*

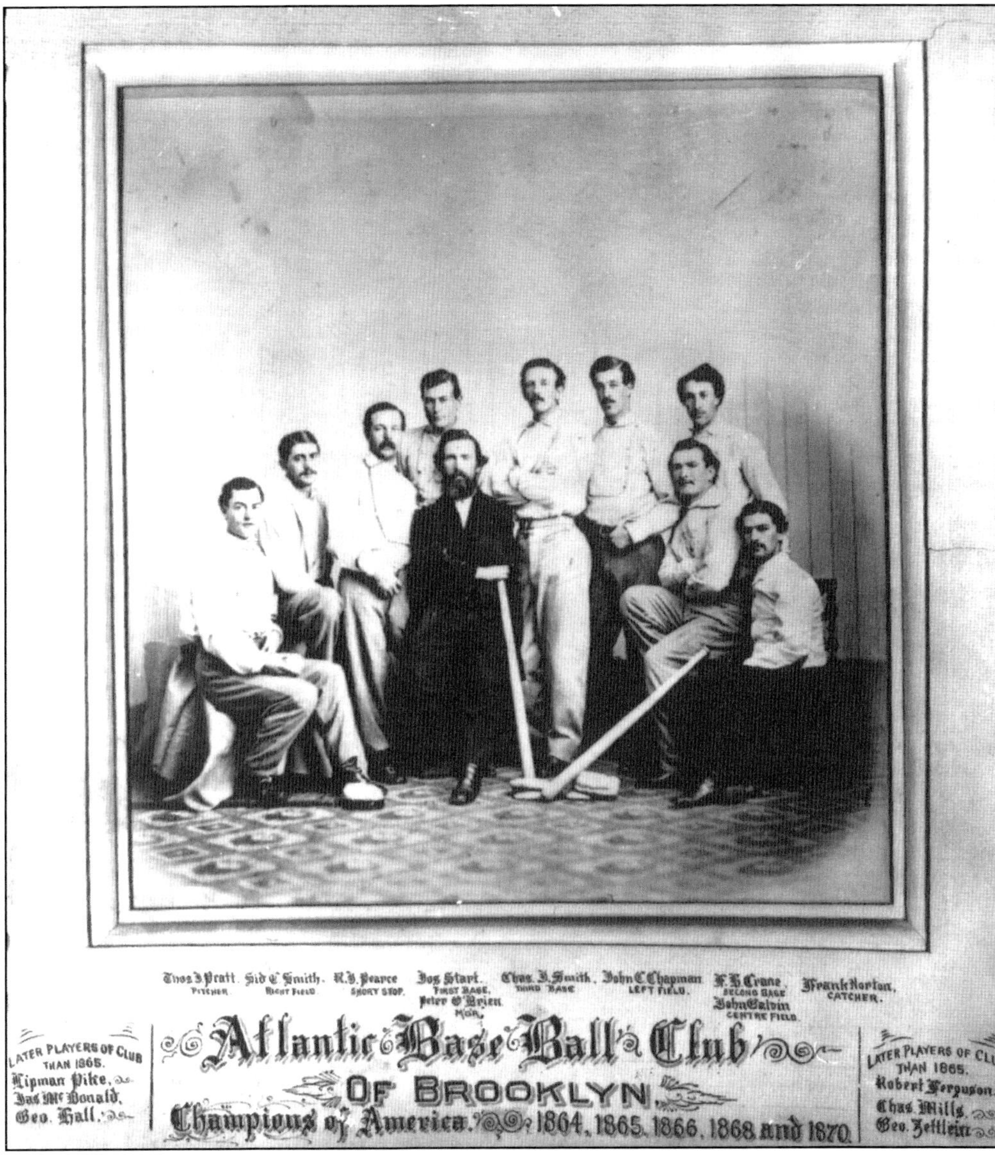

ATLANTIC BASE BALL CLUB OF BROOKLYN, CHAMPIONS OF AMERICA. *Among the Atlantic players are many innovators of the game including Dicky Pearce. The Atlantic Base Ball Club, of Brooklyn, claimed to be Champions of America in 1864, 1865, 1866, 1868, and 1870—the boasting rings out in this classic image of the Atlantic team of the late 1860s. They claim to be champions in these years, but historians and the media of the era disagree. In 1864, the Atlantic were 20–0–1 according to records, thus giving the best record. They followed that up with a 18–0 record, champions again. In 1866, the Unions of Morrisania were considered champions with a 25–3 record, followed closely by the Philadelphia Athletics with a 23–2 mark. Brooklyn sported a 17–3 record that season but still claimed to be champs. In 1868, the Philadelphia had a 47–3 record and the Atlantics had a 47–7 record. The Athletics also had two victories over the Atlantics (18–9 and 37–13). And in 1870, the Atlantics were the fifth-best team in the country (at best) behind the New York Mutuals, Cincinnati Red Stockings, Chicago White Stockings, Philadelphia Athletics, and Forest City of Rockford, all having better records than Brooklyn that season. (Source: Transcendental Graphics.)*

June 27.—Atlantic and Mutual, at Hoboken. Atlantic, 26; Mutual, 16. Umpire, Thos. Fitzgerald, Athletic Club, of Philadelphia.

July 6.—Atlantic and Nassau, of Princeton, N. J., on Atlantic ground. Atlantic, 42; Nassau, 7. Umpire, Simon Burns, Mutual Club.

July 8.—Atlantic and Empire, on Atlantic ground. Atlantic, 33; Empire, 8. Umpire. George Flanley, Excelsior Club.

July 18.—Atlantic and Resolute, on Resolute's ground. Atlantic, 18; Resolute, 1. Umpire, Thos. Fitzgerald, Athletic Club, of Philadelphia.

July 20.—Atlantic and Eagle (single game), at Hoboken. Atlantic, 45; Eagle, 12. Umpire, James Forsyth, Gotham Club.

July 26, 1864.—Atlantic and Eureka (return game), on Atlantic ground. Atlantic, 25; Eureka, 13. Umpire, John J. Grum, Eckford Club.

July 30.—Atlantic and Star, on Star ground. Atlantic, 35; Star, 16. Umpire, William Culyer, Empire Club.

August 4.—Atlantic and Star, on Atlantic ground.. Atlantic, 35; Star, 17. Umpire, M. Rogers, Resolute Club.

August 7.—Visited Philadelphia, to play the clubs of that city; registered at the American Hotel. On the ninth, the club and friends were invited to a supper given by the Keystone Club, at the St. James's Hotel. On the tenth, the Club and friends were taken in charge by the Olympic Club, and by stages proceeded to the Schuylkill Falls, and there partook of a supper. On the twelfth, they were invited to a fruit supper provided by Mrs. Col. Moore. Returned to Brooklyn on the thirteenth.

GAMES PLAYED IN PHILADELPHIA.— August 8.—Atlantic and Camden, of Camden, N. J., on Olympic ground. Atlantic, 64; Olympic, 10. Umpire, G. D. Kleinfelder, Athletic Club, of Philadelphia.

August 9.—Atlantic and Keystone, of Philadelphia, on Olympic ground. Atlantic, 65; Keystone, 10. Umpire, Joseph Patchen, Excelsior Club.

August 10.— Atlantic and Olympic, of Philadelphia, on Olympic ground. Atlantic, 58; Olympic, 11. Umpire, E. J. O'Flynn, Enterprise Club.

August 11.—Atlantic and Athletic, of Philadelphia, on Olympic ground. Atlantic, 43; Athletic, 16. Umpire, D. A. Sutton, Enterprise Club.

August 23.—Atlantic and Gotham, on Gotham ground. Atlantic, 14; Gotham, 9. Umpire, Benj. Harris, Mutual Club.

September 1.—Atlantic and Resolute, on Atlantic ground. Atlantic, 53; Resolute, 6. Umpire, D. A. Sutton, Enterprise Club.

September 12.—Atlantic and Mutual, on Atlantic ground. Atlantic, 21; Mutual, 16. Umpire, Samuel Yates, Eagle Club.

September 19.—Atlantic and Gotham, on Atlantic ground. Atlantic, 38; Gotham, 12. Umpire, J. J. Westervelt, Empire Club.

September 20.—The Club having accepted a challenge from the Young Canadian Club, of Woodstock, Canada West, to meet them at Rochester, and play a match game to test the merits of the two clubs; the Young Canadians never having been defeated, and were recognized as the champion club of Canada. The club left Brooklyn on the twentieth, arrived in Rochester on the twenty-first; registered at the Lawrence House. Alert Hose Company, No. 1, of Rochester, treated the Club in the most hospitable manner, placing their house at the Club's disposal, as the city was full of strangers, it being the time of the State Fair. About the time of leaving, received several invitations to play clubs on the route, most of which they were compelled to decline. The games played were—

September 22.—Atlantic and Young Canadian, of Woodstock, C. W. (International Champion Game), at Rochester, New York. Atlantic, 75; Young Canadian, 11. Umpire, William McMahon, of Mutual Club, of New York.

September 23.—Atlantic and Ontario of Rochester, at Rochester. Atlantic, 54; Ontario, 5.

Umpire, R. McWhinnie, Young Canadian Club. Left Rochester on the 23d for Utica, registered at Bagg's Hotel, having accepted an invitation from the Utica Club. Commenced to play on the morning of the 24th, but after playing three innings, the game was terminated by the rain. Subsequently the Atlantics were taken in charge by the Utica Club, and entertained at a superb dinner at the Central House. Left Utica on the afternoon of the 24th, and arrived in Brooklyn on the 25th.

October 19.—Atlantic and Empire, at Hoboken. Atlantic, 15; Empire, 7. Umpire, J. Seaver Page, Active Club.

OFFICERS FOR 1865.—President, William F. Babcock; Vice-President, W. H. Lockwood; Secretary, James Mowlem; Treasurer, A. H. Mumby. Fifth Annual Ball was held at Gothic Hall, January 10, 1865.

January 12, 1865.—Atlantic and Gotham, on the Capitoline Skating Pond, with skates, for a silver ball. Atlantic, 32; Gotham, 5. Umpire, W. N. Wicks, Excelsior Club.

January 16.—Atlantic and Gotham, on Sylvan Lake Skating Pond, Hoboken, with skates, Atlantic, 19; Gotham, 39. Umpire, J. J. Westervelt, Empire Club.

January 26.—Atlantic and Gotham, on Washington Skating Pond, Brooklyn, with skates. Atlantic, 50; Gotham, 30. B. Bassini, Excelsior Club, Umpire.

June 21.—Atlantic and Empire, at Hoboken. Atlantic, 21; Empire, 10. Umpire, Wm. McMahon, Mutual Club.

July 10, second nines.—Atlantic and Empire, on Atlantic ground. Atlantic, 60; Empire, 36. Umpire, G. T. Cook, Enterprise Club.

July 14.—Atlantic and Gotham, at Hoboken. Atlantic, 38; Gotham , 21. Umpire, W. McMahon, Mutual Club.

July 20.—Atlantic and Lowell, of Boston, on Atlantic ground. Atlantic, 45; Lowell, 17. Umpire, J. J. Grum, Eckford Club.

July 24.—Atlantic and Union, of Morrisania, at Morrisania. Atlantic, 15; Union, 5. Umpire, J. M. Ryder, Empire Club.

July 27.—Atlantic and Empire, on Atlantic ground. Atlantic, 65; Empire, 3. Umpire, G. Flanley, Excelsior Club.

July 29.—Atlantic and Keystone, of Phila., on Atlantic ground. Atlantic, 33; Keystone,13. Umpire, E. H. Hayhurst, Athletic Club, of Philadelphia.

August 3.—Atlantic and Mutual, at Hoboken. Atlantic, 13; Mutual, 12. Umpire, S. Yates, Eagle Club.

August 10.—Atlantic and Star, on Atlantic ground. Atlantic, 26; Star, 13. Umpire, W. H. Murtah, Enterprise. Club.

August 14.—Atlantic and Mutual, on Atlantic ground. Atlantic, 40; Mutual, 28. Umpire, J. J. Grum, Eckford Club.

August 18.—Atlantic and Eureka, at Newark. Atlantic, 21; Eureka, 20. Umpire, W. F. Hudson, Union Club, of Morrisania.

August 23.—Atlantic and Active, at Hoboken. Atlantic, 24; Active, 19. Umpire, T. Bomeisler, Eureka Club.

August 28.—Atlantic and Eagle, single game, on Atlantic ground. Atlantic, 48; Eagle, 10. Umpire, J. Delaney, Atlantic Club.

August 28.—Visited Washington, D. C., having accepted an invitation from the National Club of that city. Were the guests of the Nationals, and were quartered at the National Hotel. Played on the 29th, and left on the 30th.

August 29.—Atlantic and National, of Washington, at Washington. Atlantic, 34; National, 19. Umpire, T. S. Dakin, Excelsior Club.

August 31.—Atlantic and Eureka, on Atlantic ground. Atlantic, 38: Eureka, 37. Umpire, John J. Grum, Eckford Club.

September 21.—Atlantic and Eckford, on Atlantic ground. Atlantic, 28; Eckford, 23. Umpire,

G. Flanley, Excelsior Club.

September 23.—Left Brooklyn on a visit to Boston. Arrived in that city on the 24th, quartering at the Broomfield House. On Monday, 25th, played, and were entertained by the Lowell Club. 26th.—played the Tri-Mountain Club. 27th.—played the Harvard Club. Left Boston on the 27th for Hartford, Conn. Were met by a committee of the Charter Oak Club, and by them quartered at the Allyn House, as their guests. On the evening of the 28th left for Brooklyn.

September 25.—Atlantic and Lowell, at Boston. Atlantic, 30; Lowell, 10. Umpire, Flagg, Harvard Club.

September 26.—Atlantic and Tri-Mountain, at Boston. Atlantic, 107; Tri-Mountain, 16. Umpire, Flagg, Harvard Club.

September 27.—Atlantic and Harvard, at Boston. Atlantic, 58; Harvard, 22. Umpire, John A. Lowell, of the Lowell Club.

September 28.—Atlantic and Charter Oak of Hartford, at Hartford. Atlantic, 37; Charter, 11. Umpire, D. A. Sutton, Atlantic Club.

October 5.—Atlantic and Union, of Morrisania, on Atlantic ground. Atlantic, 58; Union, 30. Umpire, J. E. Duval, Excelsior Club.

October 13.—Atlantic and Eckford, on Eckford ground. Atlantic, 35; Eckford, 8. Umpire, E. Brown, Mutual Club.

October 30.—Atlantic and Athletic, of Philadelphia, at Philadelphia. Atlantic, 21; Athletic, 15. Umpire, T. C. Knight, Camden Club.

November 6.—Atlantic and Athletic, of Philadelphia, on Atlantic ground. Atlantic, 27; Athletic, 24. Umpire, J. J. Grum, Eckford Club.

November 27.—Atlantic and a Picked Nine, on Atlantic ground. Atlantic, 28; Picked Nine, 7. Umpire, William Culyer, Empire Club.

May 30, 1866.—Atlantic and Harvard, of Cambridge, Mass. Capitoline grounds; won by the Atlantic; score, 37 to 15, time, 3.15.

June 14.—Atlantic and Irvington, at Irvington, N. J.; Atlantic score 17 runs; Irvington, 23 runs; time, 4 hours..

June 18.—Atlantic and Peconic, Capitoline grounds; won by the Atlantic by a score of 43 to 19; time, 2.45.

July 19.—Atlantic and Peconic; score, 64 to 7, in favor of the Atlantic; time, 2.40.

July 21.—Atlantic, and Atlantic of Jamaica, L.I., on the ground of the latter; score, 38 to 4, in favor of the Atlantic; time, 2.15.

August 8.—Atlantic and Union, of Lansingburgh, on Capitoline grounds; score, 46 to 11, in favor of the Atlantic; time, 2.15.

August 18.—Atlantic and Eureka, at Newark, N. J.; won by the Eureka by a score of 30 to 10; time, 2.20.

September 9.—Atlantic and Eckford, on Union ball grounds; score, 28 to 12, in favor of the Atlantic; time, 2.25.

September 13.—Atlantic and Mutual, at Hoboken; score of Atlantic, 17 runs; Mutual score, 15 runs; time, 2.30.

September 24.—Atlantic and Irvington, Capitoline grounds; return game. Irvington score, 11 runs; Atlantic score, 28 runs; time, 2.03.

September 27. Atlantic and Eureka, Capitoline grounds; score, 30 to 20., in favor of the Atlantic; time, 2.40.

October 1.—Atlantic and Athletic, in Philadelphia. Game brought to an abrupt termination, before two innings had been played, by a disorderly assemblage.

October 2.—Atlantic and Keystone, on the grounds of the latter, in Philadelphia. Keystone, score, 18 runs; Atlantic score, 25, runs; time, 2.25.

October 3.—Atlantic and Camden, on the grounds of the latter; won by the Atlantic; score 35 to 7; time, 2.15.

October 11.—Atlantic and Star, Capitoline grounds; score 46 to 18, in favor of the Atlantic.
October 15.—Atlantic and Athletic, of Philadelphia, Capitoline grounds; won by the Atlantic; score, 27 to 17; Umpire, George Flanley, of the Excelsior club; time, 3 hours.
October 18.—Atlantic and Mutual, Capitoline grounds; in favor of the Atlantic; score, 34 to 24.
October 25.—Atlantic and Eureka; home-and-home game, on the Union ball grounds; seven innings; Eureka, 13 runs; Atlantic, 38 runs; time, 2.15.
October 29.—Atlantic and Irvington; Home-and-home game, on the Union ball grounds, Brooklyn; at the end of nine innings the score was 5 and 5; the Atlantic won on the tenth, by a score of 12 to 6; time, 2.15; Umpire, Birdsall, of the Union Club.

The Atlantic Club play on the Capitoline grounds, and practise on Monday and Thursday. They have 170 active, and 50 honorary members. Their uniform consists of light blue pants, white flannel shirt, and red and white caps. In addition to their summer club-room, they have also a handsomely furnished club-room at No. 355 Fulton street, Halsey Building. Officers for 1866:—President, William V. Babcock; Vice-President, George R. Rogers; Recording Secretary, James Mowlem; Corresponding Secretary, Sidney Smith; Treasurer, A. H. Mumby.

ECKFORD CLUB

The Eckford Base Ball Club, of Brooklyn, which has always ranked as one of the best clubs in the United States, was organized in 1855, but did not engage in any matches until 1856, when they played but two games, their competitors being the Union Club of Morrisania. We quote the following letter, from the pen of Mr. Frank Pidgeon, which was published in *Porter's Spirit*, in January, 1855, as it will convey an infinitely better idea of the Eckford's than any thing we can offer the reader. The name of Frank Pidgeon is familiar to the lovers and patrons of base ball where ever the pastime has a follower and advocate, and his merits and character are as much respected as they are widely known.

"A year ago last August, a small number of young men of that part of the city known as the Island, formed themselves into a club, for the purpose of enjoying this noble and manly game. Being shipwrights and mechanics, we could not make it convenient to practise more than once a week; and we labored under the impression that want of practice and the small number from whom to select our nine, would make it almost impossible for us to win a match if we engaged in one. However, we were willing to do the best we could, if some club would give us an invitation to play. But, alas, no such invitation came, and we began seriously to doubt if we were worth taking notice of.

"Still, we had some merry times among ourselves; we would forget business and everything else on Tuesday afternoons, go out in the green fields, don our ball suits, and go at it with a perfect rush. At such times, we were boys again. Such sport as this brightens a man up, and improves him, both in mind and body. After longing for a match, yet so dreading (not a defeat-we were sure of that) a regular 'Waterloo,' we finally, through sheer desperation, expressed a wish to play the winners in the match between the Baltic and Union Club of Morrisania. The Union won, and signified their willingness to play us. Well, we had got what we wanted—a match; and then, what?—why, we would have to do the best we could. The day came at last, on which we were to meet the conquerors of the Baltic; and nine determined, but badly-scared men, whistling to keep up their spirits, might have been seen winding their way to the Red House. It would be difficult to describe the sensations we felt that day—such an intense desire to win, and such a dread of defeat! We knew that, if badly beaten, we could never succeed in building up a club. Many of our friends would not go to see the match, because they did not wish to witness our defeat. They said that the last time our 'Island' boy spread himself, he beat

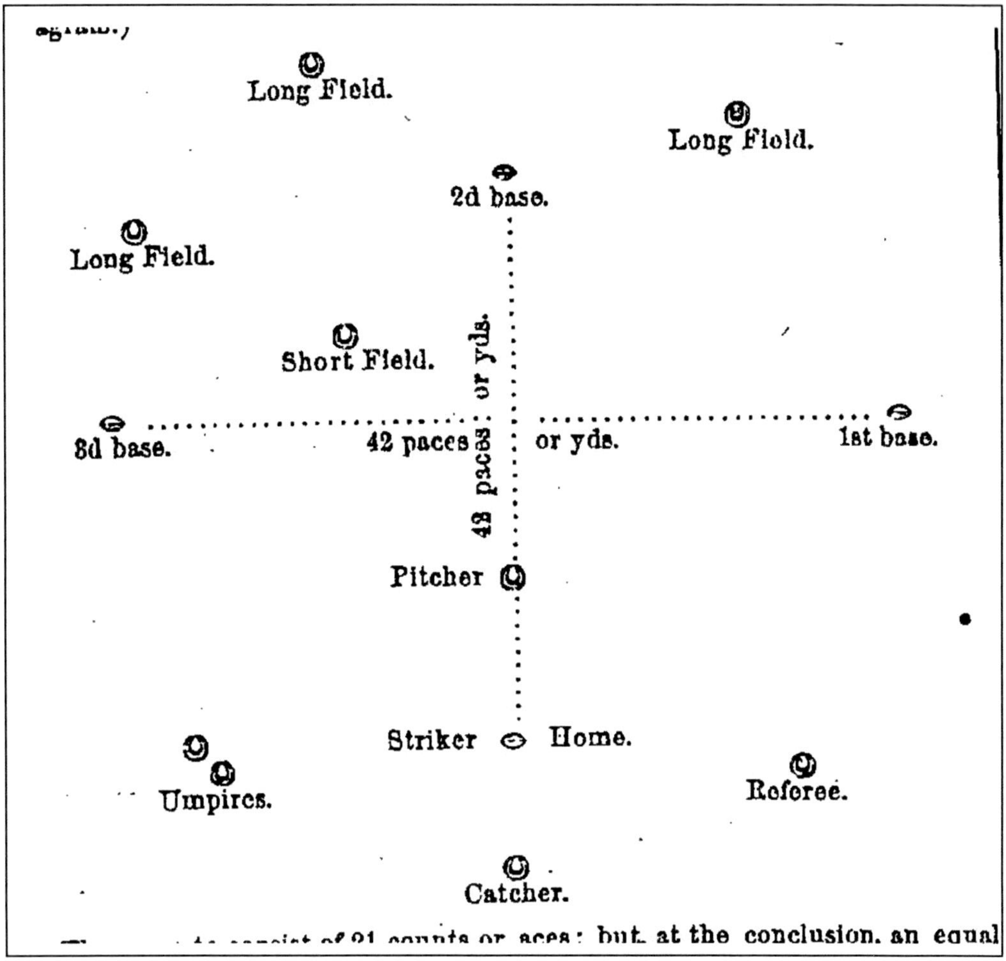

Putnam Diagram. *This diagram, published in* Porter's Spirit of the Times, *1856, shows the field set out by the "Putnam Rules." For you vintage base ball players, notice that the fielders are not in the center of the fields as they are positioned today. (Source:* Vintage Ballist.*)*

not only a club, but a nation—aye, the world! Poor GEORGE STEERS! We were boys together! Anything he did was well done, indeed. I fear many a long day will go by before we see his equal again.

"But, to the game. 'We pulled off our coats, and rolled up our sleeves; we stood up to the rack, but were very nervous—first appearance on any stage! Our first man took the bat, tipped out, great dependence placed on him. Good heaven! how unfortunate! Next man got scared; caught out. No use trying to win; do the best we can, however. Steady! boys, steady! Third man gave the ball a regular crusher. One desperate yell burst from eight throats, and I am not sure that the striker did not yell with the rest. First base, go it! Second base, come up! go again! Stay there, stay there! Another fortunate strike; man on the third base got home. Glory! One run. Ah! How proud the Eckford Club were of that run. Some ran to the Umpire's book to see how it looked on paper.

"The Innings ended with three runs for the Eckford. The Unions took the bat and made two runs —could it be possible! We could scarcely believe it. We did the best we could to keep our end up, and by that means we overdid the matter, and the result was: Eckford, 22; Union, 8. About seven o'clock that evening, nine peacocks might have been seen on their way home, with tail-feathers spread. Our friends were astonished, as well as ourselves, and all felt rejoiced at the result, except one old croaker, who insisted that 'it was all luck, and the next match would prove he was right, and that the Unions would bring out a stronger team in the next match.' We consoled ourselves, however, with the idea, that if we did not beat their team, we would send them along a pretty fast gait. On the 15th of October, we again met our gentlemanly opponents at the Red House. If we lost this match, then indeed they might say the first was all luck; but if we could only win! Every pulse beat quicker at the thought. Where there is a determination to succeed, there is seldom failure. We won, and the score stood: Union, 6; Eckford, 22. I don't exactly remember about the peacocks coming home that evening; all I know is, that the Unions fraternized with us, and we got home safe and happy, and, like true Christians, forgave the croaker. We look back with pride and pleasure to our first base ball matches, and hope that in all our future matches, whether we are the victors or vanquished, the same spirit of kindness and friendship may exist between our opponents and ourselves as now exist between the Union Club, of Morrisania, and the Eckford, of Manhattan Island.

F.P.

"New York, January, 1857"

September 17, 1856.—Union, of Morrisania, at Red House, N.Y. Eckford, 22; Union, 8.
October 15.—Union, of Morrisania, at Red House, N.Y. Eckford, 22; Union, 6.
June 16, 1857.—Eagle, of N.Y., at Greenpoint. Eckford, 20; Eagle, 34.
July 29.—Empire, of N.Y., at Greenpoint. Eckford, 35; Empire, 33.
September 15.—Atlantic, of Brooklyn, at Greenpoint. Eckford, 17; Atlantic, 21.
September , 15.—Eagle, N.Y., at Hoboken. Eckford, 22; Eagle, 23.
October 9.—Empire, of N. Y., at Hoboken. Eckford, 23; Empire, 13.
October 22.—Atlantic, of Brooklyn, at Bedford. Eckford, 11; Atlantic, 29.
August 31, 1858.—Gotham, of N.Y., at Greenpoint. Eckford, 23; Gotham, 17.
September , 4.—Putnam, of Brooklyn, at Brooklyn, E.D. Eckford, 29 Harlem, 10.
September 8.—Harlem, of N. Y., at Harlem. Eckford, 40; Harlem, 22.
September 14.—Continental, of N.Y., at Greenpoint. Eckford, 48; Continental, 18.
October 12.— Continental, of N.Y., at Greenpoint. Eckford, 13; Continental, 9.
October 19.—Gotham, of N.Y., at Hoboken. Eckford, 6; Gotham, 23.
May 2, 1859.—Gotham, of N.Y., at Greenpoint. Eckford, 17; Gotham, 10.
July 1.—Putnam, of Brooklyn. Eckford, 23; Putnam, 17.
July 8.—Atlantic, of Brooklyn, at Greenpoint. Eckford, 15; Atlantic, 25.
August 2.—Continental, at Wheat Hill. Eckford, 79; Continental, 19.
August 9.—Empire, of N.Y., at Hoboken. Eckford, 21; Empire, 8.
August 17.—Hoboken, of N.Y., at Hoboken. Eckford, 40; Hoboken, 16.
August 20.—Harlem, of N.Y., at Harlem. Eckford, 15; Harlem, 13.
September 8.— Atlantic, of Brooklyn, at Bedford. Eckford, 22; Atlantic, 16.
September 28.— Harlem, at Greenpoint. Eckford, 28; Harlem, 5.
October 7.—Hoboken, of N.Y., at Greenpoint. Eckford, 51; Hoboken, 13.
November 12.—Atlantic, of Brooklyn, at Hoboken. Eckford, 12; Atlantic, 22.
November 24.—Newburgh Club, at Greenpoint. Eckford, 58; Newburgh, 19.
April, 23, 1860.— Union, of Morrisania, at Morrisania. Eckford, 22; Union, 19.
June 13.—Putnam, of Brooklyn, at Bowronville, L.I. Eckford, 36; Putnam, 29.
June 25.—Continental, of Brooklyn, at Greenpoint. Eckford, 30; Continental, 15.
July 11.—Star, of Brooklyn, at Greenpoint. Eckford, 19; Star, 6.

July 24.—Enterprise, of Brooklyn, at Bedford. Eckford, 20; Enterprise, 10.
August 1.— Union, of Elizabeth, N.J., at Elizabeth. Eckford, 35; Union, 19.
August 8.—Empire, of N.Y., at Hoboken. Eckford, 21; Empire, 13.
August 29.—Newburgh, of Newburgh, at Greenpoint. Eckford, 36; Newburgh, 22.
September 5.— Star, of Brooklyn, at Carroll Park, Brooklyn. Eckford, 16; Star, 8.
September 10.— Union, of Elizabeth, at Greenpoint. Eckford, 47; Union, 6.
September 19.—Union, of Morrisania, at Greenpoint. Eckford, 41; Union, 5.
September 26.— Enterprise, of Brooklyn, at Greenpoint. Eckford, 31; Enterprise, 18.
October 4.—Empire, of N.Y., at Greenpoint. Eckford, 26; Empire, 10.
October 8.—Metropolitan, of N.Y., at 3rd avenue and 61st street, N.Y. Eckford, 28; Metropolitan, 10.
October 15.—Atlantic, of Brooklyn, at Greenpoint. Eckford, 15; Atlantic, 17.
October 22.—Atlantic, of Brooklyn, at Bedford, L.I. Eckford, 20; Atlantic, 15.
October 29.— Atlantic, of Brooklyn, at Greenpoint. Eckford, 11; Atlantic, 20.
June 5, 1861.—Enterprise, of Brooklyn, at Greenpoint. Eckford, 53; Enterprise, 19.
June 8.—Mutual, of N.Y., at Hoboken. Eckford, 18; Mutual,10.
July 23.—Eagle, of N.Y., at Hoboken. Eckford, 23; Eagle, 32.
August 15.—Harlem, of N.Y., at Harlem. Eckford, 26; Harlem, 16.
August 28.— Newark, of Newark, at Newark. Eckford, 18; Newark, 12.
September 5.—Exercise, of Brooklyn, at Bedford. Eckford, 27; Exercise, 20.
September 13.—Eureka, of Newark, at Newark, N.J. Eckford, 11; Eureka, 9.
September 16.—Newark, of Newark, at Greenpoint. Eckford, 24; Newark, 25.
October 1.—Exercise, of Brooklyn, at Greenpoint. Eckford, 27; Exercise, 12.
October 17.—Enterprise, of Brooklyn, at South Brooklyn. Eckford, 23; Enterprise, 26.
November 12.—Newburgh, of Newburgh, at Greenpoint. Eckford, 38; Newburgh, 17.
May 20, 1862.—Enterprise, of Brooklyn, at Greenpoint. Eckford, 19; Enterprise, 20.
July 4.—Hudson River, of Newburgh, at Newburgh, N.Y. Eckford, 74; Hudson River, 29.
July 29.—Eagle, of N.Y., at Hoboken. Eckford, 18; Eagle, 5.
August 8.—Mutual, of N.Y., at Hoboken. Eckford, 28; Mutual, 24.
August 11.—Atlantic, of Brooklyn, at Union ground. Eckford, 20; Atlantic, 14.
August 13.—Harlem, of Harlem, at Union ground. Eckford, 42; Harlem, 25.
August 18.—Atlantic, of Brooklyn, Union ground, Brooklyn. Eckford, 5; Atlantic, 39.
August 19.—Newark, of Newark, N.J., at Union ground, Brooklyn. Eckford, 35; Newark, 19.
August 29.—Union, of Morrisania, at Morrisania. Eckford, 29; Union, 11.
September 18.—Atlantic, of Brooklyn, at Union ground, Brooklyn. Eckford, 8; Atlantic, 3.
September 24.—Mutual, of N.J., at Union ground, Brooklyn. Eckford, 28; Mutual, 14.
October 7.—Union, of Morrisania, at Union ground, Brooklyn. Eckford, 13; Union, 10.
October 21.—Combination Nine, of Philadelphia, at Philadelphia. Eckford, 39; Combination, 8.
October 22.—Olympic, of Philadelphia, at Philadelphia. Eckford, 39; Olympic, 13.
October 23.—Athletic, of Philadelphia, at Philadelphia. Eckford, 32; Athletic, 25.
October 24.—Keystone, of Philadelphia, at Philadelphia. Eckford, 26; Keystone, 2.
June 17, 1863.—Athletic, of Philadelphia, at Union ground, Brooklyn. Eckford, 10; Athletic, 5.
July 22.—Mutual, of N.Y., at Hoboken. Eckford, 10; Mutual, 9.
July 30.—Union, of Morrisania, at Morrisania. Eckford, 8; Union, 4.
August 4.—Hudson River, of Newburgh, at Union ground, Brooklyn. Eckford, 50; Hudson River, 13.
August 14.—Resolute, of Brooklyn, at Union ground, Brooklyn. Eckford, 16; Resolute, 5.
September 2.—Atlantic, of Brooklyn, at Bedford, L.I. Eckford, 31; Atlantic, 10.
September 8.—Atlantic, of Brooklyn, at Union ground, Brooklyn. Eckford, 21; Atlantic, 11.
September 16.—Resolute, of Brooklyn, at Union ground, Brooklyn. Eckford, 24; Resolute, 8.

September 24.—Union, of Morrisania, at Union ground, Brooklyn. Eckford, 29; Union, 5.
June 7, 1864.—Combination Ten, at Capitoline ground, Brooklyn. Eckford, 18; Combination, 24.
July 21.—Newark, of Newark, at Newark. Eckford, 37; Newark, 22.
August 22.—Mutual, of N.Y., at Hoboken. Eckford, 17; Mutual, 29.
August 30.—Eagle, of N.Y., at Hoboken. Eckford, 14; Eagle, 16.
October 10.—Mutual, of N.Y., at Union ground, Brooklyn. Eckford, 19; Mutual, 23.
June 21, 1865.—Union, of Morrisania, at Morrisania. Eckford, 18; Union, 27.
June 30.—Newark, of Newark, at Union ground, Brooklyn. Eckford, 22; Newark, 5.
July 14.—Eagle, of N.Y., at Union ground, Brooklyn. Eckford, 38; Eagle, 7.
August 2,.—Empire, of N.Y., at Hoboken. Eckford, 48; Empire, 35.
August 9.—Union, of Morrisania, at Union ground, Brooklyn. Eckford, 22; Union, 34.
August 22.—Keystone, of Philadelphia, at Union ground, Brooklyn. Eckford, 16; Keystone, 18.
August 25.—Mutual, of N.Y., at Union ground, Brooklyn, Eckford, 10; Mutual, 19.
August 28.—Enterprise, of Brooklyn, at Union ground, Brooklyn. Eckford, 21; Enterprise, 20.
September 5.—Gotham, of N.Y., at Hoboken. Eckford, 18; Gotham, 9.
Septneber13.—Enterprise, of Brooklyn, at Bedford, L.I. Eckford, 26; Enterprise, 25.
September 21.—Atlantic, fo Brooklyn, at Bedford, L.I. Eckford, 23; Atlantic, 28.
September 28.—Mutual, of N.Y., at Hoboken. Eckford, 23; Mutual, 11.
October 10.—Empire, of Brooklyn, at Union ground, Brooklyn. Eckford, 38; Empire, 8.
October 13.—Atlantic, of Brooklyn, at Union ground, Brooklyn. Eckford, 8; Atlantic, 35.
May 4, 1866.—Picked Nine, at Union ground, Brooklyn. Eckford, 50; Picked Nine, 4.
June 6.—Union, of Morrisania, at Union ground, Brooklyn. Eckford, 11; Union, 15.
June 20.—Enterprise, of Brooklyn, at Capitoline ground, Brooklyn. Eckford, 39; Enterprise, 21.
July 2.—Irvington, of Irvington, at Irvington, N.J. Eckford, 22; Irvington, 37.
July 4.—M.M. Van Dyke, at Union ground, Brooklyn. Eckford, 60; M.M. Van Dyke, 5.
July 24.—Eagle, at Hoboken. Eckford, 38; Eagle, 33.
August 1.—Empire, at Hoboken. Eckford, 53; Empire, 23.
August 22.—Active, at Hoboken. Eckford, 16; Active, 19.
August 24.—Oriental, at Greenpoint. Eckford, 33; Oriental, 12.
August 28.—Unionville, of New Utrecht, at Union ground, Brooklyn. Eckford, 56; Unionville, 20.
September 4.—Empire, at Union ground, Brooklyn. Eckford, 32; Empire, 19.
September, 3.—Enterprise, of Manhasset, L.I., at Manhasset, L.I. Eckford, 34; Enterprise, 10.
September 10.—Enterprise, of Brooklyn, at Union ground, Brooklyn. Eckford, 17; Enterprise, 22.
September 12.—Irvington, at Union ground, Brooklyn. Eckford, 13; Irvington, 20.
September 19.—Atlantic, at Union ground, Brooklyn. Eckford, 12; Atlantic, 28.
October 1.—Active, at Union ground, Brooklyn. Eckford, 21; Active, 6.
October 10.—Union, at Union ground, Brooklyn. Eckford, 58; Union, 29.
October 11.—Mutual, at Hoboken. Eckford, 10; Mutual, 18.
October 18.—Union, at Morrisania. Eckford, 9; Union, 20.
October 19.—M.M. Van Dyke, at Union ground, Brooklyn. Eckford, 57; M.M. Van Dyke, 12.
October 24.—Oriental, at Union ground, Brooklyn. Eckford, 27, Oriental, 9.

Location of play-grounds: From 1855 to 1862 on the Manor House grounds, at Greenpoint, L.I. From that to the present , on the Union ball ground, Brooklyn, E.D. Practice days: Tuesday and Friday. Uniform: grey pants, white shirt, white cap with red star, and red worsted belt. Active and honorary members, 150. The Eckford annual balls have been given as follows: January 20, 1861, at the Odeon. January 25, 1864, at Union Hall. January 26, 1865, at

Union Hall. January 4, 1866, at the Odeon. Officers of the club since its institution: 1855 President, Francis Pidgeon; Vice-President, Wm. Logan; Secretary, H.F. Metzler. 1856, President, Wm. H. Haight; Vice-President, H.C. Calkins; Secretary, H.F. Metzler. 1857 President, W.H. Haight; Vice-President, H.C. Calkins; Secretary, H.F. Metzler. 1858, President, Peter Tostevan; Vice-President, W.H. Bell; Secretary, Francis Pidgeon. 1859, President, Louis Guiledeau; Vice-President, W. H. Bell; Secretary, John J. Grum. 1860, President, Francis Pidgeon; Vice-President, George Lamphear; Secretary, M.L. Mann; Treasurer, E.F. Jenkins. Mr. Jenkins held the position of Treasurer up to the close of 1865. For 1861, President, Francis Pidgeon; Vice-President, George Lamphear; Secretary, D.J. McAuslan. 1862, President, E.F. Jenkins; Vice-President, John J. Crum; Secretary, D.J. McAuslan. 1863, President, Francis Pidgeon; Vice-President, John J. Grum; Secretary, Wm. M. Brown. 1864, President, John J. Grum; Vice-President, Henry Manolt; Secretary, Wm. J. Watson. 1865, President, R.W. Kenyon; Vice-President, W. M. Brown; Secretary, M.M. Simonson. 1866, President, George Wildey; Vice-President, W. M. Brown; Secretary, Guy F. Gosman; Treasurer, Joseph L. Vanderbilt.

CONTEST CLUB

The Contest Base Ball Club, of Brooklyn, was organized in 1857, being the first junior club organized in Brooklyn. They held the championship of the juniors from 1857 to 1861, when they were defeated by the Mohawks, being the first and only defeat in a home-and-home game that they suffered since organization. Last year the Club was reorganized by the old members, and in the latter part of 1865 they stood at the head of the juniors. They played eight home-and-home games, —each time carrying off the ball as a memento of victory. The Unknowns and Monmouths received challenges from them, which they refused to accept, so that the Contests think their title as champions of the juniors could easily be substantiated if they desired to claim it, but they do not, as they now belong to the seniors. They have upwards of forty members, and are in an extremely flourishing condition. They practice every Tuesday, Thursday, and Saturday on the Contest grounds, corner of Twelfth street and Third avenue.

The annual election for officers for 1866 was held in April, when the following were chosen:—President, Charles Hough; Vice-President, George Tompkins; Secretary, J. Boerum; Treasurer, Silas Boone; Corresponding Secretary, F. Boone.

July 7, 1866.—Contest and Greenwood, on the Contest's ground. Score, 57 to 13, in favor of Contest.

July 17.—Contest and Excelsior. Score, 34 to 5, in favor of Excelsior.

August 10.—Contest and Irvington. Carroll Park grounds. Score, 22 to 14, in favor of Irvington.

August 30.—Contest and Irvington, at Irvington, N.J. Score, 29 to 14, in favor of Irvington.

Nov. 17.—Contest and Pacific, of New Utrecht, L. I. Score, 15 to 14, in favor of Contest. Seven innings.

POWHATAN CLUB

The Powhatan Base Ball Club, of Brooklyn, was organized September 14, 1858, with the following officers: President, Edward Simpson; Vice-President, Edward Bartlett; Secretary, George H. Tourney; Treasurer, William Williamson.

We append summary of the games played by the Club:

November 11, 1858.—Powhatan, 36; Unknown, 10; played at Brooklyn.

July 23, 1859.—Powhatan and Resolute. Powhatan, 17; Resolute, 14.
August 19.—Powhatan and Oakland. Powhatan, 13; Oakland, 13; ten innings.
August 31.—Powhatan and Pacific. Powhatan, 37; Pacific, 22.
September 7.—Powhatan and Constellation. Powhatan, 24; Constellation, 19.
September 26.—Powhatan and Constellation. Powhatan, 22; Constellation, 10.
October 4, 1859.—Powhatan and Enterprise; played at Bedford; Powhatan, 11; Enterprise, 13.
October 11.—Powhatan and Pacific. Powhatan, 27; Pacific, 4.
October 18.— Powhatan and Lone Star, at Jersey City; Powhatan, 14; Lone Star, 12.
November 9.—Powhatan and Enterprise. Powhatan, 8; Enterprise, 15.
July 2, 1860.—Powhatan and Oakland. Powhatan, 35; Oakland, 10.
July 25.—Powhatan and Quickstep, at Bergen, N.J. Powhatan, 36; Quickstep, 9.
August 6.—Powhatan and Lone Star, at Jersey City. Powhatan, 48; Lone Star, 6.
August 22.—Powhatan and Oriental. (For the championship of the Juniors.) Played at Greenpoint. Powhatan, 16; Oriental, 11.
September 11.—Powhatan and Buena, at Morrisania. Powhatan, 20; Buena, 6.
September 18.—Powhatan and Quickstep. Powhatan, 33; Quickstep, 13.
October 9.—Powhatan and Oriental. Home-and-home game for the championship. Powhatan, 19; Oriental, 10.
May 21, 1861.—Powhatan and Star. Powhatan, 11; Star, 46.

In 1861 the Club became in a measure disorganized, on account of so many members entering the army. In September, 1865, the Powhatan reorganized, with the following officers: President, Wm. Williamson; Vice-President, A.H. Wray, Secretary, James Thompson; Treasurer, Thos. F. Mason.

July 27, 1866.—Powhatan and Greenwood. Powhatan, 23; Greenwood, 5.
August 17.—Powhatan and Mohawk. Powhatan, 17; Mohawk, 42.
August 28.—Powhatan and Atlantic, of Jamaica. Capitoline grounds. Powhatan, 51; Atlantic, 27.
September 4.—Atlantic (of Jamaica) and Powhatan (at Jamaica). Atlantic, 14; Powhatan, 9.
September 8.—Powhatan and Independent. Powhatan, 36; Independent, 19.
September 22.—Powhatan and Unionville, at Unionville, L.I. Powhatan, 41; Unionville, 15.
October 4.—Powhatan and Peconic, at Bedford. Powhatan, 28; Peconic, 27.
October 31.—Powhatan and Unionville, on Union Ball Ground. Powhatan, 16; Unionville, 9.

PACIFIC CLUB

The Pacific Base ball Club, of New Utrecht, L.I., was organized November 29, 1865. The first officers consisted of : President, J. Van Brunt, Jr.; Vice-President, Simon W. Dubois; Treasurer, Peter A. Hegeman; Secretary, Walter A. Brown. Number of members, fifty. Uniform; dark blue pants, white flannel shirt, blue cap, trimmed with red. Ground at Fort Hamilton. The following are the games the club has played:

July 14, 1866.—Pacific and Unionville, on the ground of the latter. Won by the Unionville, by 43 to 27.
July 21.—Pacific and Enterprise, at New Utrecht; 30 to 15, in favor of Enterprise.
October 24.—Pacific and Enterprise; won by Enterprise, whose score was 52 to 19.
November 10.—Pacific and Unionville, on the ground of the former; Unionville, 26; Pacific, 47.
November 17.—Pacific and Contest; seven innings; won by Contest; score. 15 to 14.

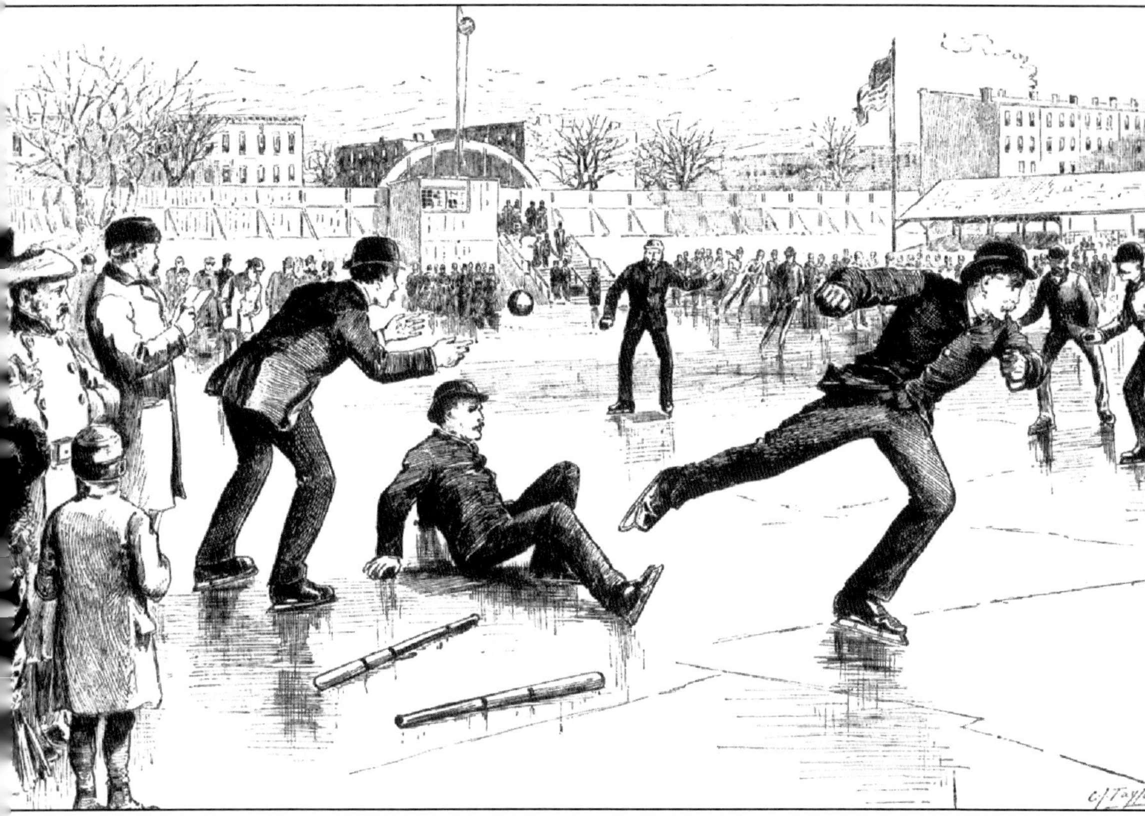

HARPER'S WOODCUT OF "BASEBALL ON SKATES." *These games are played on ice with skates, like a regular ball game. These came about through a combination of winter boredom and promoters' need for a winter gate. (Source: Transcendental Graphics.)*

ATLANTIC CLUB

The following is a summary of the games played by the Atlantic Base Ball Club of Jamaica, L.I., which was organized in August, 1855, and joined the National Association in 1860.

July 21, 1858.—Atlantic and Osceola, at Jamaica. 50 to 30, in favor of Atlantic.
August 10.—Atlantic and Pastime, at Bedford. 19 to 28; won by Pastime.
September 15.—Atlantic and Pastime. 24 to 14, in favor of Atlantic.
October 14.—Atlantic and Osceola, at Brooklyn. 15 to 7, in favor of Osceola.
July 8, 1859.—Atlantic and Pastime; played at Brooklyn. 13 to 25, in favor of Pastime.
July 18.—Atlantic and Osceola. 16 to 14, in favor of Osceola. Home-and-home game.
August 17.—Atlantic and Washington, at Mineola, L.I. 21 to 18, in favor of Atlantic.
September 14.—Atlantic and Hamilton. Won by Hamilton; score, 24 to 18.
September 28.—Atlantic and Hamilton. 19 to 22, in favor of Hamilton.
Atlantic and Astoria. In favor of Atlantic by 23 to 14.
August 31, 1860.—Atlantic and Exercise. Won by Atlantic, by 15 to 13.
July 4, 1862.—Atlantic and Constellation. Won by Atlantic, by 35 to 23; played at Jamaica.
July 30.—Atlantic and Constellation, at Brooklyn. Won by Constellation, by 24 to 15.
August 22.—Atlantic and Constellation. Home-and-home game; at Bedford. Score, 24 to 8, in favor of Atlantic.
September 7.—Atlantic and Pastime. Won by the Atlantic, by 33 to 24. Played on the Pastime ground.
July 21, 1866.—Atlantic, of Brooklyn, and Atlantic, of Jamaica, on the grounds of the latter. Score, 38 to 4, in favor of the Atlantic, of Brooklyn.
August 28.—Atlantic and Powhatan, in Brooklyn. Score, 51 to 26, in favor of Powhatan.
September 4.—Atlantic and Powhatan, at Jamaica. Score, 14 to 9, in favor of Atlantic.

The grounds are located at Beaver Pond, Jamaica, Long Island. Uniform— Dark blue pantaloons; white flannel jacket; cap, light grey.

OFFICERS FOR 1866.—President, Alexander Hagener; Vice-President, Theodore Rogers; Secretary, T. J. Cogswell; Treasurer, J.V.S. Wooley.

UNA CLUB

The Una Base ball Club, of Mount Vernon, N.Y., was organized April 1, 1865, with the following officers:

S.P. Moore, President; Wm. H. Howe, 1st Vice-President; Wm. A. Huestace, 2d Vice-President; J.S. Fleming, Recording Secretary and Treasurer; J. Stevens, Corresponding Secretary.

The Una Club numbers ninety members. Uniform: white cap, red star in centre; white shirt, blue trimming; dark blue pants.

The following is a summary of the games played by the Una Base Ball club since their organization:

May 19, 1866.—With Union, of Morrisania, at Morrisania; score, 25 to 11, in favor of the Union.
June 16.—With Active, at Hoboken; score, 23 to 17, in favor of Active.
June 27.—With Constellation, at Brooklyn; score, 42 to 9, in favor of Una Club.
July 4.—With Nonpareil, of City Island, on Nonpareil ground; score, 49 to 9, in favor of Una.
July 25.—With Eclectic, at Hoboken; won by Eclectic; score, 25 to 23.
August 3.—With Union, of Morrisania, on Una's ground; score, 27 to 18, in favor of Union.

August 18.—With Active; return game, at Mount Vernon; won by Active; score, 43 to 22.

Sept. 3.—With Constellation; return game,, at Mount Vernon; score, 39 to 23, in favor of Una Club.

Oct. 3.—With Eclectic; return game, at Mount Vernon; Una won; score, 37 to 8.

Oct. 10.—With Resolute, of Elizabeth, N.J., on the ground of Resolute; won by the Una; score, 30 to 39.

Oct. 17.—With Stamford Club, at Mount Vernon; score, 25 to 15, in favor of Una.

Oct. 26.—With Eclectic; home-and-home game; on the ground of the Union Club, at Morrisania; won by the Eclectic, by 29 to 21.

Nov. 3.—With Stamford Club, at Stamford, Conn; won by the Una Club; score, 29 to 8.

SURPRISE CLUB.

The Surprise Base Ball Club, of West Farms, N.Y., was organized Sept. 20, 1865, with the following officers: John W. Bolton, President; John Valentine, Vice-President; A D. Pettit, Secretary. Delegates—John W. Bolton and James W. Graff.

October 19, 1865, with Metamora, of Fordham. Score, Surprise, 7; Metamora, 11.

November 3, 1865, with Una, of Mount Vernon. Score, Surprise, 27; Una, 28.

November 11, 1865, with Una, of Mount Vernon. Score, Surprise, 19; Una, 51.

May 24, 1866.—With Union, of Morrisania. Surprise, 4; Union, 52.

June 21.—With Mohawk, of Brooklyn. Surprise, 10; Mohawk, 40.

July 20.—With Union, of Morrisania. Score: Surprise, 9; Union, 46.

September 5.—With Ambidexter Club, of New Rochelle. Surprise, 20; Ambidexter, 14.

September 21.—With Harlem Club, of Harlem. Surprise, 6; Harlem, 13.

October 18.—With Arctic Club, of Brownsville. Surprise, 23; Arctic, 26.

October 25.—With Arctic Club. Surprise, 42; Arctic, 17.

November 7.—With Athlete, of Washington Heights. Surprise, 23; Athlete, 17.

UNIFORM.—White flannel shirt, trimmed with blue; blue flannel pants; blue cap

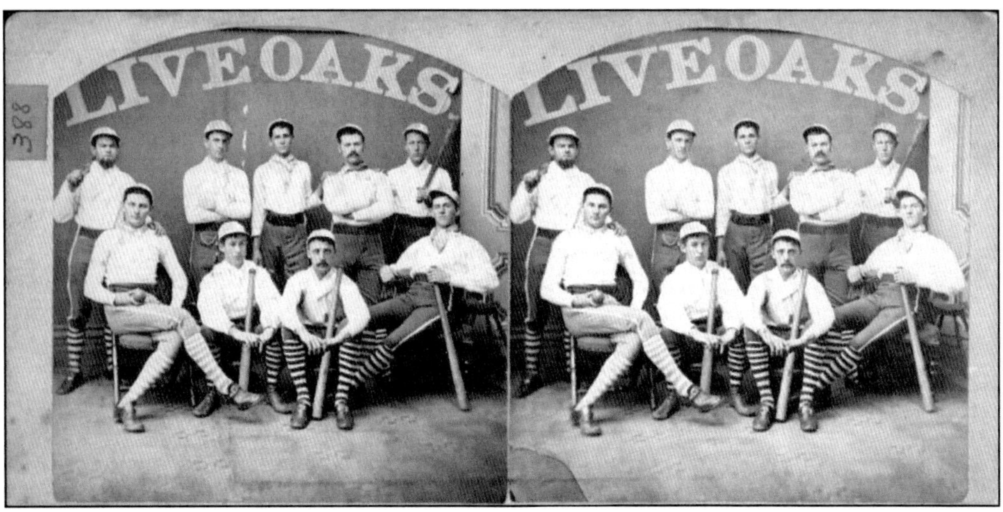

STEREOGRAPHIC PICTURE OF LIVE OAK BALL CLUB, ROCHESTER, NEW YORK. *This image is believed to be the 1858 club. The long stockings look great on the ball players in the front row. (Source: Transcendental Graphics.)*

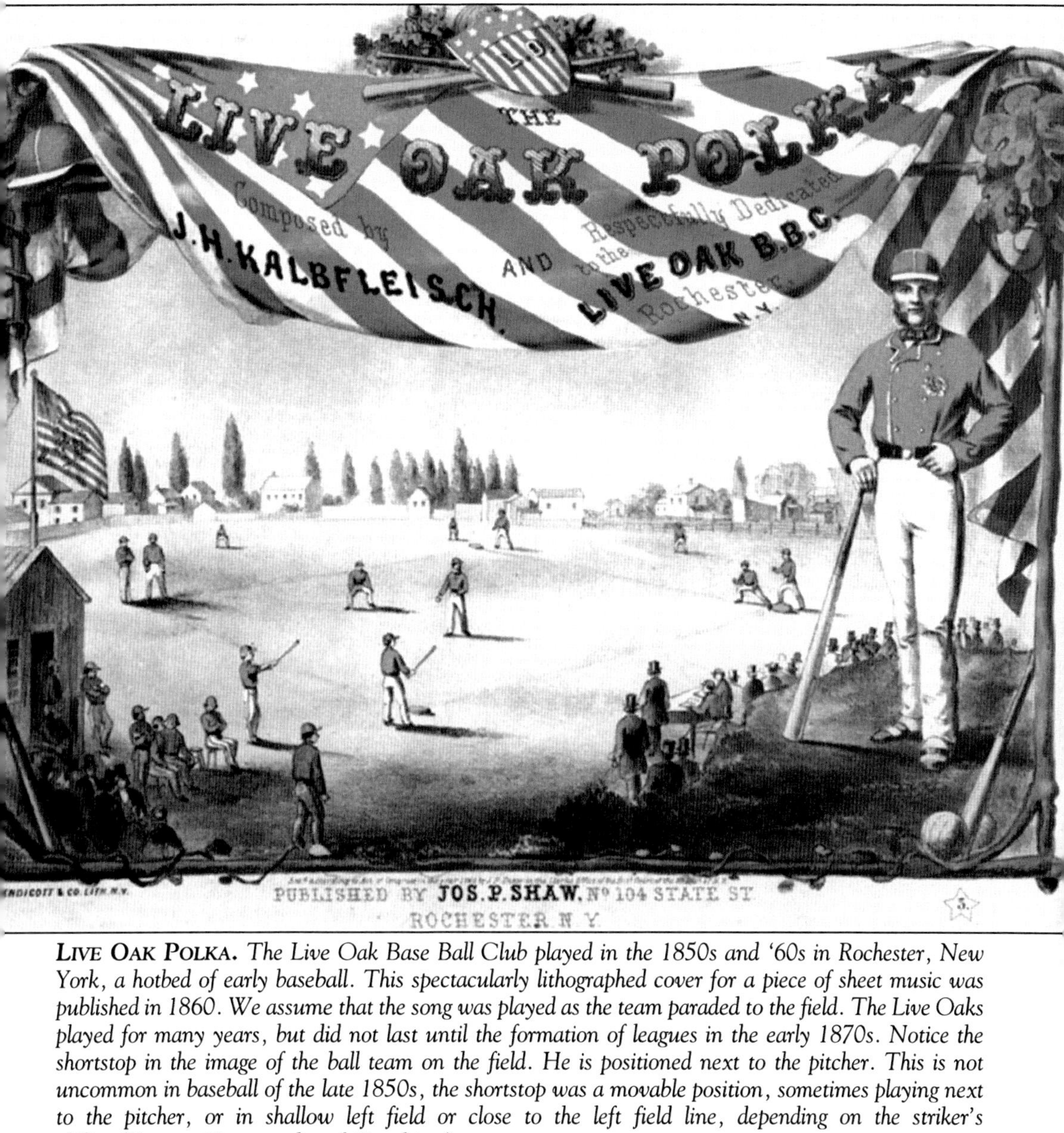

LIVE OAK POLKA. *The Live Oak Base Ball Club played in the 1850s and '60s in Rochester, New York, a hotbed of early baseball. This spectacularly lithographed cover for a piece of sheet music was published in 1860. We assume that the song was played as the team paraded to the field. The Live Oaks played for many years, but did not last until the formation of leagues in the early 1870s. Notice the shortstop in the image of the ball team on the field. He is positioned next to the pitcher. This is not uncommon in baseball of the late 1850s, the shortstop was a movable position, sometimes playing next to the pitcher, or in shallow left field or close to the left field line, depending on the striker's ability.(Source: Transcendental Graphics.)*

with white star; black leather belt. Ground located at East Tremont, Westchester County, N.Y. Number of members—48 active, 2 honorary.

UNDERCLIFF CLUB.

The Undercliff Base Ball Club, of Cold Spring, New York, was organized August 10, 1865, with the following officers:

Jackson O. Dykeman, President; Hamilton Jaycox, Vice-President ; Wm. K. Lawson, Secretary; Seymour B. Nelson, Treasurer.

Reorganization of club, April 10, 1866. Officers elected for the year 1866: Wm. A. Ladue, President; Hamilton Jaycox, Vice-President; Wm. K. Lawson, Secretary; Joseph Morrison. Treasurer.

RESULT OF GAMES FOR 1865.— August 12—Undercliff and Highland, at Cold Spring, N.Y.; won by Undercliff, by a score of 49 to 33.

August 19.—Undercliff and Highland at Cold Spring; score, 31 to 23, in favor of Undercliff.

August 30.—Undercliff and Poughkeepsie, at Cold Spring; score, 33 to 26, in favor of Poughkeepsie.

Sept. 5.—Undercliff and Poughkeepsie, at Poughkeepsie; won by Undercliff, by a score of 37 to 30.

Sept. 13.—Undercliff and Poughkeepsie, at Cold Spring; won by the latter, by a score of 33 to 23.

Sept.29.—Undercliff and Lorillard, at Rhinebeck; score, 62 to 43, in favor of the Lorillard.

Nov. 9.—Undercliff and Petroleum, at Fishkill Village; won by the former, by 30 to 21.

May 26, 1866.—Undercliff and Cedar Grove, at Cold Spring; score, 89 to 23, in favor of Undercliff.

July 20.—Undercliff and Hudson River, of Newburgh, at Cold Spring; Hudson River, 23; Undercliff, 21.

August 8.—Undercliff and Lone Star, at Matteawan; score in favor of Undercliff, by 19 to 18.

August 15.—Undercliff and National, of Albany, at Cold Spring; National, 81; Undercliff, 30.

The uniform of the club consists of white cap, white shirt, and blue pants. Their practice-ground is located a short distance from the village of Cold Spring, adjoining the residence of the late General George P. Morris. Number of members, about fifty.

HUDSON RIVER CLUB.

NEWBURGH, April 23, 1866.

MR. CHAS. A. PEVERELLY:

DEAR SIR—It is impossible for the Hudson River Basse Ball Club to give any satisfactory account of its origin and history. The few data that I am able to obtain, you are welcome to; but they are rather meagre to prove very satisfactory.

The Hudson River Base Ball Club, of Newburgh, was organized in the spring of 1859. William C. Miller was President for the years of 1859, 1860, 1861, 1862, and 1863; David A. Scott, Surrogate of Orange county, for 1864, 1865, and 1866. Vice-President, Captain Henry Robinson, for 1859 and 1860; Dr. L.S. Straw, 1861 and 1862; Wm. L. Smith, 1863 and 1864; W.H. Kelly, 1865 and 1866. Secretaries— A.S. Cassidy, 1859, 1860, 1861, 1862, and 1863; W.H. Kelly, 1864; A.S. Mapes, deceased, 1865; L.B. Halsey, 1866. We have played in Albany,

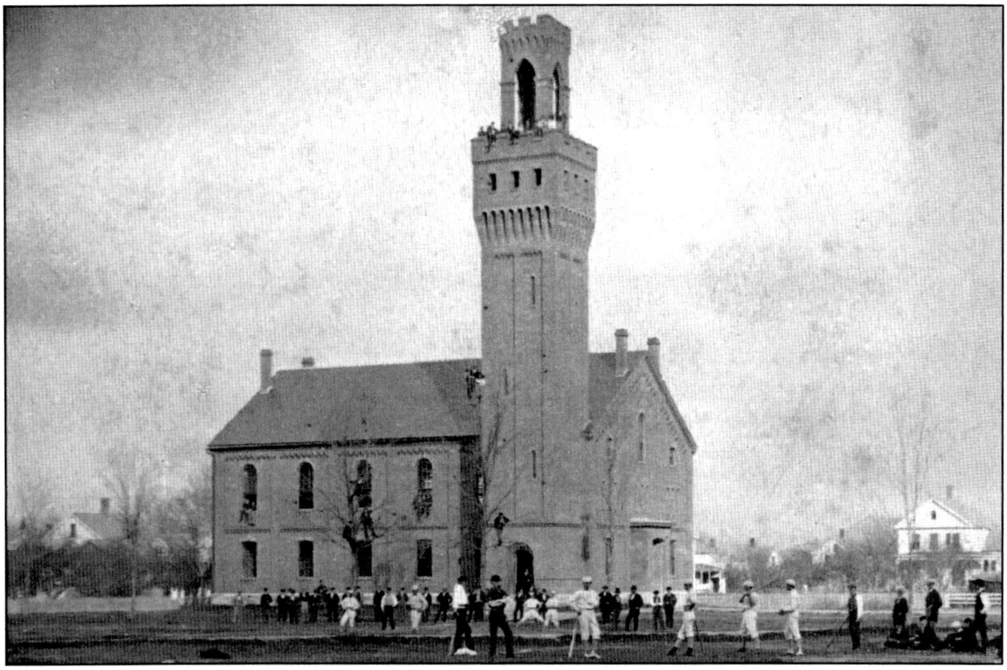

GAME AT EAST HAMPTON. *A Game at East Hampton, Long Island, is pictured c. 1861. Games were usually played in a town square or in close proximity to places like churches, hotels, or town halls, for entertainment purposes after the match. Home teams always hosted a gala after the match was over; awards would be given and speeches would be made. (Source: Transcendental Graphics.)*

Saugerties, Kingston, Poughkeepsie, New York and Brooklyn. We have not been defeated in a return game by any club outside of New York and Brooklyn. In those cities we have lost games with the Excelsior, Star, Eckford, Mutual, and Gotham; which clubs we have never defeated in any game. The Unions, of Morrisania, have won a home-and-home match. We have won from the Empire, Eagle, Enterprise, Resolute, and Mystic Clubs. The nine for 1865 were as follows: catcher, James Boyd; pitcher, W.H. Kelly; first base, Samuel Miller; left field, A. G. Mapes, deceased; centre field, Watson Fisher; right field, H.C. Milspaugh. Mapes was a great loss, both to efficiency of the nine, and to the welfare of the club. He was widely known as a ball-player, and was not to be excelled in his position by any one. Our grounds are situated at the corner of South and Johnson streets, in Newburgh, Orange county, New York. We practice every Tuesday and Friday of each week. Uniform—white shirt and cap; blue pants. We frequently receive clubs from the cities of New York and Brooklyn, and we cordially extend a general invitation to all clubs in good standing to visit our beautiful city in the future. In 1865, we were the guests of the Enterprise, Mystic, Gotham, and Mutual Clubs, respectively. We have forty active members, ten honorary. The organization has always commanded the respect and esteem of our citizens, and now stands, very high in this community.

LEWIS B. HALSEY , Secretary.

The following are the principal games in which the club has engaged during the past season:

July 4, 1866.—Hudson River and Eclectic, of New York, at Mattewan, for silver ball. Won by the Hudson River, by 26 to 14.

July 20.—With Undercliff, at Cold Spring. Score in favor of Hudson River, by 23 to 21.

September 29.—With Union, of Lansingburgh, at Poughkeepsie, for silver ball. Won by Union; score, 18 to 17.

October 20.—With Union, of Morrisania, on the ground of the latter. Score, 43 to 4, in favor of the Union Club.

NATIONAL CLUB.

The National Base Ball Club of Albany, N.Y., was organized May 6, 1864, with the following officers:—President, H.A. Carpenter; Vice-President, C. C. Alden; Secretary, Edward A. Server; Treasurer, Edward A. Durant. The Nationals engaged in the annexed games during 1864:

June.—With Live Oak. Score, Live Oak, 34; National, 31.
August.—With Eckford. Score, Eckford, 40; National, 29.
August.—With Live Oak. Score, National, 27; Live Oak, 43.
September.—With Mohawk. Score, National, 55; Mohawk, 31.
October .—With Mohawk. Score, Mohawk, 10; National, 28.
October.—With Enterprise, of Troy. National, 45; Enterprise, 20.

The following officers were elected in 1865:—President, J. Townsend Lansing; Vice-President, George Leonard; Secretary, Edward A. Server; Treasurer, Thomas W. Cantwell.

January, 1865.—With Knickerbocker, on skates. Knickerbocker, 24; National, 5.
February.—With Washington, of Troy, on skates. Washington, 10; National, 21.
February.—With Washington, of Troy on skates. National, 33; Washington, 33.
June 15.—With Knickerbocker, at Albany. Knickerbockers, 53; Nationals, 15.

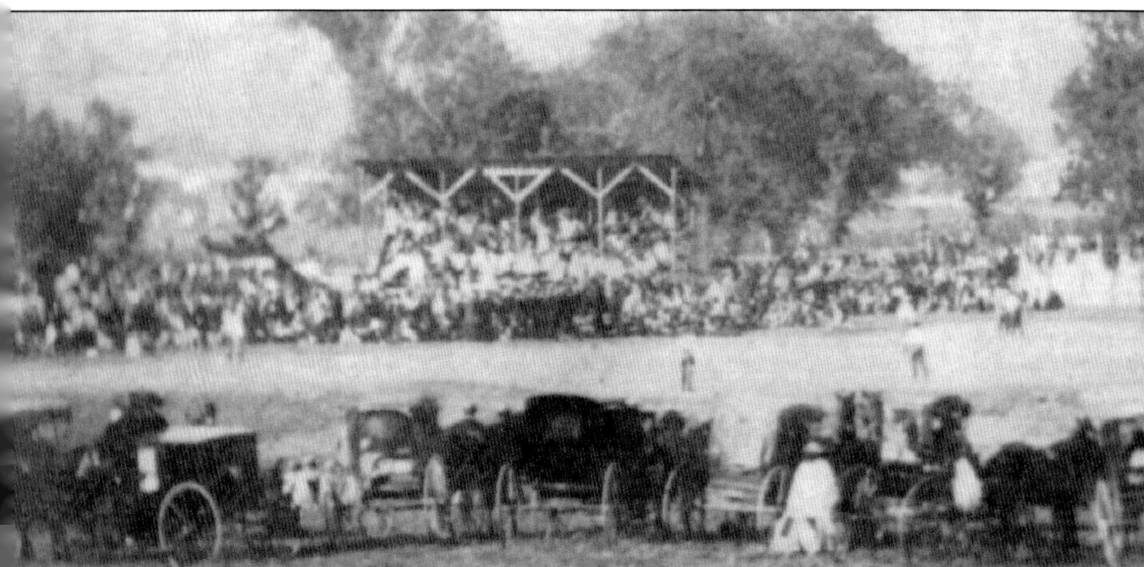

A GAME AT NEWBURGH, NEW YORK, FEATURING THE HUDSON RIVER CLUB. *This Beautiful picture of a typical game scene of the late 1860s features the Hudson River Club of Newburgh, New York. To the left, you can see a primitive grandstand. The wagons help form the shape of the field. The*

July 3.—With Utica City, of Utica, at Utica. Utica City, 75; Nationals, 17.
July 22.—With Indianola, at Albany. Indianola, 38; Nationals, 50.
July 26.—With Enterprise, of Troy, at Troy. Enterprise, 37; Nationals, 21.
August 9.—With Enterprise, of Troy, at Albany. Enterpris 24; Nationals, 15.
August.—With Columbia, of Chatham, at Chatham. Columbias, 20; Nationals, 22.
August 24.—With Eckford, at Albany. Eckfords, 20; Nationals, 27.
September 5.—With Eckford, at Albany. Eckfords, 18; Nationals, 25.
October 12.—Hiawatha, of Utica, at Albany. Hiawatha, 18; Nationals, 26.
October 26.—Knickerbocker, at Albany. Knickerbocker, 21; Nationals, 24.
November 2.—With Knickerbocker, at Albany. Knickerbockers, 20; Nationals, 6.
November 8.—With Albany, at Albany. Albany, 13; Nationals, 45.
November 16.—With Live Oak, at Albany. Live Oaks, 15; Nationals, 13.
November 25.—With Live Oak, at Albany. Live Oaks, 14; Nationals, 33.

The annual election for 1866 resulted as follows:—President, J.T. Lansing; Vice-President, N.B. Clement; Recording Secretary, J. E Soule; Corresponding Secretary, D. W. Johnson, Treasurer, W. H. McClure.

January 23, 1866.—With Knickerbocker, at Albany. National, 36; Knickerbocker, 9.
June 1.—With Live Oak, at Albany. National, 42; Live Oak, 16.
June 22.—With Albany, at Albany. National, 50; Albany, 38.
June 30.—With Pioneer, at Albany. National, 57; Pioneer, 6.
July 19.—With Victory, of Troy, at Troy. National, 42; Victory, 27.
August 2.—With Knickerbocker, at Albany. National, 17; Knickerbocker, 22.
August 6.—With Wide Awake, of Green Island, at Albany. National, 59; Wide Awake, 8.
August 14.—With Lorillard, of Rhinebeck, at Rhinebeck. National, 38; Lorillard, 11.
August 14.—With Fremont, of Fishkill, at Fishkill. National, 113; Fremont, 15.
August 15.—With Undercliff, of Cold Spring, at Cold Spring. National, 81; Undercliff, 20.

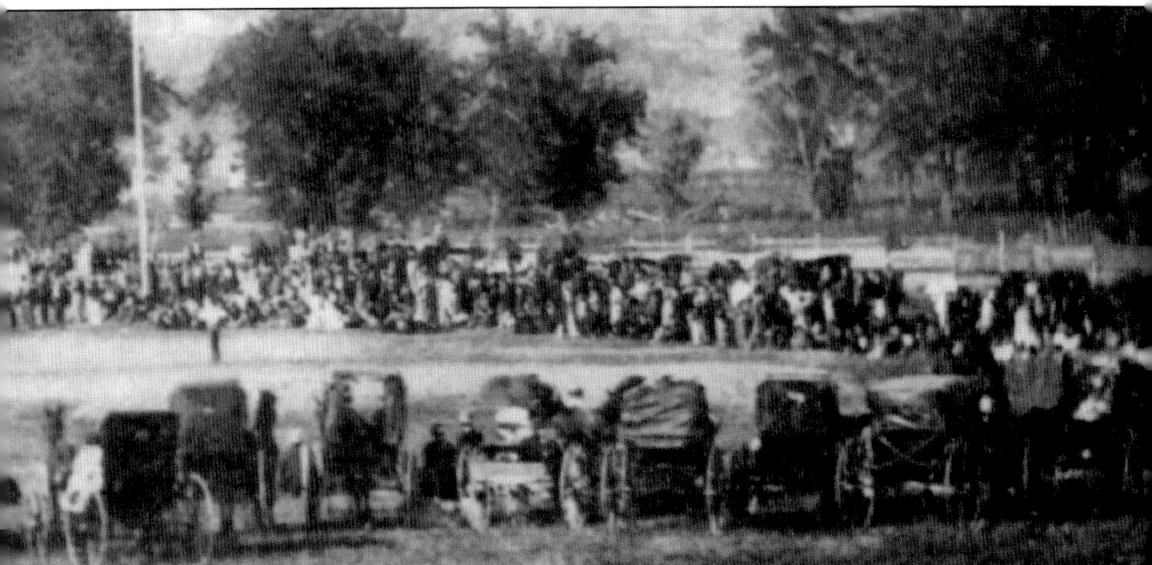

Hudson River Club was very competitive against the bigger New York clubs. A game like this could easily draw 1,000 people, as can be seen by this image. (Source: Transcendental Graphics.)

August 16.—With Union, of Morrisania, at Morrisania. National, 18; Union, 53.
August 17.—With Excelsior, of Brooklyn, at Brooklyn. National, 29; Excelsior, 48.
August 22.—With Columbia, of Chatham, at Albany. National, 60; Columbia, 20.
August 23.—With Hiawatha, of Utica, at Albany. National, 24; Hiawatha, 7.
September 3.—With Union, of Lansingburgh, at Albany. National, 23; Union, 18.
September 5.—With Knickerbocker, of Albany, at Albany. National, 8; Knickerbocker, 21.

The first nine of the National consists of Sprague, third base; Bush, catcher; Ross, right field; Waddell, pitcher; Wolverston, short stop; Lansing, first base; McClure, second base; Ertzberger, left field; and Johnson, centre field.

UTICA CLUB.

The Utica Base Ball Club of Utica, N.Y., was organized April 18, 1859. The following is a list of the officers of the Club since its organization:

Officer for 1859.—President, Samuel Barnum; Secretary Wm. J. Doolittle; Treasurer, Samuel Y. Lane.

Officers for 1860.—President, N.C. White; Secretary, M. G. Thomson; Treasurer, S. Y. Lane.

Officers for 1861.—President, N. C. White; Secretary, M.G. Thomson; Treasurer, James Murdock.

Officers for 1862.—President, G.J. Sicard; Secretary, M.G. Thomson; Treasurer, James Murdock.

Officers for 1863.—President, Geo. J. Sicard; Secretary, M.G. Thomson; Treasurer, James Murdock.

Officers for 1864.—President, J.C. McIntosh; Secretary, G. J. Curran; Treasurer, Wm. J. Doolittle.

Officers for 1865.—President, Henry Griffin; Vice-President, Lewis H. Babcock; Corresponding Secretary, L.M. Thomson; Recording Secretary, Horace E. Day; Treasurer, John S. Hill.

The club-grounds are situated near the New York Central Railroad depot, on the bank of the Mohawk River, three miles from Baggs' Hotel and the depot. The club has seventy-five active, and thirty honorary members. Since their organization, the club has played over fifty games, losing but thirteen. Delegates to "National Association of Base Ball Players," Messrs. M. Callender and E.E. Millard.

KNICKERBOCKER CLUB.

The Knickerbocker Base Ball Club, of the City of Albany, was organized on the 13th day of September, 1860. The officers of the Club for 1860 and 1861 were: President, J.L. Babcock; Vice-President, R.V. DeWitt, Jr.; Recording Secretary, W.R. Seymour; Corresponding Secretary, A.B. McDonald; Treasurer, W.H. Haskell.

September 22, 1860.—With Mohawk, at Schenectady. Knickerbocker, 32; Mohawk, 23.
September 28.—With Preams, at Troy. Knickerbocker, 28; Preams, 24.
October 27.—With Mohawk, at Schenectady. Knickerbocker, 17; Mohawk, 30.
November —,— With Champion, at Albany. Knickerbocker 22; Champion, 8.
October 8, 1861.—With Victory, of Troy. Knickerbocker, 17; Victory, 19.
October 29.—With Knickerbocker, of Troy. Knickerbocker, 38; Knickerbocker of Troy, 18.

OFFICERS FOR 1862.— President, Hon. A.D. Robinson; Vice-President, W. H.

Haskell; Corresponding Secretary, H. C. Steele; Recording Secretary, F.P. Olcott; Treasurer, R. Headlam.

November 9.—Champion, of Albany. Knickerbocker, 16; Champion, 10.
June 6.—With Victory, of Troy. Knickerbocker, 20; Victory, 28.
July 15.—With Victory, of Troy. Knickerbocker, 74; Victory, 35.
——-.With Utica Club, at Utica. Knickerbocker, 37; Utica, 42.
——-.With Utica Club, at Albany. Knickerbocker, 33; Utica, 18.
November 6.—With Victory, at Albany. Knickerbocker, 29; Victory, 20.

OFFICERS FOR 1863.—President, R.V. DeWitt, Jr.; Vice-President, A. Strever; Corresponding Secretary, M.V.B. Winne; Recording Secretary, G.H. Turner; Treasurer, A.B. Lathrop.

June 22, 1863.—With Victory, at Saratoga. Knickerbocker, 20; Victory, 21.
July 22.—With Victory, at Troy. Knickerbocker, 25; Victory, 27.
September 5.—With Conqueror, at Cricketville. Knickerbocker, 31; Conqueror, 36.
September 11.—With Conqueror, at Albany. Knickerbocker, 40; Conqueror, 21.
September 12.—With Utica, at Utica. Knickerbocker, 24; Utica, 17.
September 30.—With Utica, at Utica. Knickerbocker, 24; Utica, 14.

OFFICER FOR 1864.—President, M.V.B. Winne; Vice-President, A.M. Comb; Corresponding Secretary, W.D. Wendell; Recording Secretary, G.P. Whitney; Treasurer, A.B. Lathrop.

June 16.—With Eckford, at Albany. Knickerbocker, 26; Eckford, 18.
July —. With Eckford, at Albany. Knickerbocker, 27; Eckford, 8.
July 16.—With Union College, at Albany. Knickerbocker, 37; Union College, 8.
August 4.—With Mutual, of New York. Knickerbocker, 16; Mutual, 24.
August 24.—With Hudson River Club, at Albany. Knickerbocker, 51; Hudson River, 11.
August 25.—With Empire, of New York, at Albany. Knickerbocker, 18; Empire, 32.
August 32.—With Mutual, of New York, at Albany. Knickerbocker, 29; Mutuals, 36.
September 22.—With Union Club, of Green Island, at Albany. Knickerbocker, 35; Union Club, 15.
October 4.—With Union Club, of Green Island, at Albany. Knickerbocker, 24; Union Club, 14.
October 8.—Utica Club, at Albany. Knickerbocker, 32; Utica, 28.
October 26.—With Utica Club, at Utica. Knickerbocker, 22; Utica, 31.

—.With Enterprise, of Troy, at Albany. Knickerbocker, 48; Enterprise, 11.
November 22.—Resolute, of Brooklyn, at Albany. Knickerbocker, 11; Resolute, 16.

OFFICERS FOR 1865.—President, Jacob C. Cuyler; Vice-President, W.H. Davis; Corresponding Secretary, W.R. Dorlon; Recording Secretary, J.S. Hurdis; Treasurer, G.E. Latham.

January 13, 1865.—With National (on skates), at Albany. Knickerbocker, 24; National, 5.
January 20.—With Eckford (on skates), at Albany. Knickerbocker, 25; Eckford, 10.
June 15.—With National, at Albany. Knickerbocker, 53; National, 15.
June 20.—With Eckford, at Albany. Knickerbocker, 28; Eckford, 13.
June 24.—With Williams College, at Albany. Knickerbocker, 6; Williams College, 18.
June 29.—With Eckford, at Albany. Knickerbocker, 35; Eckford, 11.

July 15.—With Utica, at Utica. Knickerbocker, 27; Utica, 15.
August 4.—With Union Club, of Lansingburgh, at Albany. Knickerbocker, 32; Union Club, 16.
August 28.—With Columbia, at Chatham. Knickerbocker, 32; Columbia, 9.
August 31.—With Conquerors, at Albany. Knickerbocker, 36; Conqueror, 1.
September 7.—Eureka, of South Adams, at Chatham. Knickerbocker, 55; Eureka, 17.
September 21.—With Resolute Club, of Brooklyn (for silver ball), at Kingston, New York. Knickerbocker, 13; Resolute, 12.
September 28.—With Trojan, at Albany. Knickerbocker, 33; Trojan, 15.
October 5.—With Utica, at Albany. Knickerbocker, 13; Utica, 8.
October 26.—With National, at Albany. Knickerbocker, 21; National, 24.
November 2.—With National, at Albany. Knickerbocker, 20; National, 6.
November 15.—With Hudson River Club, of Newburgh, at Albany. Knickerbocker, 18; Hudson River, 24.

OFFICERS FOR 1866.—President, T.L. Godwin; Vice-President, E. S. Foster; Recording Secretary, W. R. Dorlon; Corresponding Secretary, G.P. Whitney; Treasurer, Charles B. Porter, Jr.

July 4, 1866.—National, of Poughkeepsie, at Albany. Knickerbocker, 39; National, 15.
August 1.—With Live Oak, at Albany. Knickerbocker, 43; Live Oak, 11.
August 22.—With Hiawatha, at Albany. Knickerbocker, 47; Hiawatha, 15.
——2, —With National, at Albany. Knickerbocker, 22; National, 17.
September 5.—With National, at Albany. Knickerbocker, 24; National, 8.
October 2.—With Niagara, of Buffalo. Knickerbocker, 18; Niagara, 29.

The Van Rensselaer Skating Park is used by the Club for a ground, and is situated about one-quarter of a mile north of the city of Albany. The practice-days of the club are Mondays, Thursdays, and Saturdays. The uniform consists of blue pants, white shirts, and white caps, with enamelled belt, with the words "Knickerbocker Base Ball Club" in white letters. Number of active members, sixty-two; honorary members, seventy-nine.

AMERICUS CLUB.

The Americus Base Ball Club of Newark, N.J., was organized on the first day of August, 1864, by seventeen young men who were connected with the Americus Engine Company, Number eight, of Newark. The first officers were elected August 1, 1864.—William E. Greathead, President; Fred. H. Pilch, Vice-President; A. P. Mayhew, Treasurer; D.W.C. Joralemon, Secretary.

The officers for 1865, were: Fred. H. Pilch, President; D.W.C. Joralemon, Vice-President; A. P. Mayhew, Treasurer; T. Jeff. Marshall, Secretary.

For 1866: J.D. Leonard, President; A. P. Mayhew, Vice-President; F.H. Pilch, Recording Secretary; J.T. Leonard, Corresponding Secretary; G.W. Hubbard, Treasurer.

Games played by the Americus Club.

August 23, 1865, with the Mystic, of Harlem. Won by the Mystic by a score of 48 to 30.
September 6, with the Mystic, at the Red House, Harlem. Won by the Mystic, by 39 to 5.
September 25, with the Eclectic of New York, at Newark; lost by a score of 44 to 6.
October 5, with the Eureka of Newark. Eureka, 85; Americus, 12. October 12, with Eclectic; played in Hoboken. Eclectic, 18; Americus, 12.

During 1866 the Americus Club engaged in the following games: June 8, with Eclectic of New York, at Hoboken. Score 40 to 11, in favor of Eclectic. June 22, game with Eureka. Score 67 to 7, in favor of Eureka. June 26, Americus and National of Jersey City. Won by Americus, by 54 to 42. July 11, Americus and Star of New Brunswick. Score, 48 to 38, in favor of Americus. July 28, Americus and Social of New York, at Newark, N.J. Score, 28 to 21, in favor of Americus. August 7, Americus and National of Jersey City. Won by Americus of Jersey City. Won by Americus, by 47 to 33. August 15, Americus and Star of New Brunswick, at the latter place. Star won; score, 24 to 19. September 5, Americus and Social of New York, at Hoboken. Score, 28 to 20, in favor of Americus. September 14, Americus and Resolute, at Elizabeth, N.J. Score, 16 to 11, in favor of Resolute. September 19, Americus and Eclectic at Hoboken. Americus 28 to 20. September —, Americus and Star, at New Brunswick. Star 56 to 18. October 2, Americus and National, at Jersey City. Americus, 30; National, 21. October 19, Americus and Newark. Score, Newark, 12; Americus, 32. October 27, Americus and Endeavor. Won by Americus, by 38 to 14. November 17, Americus and Eclectic, at Hoboken. Won by the Eclectic by 25 to 17.

OLYMPIC CLUB.

The Olympic Base Ball Club, of Paterson, N.J., was organized June 1, 1864. Its first officers were, President, Simon J. Carroll; Vice-President, Michael Morris; Secretary, James McMannus; Treasurer, James Rossiter. Officers for 1865.—President, Peter Toole; Vice-President, Peter Chapman; Secretary, Simon J. Carroll; Treasurer, Michael Toomey. Officers of 1866.—President, Samuel McKiernan; Vice-President, Richard Sammond; Secretary, Arthur Fitzgerald; Treasurer, Michael Toomey.

The Olympic grounds are located at the Red Woods, near the Passaic Falls. Their uniform consists of blue pants, white shirt, red and blue caps, and black belt. Forty members. The following is a summary of the games played by the club since their organization:

June 17, 1864.—Olympic and Empire. Score, 29 to 15, in favor of Olympic.
August 10.—Olympic and Active. Score, 23 to 12, in favor of Olympic.
September 24.—Olympic and Excelsior. Won by Olympic; score, 19 to 13.
July 19, 1865.—Olympic and Picked Nine. Won by Olympic, by 36 to 15.
August 8.—Olympic and Gotham, of New York, at Hoboken. Won by Gotham, by 77 to 18.
August 20.—Olympic and Hudson River, at Newburgh. Won by Hudson River, by 42 to 13.
August 25.—Olympic and Active, at Paterson. Won by Active, by 30 to 32.
September 6.—Olympic and National, at Jersey City. Won by Olympic, 47 to 25.
September 13.—Olympic and Active. Tie game; 33 to 33.
September 25.—Olympic and Gotham, of New York. Won by Gotham, by 35 to 29.
July 19, 1866.—Olympic and Eagle, of New York, at Paterson. Won by Olympic; 28 to 24.
August 20.—Olympic and Eclectic, of New York, at Paterson. Won by Olympic,; 21 to 9.
September 5.—Olympic and Irvington, at Paterson. Won by Olympic; 20 to 16.
September 19.—Olympic, and Star, of New Brunswick. Won by Olympic; 27 to 20.
November 21.—Olympic and Eclectic, at Hoboken. Won by Olympic,; 17 to 15.

KEARNEY CLUB.

The Kearney Base Ball Club, of Rahway, N.J., was organized August 1, 1865, with the following officers: Jos. T. Crowell, President; Geo. Brumhall, Vice-President; Garret Berry, Treasurer; Phillip E. Tufts, Secretary. Delegates to National Convention, Colonel J.R. Harma and Dr. G.A. Hoffman.

Games played: September 1, 1865.—At Elizabeth, N.J., 9 innings. Kearney, 30; Union, of Elizabeth, 11. September 12.—At New Brunswick, N.J., 9 innings. Kearney, 31; Hopeful, of N.B., 34. September 15.—At Rahway, N.J., 9 innings. Kearney, 51; National, of

Morristown, N.J., 14. September 26.— At Morristown, N.J., 6 innings. Kearney, 43; National, of Morristown, 22. September 28.—At Rahway, N.J., 9 innings. Kearney, 24; Hopeful, of New Brunswick, 10. October 6.—At Newark, N.J., 8 innings. Kearney, 40; Uncas, of Spuyten Duyvil, 20. October 11.—At East Orange, N.J., 9 innings. Kearney, 16; Union, of East Orange, N.J., 22. October 20.—At Rahway, N.J., 9 innings. Kearney, 20; Union, of East Orange, 19. October 24.—At Rahway, N.J., 5 innings. Kearney, 23; Resolute, of Brooklyn, 14. October 31.—At Newark, N.J., 9 innings. Kearney, 33; Union, of East Orange, 17.

July 10, 1866.—At Rahway. Eureka, of Newark, 45; Kearney, 6. July 20.—At Rahway. Fulton Market, of New York, 14; Kearney, 45. July 27.— At Newark, N.J., Eureka, 36; Kearney, 5. August 21,.—At New York. Fulton Market, 39; Kearney, 16. October 29.—At Rahway. Fulton Market, 71; Kearney, 14; 7 innings.

The officers of the Kearney Club for 1866, are: President, Colonel J.R. Harma; Vice-President, George Bramhall; Treasurer, Scott Laing; Secretary, P.E. Tufts. The Club has upon its roll, forty active, and seven honorary. The uniform consists of blue pants, white shirt with red star on collar, and white cap with red star. Practice-ground, at head of Seminary street, Rahway, N.J.

LIBERTY CLUB.

The Liberty Base Ball Club of New Brunswick, N.J., was organized March 1, 1857; was disbanded during the civil war, and was reorganized September 15, 1865. Its first officers were: President, W.C. Hildebrant; Vice-President, William Shooks; Secretary, J.F. Elkin; Treasurer, J. Van Nest.

Their two first games were with the Amity Club, of Rahway, N.J., both of which were won by the Liberty. The third, was with the Hamilton, of Jersey City, which was won by the latter. Then followed two more games with the Amity Club, the Liberty Nine winning both. September 27, 1860.—The Liberty played with the Atlantic, of Brooklyn, at New Brunswick; the Atlantic winning by 15 runs. October 8th, following, they again met the Atlantic Club, a tie game being the result. This game was followed by trials with the Amity and Union, of Elizabeth, N.J., no record being kept of either game. Then came a game with the Star Club of New Brunswick, the Liberty proving victorious by 13 runs. July 11, 1859, played with the Union, of Elizabeth; result, in favor of Liberty, by 34 runs. August 1. 1859; game with Independent, of Somerville. Won by Liberty; score, 35 to 44. August 12, 1859.—Lost a game with the Newark Club of New Brunswick, N.J., by score of 22 to 16. The Liberty Club also received two defeats from the Atlantic, of Brooklyn, by score of 24 to 8, at New Brunswick, N. J., and 61 to 14, at Bedford. October 5, 1859.—Game with the Union, of Elizabeth; score, in favor of Liberty by 50 to 21. October 28, 1859.—Played with Live Oak Club, at Orange, N.J. Won by Liberty, by a score of 25 to 24. November 7, 1859.—Game with the Newark Club, at Rahway. Score, 26 to 18, in favor of Liberty.

July 7, 1866.—National, of Washington, and Liberty, at New Brunswick, N.J. Won by the National, by 29 to 9. August 17. The Liberty played a game with the Gotham of New York, at New Brunswick, N.J. Won by the Liberty, by 41 to 29. August 31.—Gotham and Liberty, at Hoboken; 24 to 23, in favor of Liberty. September 7.—The Liberty Club visited Philadelphia, and played with the Athletic of that city. Score, 53 to 9, in favor of the Athletic Club.

The officers of the Liberty Club for 1866, are: President, J.C. Croman; Vice-President, C.S. Williams; Secretary, J.H. Leupp; Treasurer, N. Cortelyou. The Club has now upon its roll fifty active, and twenty-five honorary members. Their uniform consists of blue flannel pants, white shirt, and blue cap.

In the spring of 1861, Mr. John A. Lowell, and several of the members of the Bowdoin Base Ball club, proposed to some of the young players of Boston that they form a Club to play the New York game (as it was then called) of Base Ball, and promised to help them, and also to give them a set of implements, provided they obtained sufficient names down to start with. Mr. Geo. G. Richards (the first President) and Mr. James D. W. Lowell started a paper, which was soon filled. The first meeting was held at the office of Mr. Lowell, on the 18th of March, 1861. Mr. Lowell occupied the Chair, and as a compliment to him, it was moved by Mr. Richards that the Club be named the Lowell Base Ball Club.

The young men who composed the Club were mostly members of the Latin, English, High and Chauncey Hall Schools; and though some of them had played the old Massachusetts game, as it was called, they were not much acquainted with the points of the New York game, except what they had seen by the Trimountain Club (who started the game in New England) and the Bowdoins.

On the 16th of October, 1861, they visited Medford, and had their first match, and were successful. On the 29th of May, 1863, the Lowell played with the Trimountain, and were successful, by the score of 37 to 1.

Their next match was played with the Harvard College nine, and created considerable excitement amongst the ball players around Boston as to who should win, as the Lowells had been successful in all their matches, and also the Harvards in theirs. The match was played on the 9th of July, 1864, and was won by the Lowells.

A little later in the season, Mr. Lowell offered as a prize a beautiful silver ball, to be held by the winner till won by a better club. The first match for it was between the Trimountains, of Boston, and Osceolas, of Portland, Me., and was won by the Trimountains.

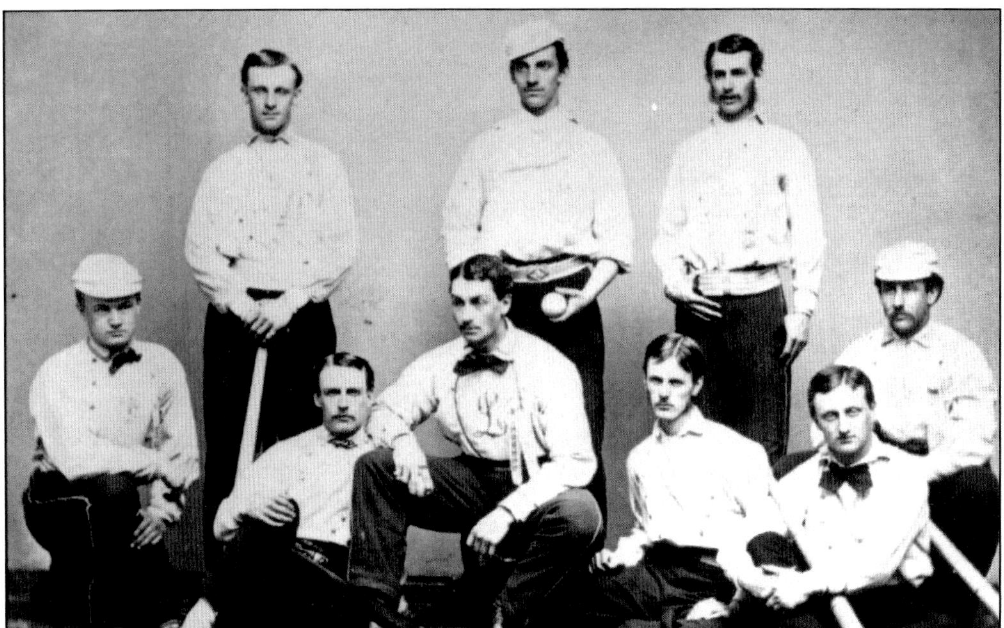

LOWELLS OF BOSTON. *This is a photograph from one of the top mid-nineteenth century New England teams, the Lowell Base Ball Club of Boston. They were one of the first teams near Boston to adopt the rules used by teams in New York and to the South. The Harvard University and Tri-Mountain clubs were their main rivals. (Source: Transcendental Graphics.)*

Then the Lowells challenged the Trimountains and won it from them, on the 4th of October, 1864. The Lowells were then challenged by the Hampshire Club, of Northampton, Mass., and the game was won by the Lowell, on the18th of Oct., 1864. The Harvards next challenged the Lowells for the champion silver ball. The game was played on the 15th of July, 1865, and was won by the Harvards, who had the honor of winning the first ball from the Lowells.

For some time the Lowells had been thinking of visiting New York, and on the 18th of July they left Boston to play with the Resolute, Atlantic, and Excelsior Clubs, of Brooklyn. They were received in New York by Mr. Mortimer Rogers, on the arrival of the train, and breakfasted at Taylor's. They quartered at the "International," and in the afternoon were met by members of the Resolute Club, and escorted over to Brooklyn, where they had a game with them, and were defeated by a score of 33 to 14. That did not look very encouraging for the next day's play with the champion Atlantics.

On the afternoon of the 20th, they were met at the Hotel by members of the Atlantic, and escorted to the Capitoline grounds, where they played with them, and were defeated. After the game, the Atlantics entertained them in good style. The next day they played with the Excelsior, and though they led at the start, the Excelsiors finally defeated them. A collation in the large hall on the grounds succeeded the game, when the Lowells were escorted to New York. The next morning the Lowells started for home, and though they did not carry a trophy with them, they were highly pleased with the hospitable manner in which they were treated during their visit.

The Atlantic Club, of Brooklyn, arrived in Boston the 24th of September, 1865, and were received by the Lowells, and escorted to the Bromfield House. On Monday afternoon the Atlantic played the Lowell, and won by a score of 30 to 10. In the evening they were taken to the fair of the Massachusetts Charitable Mechanics' Association, in Faneuil and Quincy Halls. After the game between the Atlantics and Harvards, played on the 27th, the Lowells escorted the Atlantics to the Worcester depot.

The next game of the Lowells was with the Harvards, on the 30th of September, 1865. The result was a victory for the Lowells, who regained the champion silver ball from the Harvard Club. The Harvard next challenged the Lowell for the silver ball, and the result was a victory for the Harvard nine, This game, played on the 20th of October, ended the season of 1865.

The following is a summary of the Lowell's games since their organization:

October 16, 1861.—Lowell and Medford; Lowell, 17; Medford, 10.
May 29, 1863.—Lowell and Trimountain; Lowell, 37; Trimountain, 1.
July 9, 1864.—Lowell and Harvard; Lowell, 55; Harvard, 25.
October 4.—Lowell and Trimountain. Lowell, 33; Trimountain, 18. October 18.—Lowell and Hampshire. Lowell, 83; Hampshire, 10.
June 17, 1865.—Lowell second nine and Granite first nine. Lowell, 27; Granite, 25.
July 15.—Lowell and Harvard. Lowell, 17; Harvard, 28.
July 19.—Lowell and Resolute, of Brooklyn. Lowell, 14; Resolute, 33.
July 20.— Lowell and Atlantic, of Brooklyn. Lowell, 31; Excelsior, 39.
Sept.9.—Lowell second nine and Tuft's College first nine. Lowell, 82; Tuft's College, 26.
Sept. 20.—Lowell and Trimountain. Lowell, 29; Trimountain, 27.
Sept. 25.—Lowell and Atlantic. Lowell, 10; Atlantic, 30.
Sept. 30.—Lowell and Harvard. Lowell, 40; Harvard, 37.
October 20.—Lowell and Harvard. Lowell, 37; Harvard, 73.
October.—Lowell and Shawmut.. Lowell, 34; Shawmut, 11.
October.—Lowell and Itasca. Lowell, 33; Itasca, 11.

The Lowell Club had the most successful season in 1866 they ever experienced, and had a stronger nine than ever before. They regained the championship of New England from the Harvard Club, and their first nine won the ball in every contest in which they engaged.

June 2, 1866.—Defeated the Fly-Away Club; score, 121 to 14. June 16—defeated the Granite Club; score 67 to 30. June 18—defeated the Mount Tom Club; score, 51 to 23.

July 4—defeated the Eon Club; score, 33 to 23. July 14—defeated the Harvard Club; score 37 to 27. July 25—defeated the Phillips Academy Nine; 32 to 20. Sept. 10—defeated the King Phillip Club; score, 75 to 17. Sept. 18—defeated the Independent Club; score, 36 to 18. Sept. 29—defeated the Granite Club; score, 47 to 11.

List of officers since the Club's foundation. For 1861: President , Geo. G. Richards; Vice-President, Samuel Bradstreet, Jr.; Secretary, Geo. S. B. Sullivan; Treasurer, Wm. French.

For 1862: President, Geo. G. Richards; Vice-President, Dudley R. Child; Secretary, T. Spencer Adams; Treasurer, Gerrit S. Miller. For 1863: Secretary, T. Spencer Adams, Treasurer, Geo. G. Richards. For 1864: President, Gerrit S. Miller; Vice-President, Wm. B. Joslin; Secretary, T. Spencer Adams; Treasurer, Frank G. Peabody. For 1865: President, Geo. B. Wilder; Vice-President, Edward S. Arnold; Secretary, T. Spencer Adams; Treasurer, Edward B. Kimball. For 1866: President, Wm. C. Page; Vice-President, J. Frank Gardner; Secretary, Chas. L. Fuller; Treasurer, Wm. Henry Alline. The Lowell play-ground is on Boston Common. Their uniform is white cap, trimmed with blue; white flannel shirt, and dark blue pants, with scarlet stripe. Number of members, active and honorary, about one hundred.

HARVARD CLUB.

The Harvard Base Ball Club of Cambridge, Massachusetts, is composed of the students of Harvard University, and was organized October 12, 1864.

The following list of officers was chosen: F. Wright (class of 1866), President; J.B. Ames (class of 1867), Vice-President; D.B. Abercrombie (class of 1866), Secretary and Treasurer.

The Club is made up of the best players from the Class Clubs, which generally comprise about one-half of each class—fifty or sixty in number.

The Harvard's first game was played in Boston, June 17, 1865, with the Trimountains, of Boston.—Harvard, 60 runs; Trimountain, 32 runs. July 1.—Harvard and Trimountain, on Boston Common. Harvard, 27 runs; Trimountains, 17 runs. July 4.—Harvard and Granite Club, of Holliston, Mass., at Holliston. Harvard, 44 runs; Granite, 14 runs. July 16.—Harvard and Lowell, of Boston, on Boston Common. Harvard, 28 runs; Lowell, 17 runs. Umpire, Mr. Chandler, of Trimountains. By this game the championship of New England was won by the Harvard Club. July 19.,—Harvard and Williams, of Williams College, Williamstown, Mass., at Williamstown. Harvard, 36 runs; Williams, 30 runs. July 28.—Harvard and Charter Oak, of Hartford, Conn., at Worcester, Mass. Harvard, 35 runs; Charter Oak, 13 runs. September 7.—Harvard and Atlantic , of Brooklyn, N.Y., on Boston Common. Harvard, 22 runs; Atlantic, 58 runs. September 30.—Harvard and Lowell, of Boston, on Boston Common. Harvard, 37 runs; Lowell, 40 runs. By this match the championship of New England was lost. October 20.—Harvard and Lowell, of Boston, on Boston Common. Harvard, 73 runs; Lowell, 37 runs; eight innings. By this game the championship was again obtained.

May, 1866.—Harvard and Orient. Harvard won by 97 to 11.May.—Harvard and Beacon. Won by Harvard, by 77 to 11. May 1.—Harvard and Trimountain. Won by Harvard, by 55 to 33. May 30—Harvard and Atlantic, at Brooklyn. Score, 37 to 15, in favor of Atlantic. May 31, Harvard and Eureka, at Newark, N.J. Eureka, 42; Harvard, 39. June 1.—Harvard and Excelsior, at Brooklyn. Won by Excelsior, by 46 to 28. June 2.—Harvard and Active, of New York, at Hoboken. Won by Active, by 24 to 15. July 4.—Harvard and Charter Oak, at Hartford. Score in favor of Harvard, by 16 to 14. July 14.—Harvard and Lowell, at Boston. Won by the Lowell, 37 to 27. July 17.—Harvard and Beacon. Won by Harvard, by 56 to 20.

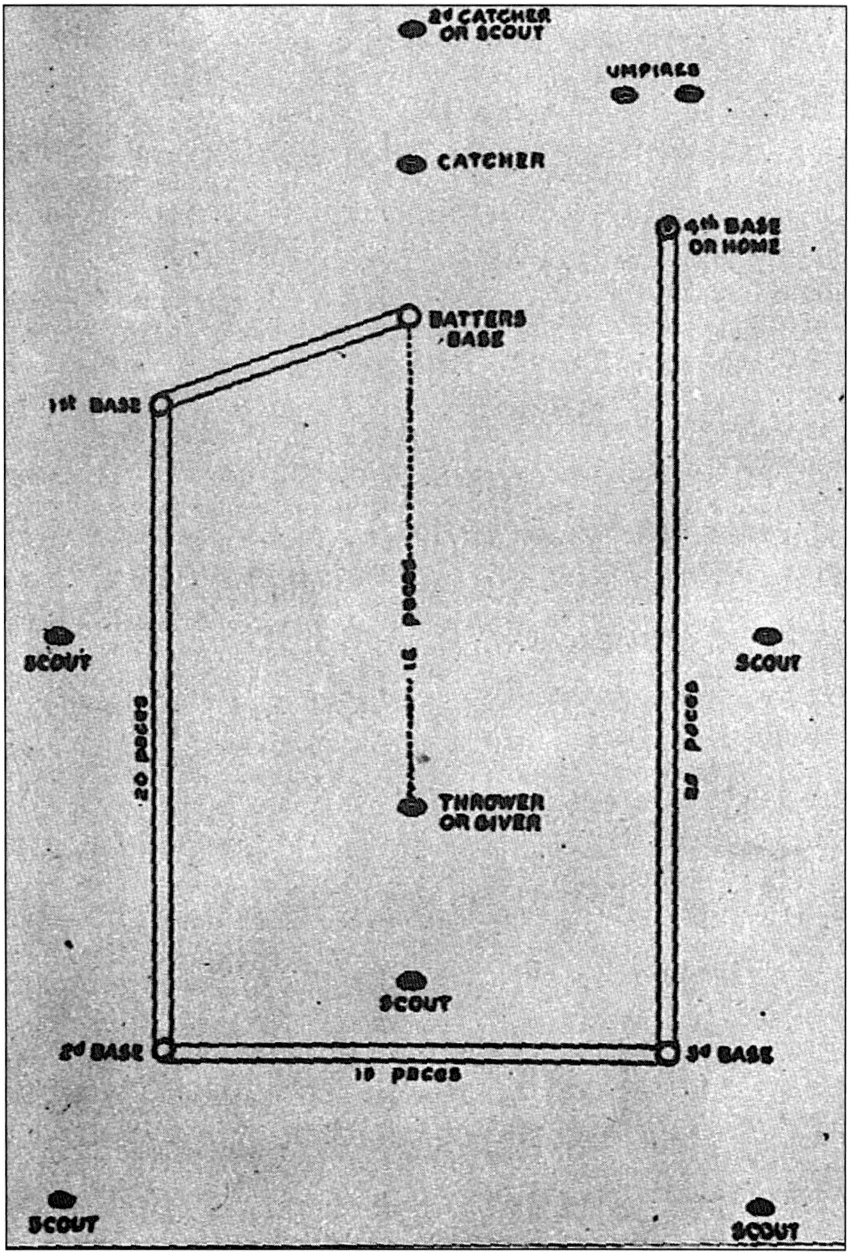

MASSACHUSETTS GAME DIAGRAM. *This diagram of the Massachusetts Game of Baseball dates to 1858. The Dedham rules were written in 1858 to establish the Massachusetts Association of Base ball Players. The Massachusetts game was more similar to town ball then the New York game, the chief difference being 60 foot bases as opposed to 90 for baseball and 40 for town ball.The Massachusetts game was a short lived success. After the original six Massachusetts association teams were organized, the Civil War hit, essentially putting an end to the Massachusetts game The Civil War helped spread the National Game (New York) and the Massachusetts game was gone by the late 1860s. Once the Trimountains switched from their Massachusetts game to the New York game, teams from small towns continued the tradition for the next few years, before succumbing to (New York) base ball fever. (Source:* Vintage Ballist.*)*

July 26.—Harvard and Williams College, at Worcester. In favor of the latter by 39 to 37. October 13.—Harvard and Beacon. Beacon score, 18; Harvard score, 53. October 27.—Harvard and Trimountain. In favor of Harvard by a score of 33 to 16.

During their visit to New York and Brooklyn, in May, 1866, the Harvard Club created the most favorable impression, and were spoken very highly of by all of the metropolitan press. The uniform of the Club is of light grey throughout, trimmed with magenta. Their play-grounds are located in Cambridge, on the College Delta.

EON CLUB

The Eon Base Ball Club, of Portland, Me., was organized May 29, 1865, and joined the National Association in the autumn of that year. Previous to July 4, 1866, the Eon Club had played eleven first nine games, winning all but one of them. The club room, score book, and other property and records of the club perished in the disastrous conflagration which visited Portland on the 4th of July, 1866. Since then the Eons have played five games, as follows: July 4, 1866, Eon and Lowell, of Boston. Won by the Lowell by a score of 33 to 23. On the 1st of August, the Eon played with the Portland, winning by a score of 39 to 3. September 5, they played with the Athletic, winning the ball by a score of 21 to 11. On October 4, 1866, they played their return game with Athletic, of Portland, whom they defeated for the second time by a score of 38 to 25. The Eon uniform consists of dark blue pants, white shirt and cap, with blue trimming. They practice on the Arsenal grounds, on the western promenade. Number of members about forty. Officers for 1865: President, L.A. Foster; Vice-President, A.H. Evans; Secretaries, E.C. Ascensio and F.W. Smith; Treasurer, Robinson Williams. Officers for 1866: President, J.H Smith; Vice-President , G.T. Means; Secretary, Andrew Geyer; Treasurer, Robinson Williams.

CHARTER OAK CLUB.

The Charter Oak Base Ball Club, of Hartford, Conn., was organized June 23, 1862, with the following officers: President, Gershom B. Hubbell; Vice-President, J.B. Burbank; Secretary and Treasurer, C.A. Jewell. Mr. Hubbell has been re-elected to the Presidency at every election since, and has contributed materially in gaining for the club its present prominent place in the base ball world. Mr. William R. Hills, the worthy Vice-President of the club, has served many years in the Charter Oak's ranks.

The Charter Oak has played the following first nine matches: August 17, 1864, at Hartford, Connecticut. Charter Oak, 28, and Collinsville, 7. November 2.—At Hartford. Charter Oak, 44; and Yale, of New Haven, Conn., 32.

June 10, 1865.—At Hartford. Charter Oak, 22; and Agallian, 12. June 24.—At Hartford. Charter Oak, 48; and Mechanics, 17. July 1.—At New Haven. Charter Oak, 39; and Yale, 12. July 28.—At Worcester. Charter Oak, 13; and Harvard, 35. September 16.—At Hartford. Charter Oak, 27; and Mechanics, 3. September 23.—Forfeit by the Mechanics' Club, of Hartford. This club challenged the Charter Oak for the "Charter Oak Bat," emblem of the championship of the State, which they held; the time was agreed upon, but they did not "come to time." September 28.—At Hartford. Charter Oak, 11; and Atlantic, of Brooklyn, N.Y., 37. September 30.—At Waterbury. Charter Oak, 30; and Waterbury, of Waterbury, Conn., 22. October 4.—At Hartford. Charter Oak, 72; and First Connecticut Artillery Regiment, 9. October 13.—At Hartford. Charter Oak, 24; and Eureka, of Newark, N.J., 31.

The Charter Oak Club opened the season of the 1866 by a game for the championship of the State, with the Yale, of New Haven. Won by Charter Oak, by 18 to 15. June 13.—With Yale, return game, at New Haven, Score, 22 to 10, in favor of Charter Oak. June 23.—Charter

Oak and Chester, of Norwich, at Hartford. Score, 59 to 15, in favor of Charter Oak. July 4.—Charter Oak and Harvard, at Hartford. Won by the Harvard, by 16 to 14. July 5.—Charter Oak and Waterbury, at Waterbury. Won by Charter Oak, by 25 to 5. July 20.—Charter Oak and Chester, at Norwich.. Won by the Chester Club, by a score of 51 to 32; eight innings. July 26.—Charter Oak and Union, of Morrisania, at Hartford. Score, in favor of the latter, by 32 to 20. July 28.—Charter Oak and Waterbury; return game. Won by Charter Oak; score, 25 to 21.; seven innings. September—,—Charter Oak and Pioneer, at Springfield, Mass. Won by the Pioneer, by 45 to 37; eight innings. September 29.—Charter Oak and Chester, home-and-home game, at New Haven. Won by Charter Oak, by 39 to 22. Having defeated every State club which has played with them, the Charter Oaks retain their title as State Champions, and the State emblem, a beautiful Charter Oak Miniature Bat. During the season the Charter Oaks have played nine matches with association clubs, and have made 252 to their opponents' 187; have won six and lost three games. The uniform of the club is blue pants, and white cap and shirt. Practice and playing ground in the Hartford Park.

WATERBURY CLUB.

The Waterbury Base Ball Club of Waterbury, Conn., was organized in August, 1864, with the following officers: George H. Pendleton, President; H.S. Peck, Vice-President; Henry Church, Secretary.

Officer for 1865 and 1866: Henry S. Peck, President; Cornelius E. Terry, Vice-President; Charles S. Treadway, Secretary and Treasurer.

First game, June, 1864.—Played the Mechanics' Club of Hartford. Mechanics, 49; Waterbury, 9.

September 30.—Waterbury and Charter Oak, at Hartford. Charter Oak, 30; Waterbury, 22.

October 18, 1865.—Waterbury and Monitor. Monitor won by 30 to 25.

October 21.—Waterbury and Plymouth. Score, 19 to 9, in favor of the Waterbury.

November 1.—Waterbury and Yale, at New Haven. Won by Yale, by 35 to 30.

November 8.—Waterbury and Yale. Waterbury, 30; Yale, 52.

July 5, 1866.—Waterbury and Charter Oak, at Hartford, Conn. Score, 25 to 5, in favor pf Charter Oak.

July 25.—Waterbury and Charter Oak; won by the latter, by 25 to 21.

The Waterbury club games in New York.—The following are the scores of the games in which the Waterbury (Conn.) Club engaged in their visit to New York and Brooklyn: Monday, September 17, at Hoboken—Eagles, of New York; score, Eagle, 20; Waterbury, 31. Tuesday, September 18, at Capitoline grounds, Brooklyn—Enterprise, of Brooklyn, 37; Waterbury, 21. Wednesday, September 19, at Hoboken—Empire, of New York, 21; Waterbury, 26. Friday, September 21, at Morrisania—Union, of Morrisania, 19; Waterbury, 8— the rain putting an end to the game at the end of the third innings.

The Waterbury Club numbers about 60 active, and 50 honorary members.

UNCAS CLUB.

The Uncas Base Ball Club, of Norwich, Conn., was organized May 2, 1865. The following is a record of their games for 1865 and 1866:

July 1, 1865.—Uncas and Norwich Free Academy. Won by Uncas; 25 to 15. September 6.—Uncas and Chester, of Norwich. Uncas, 15; Chester, 29. September 12.—Uncas and Chester. Uncas, 31; Chester, 37. September 27.—Uncas and Chester, for a prize of

$25 offered by the New London Co., Ct., Agricultural Society. Won by the Chester, by 47 to 33.

July 19, 1866.—Uncas, 75; Oceanic, of Mystic Bridge, 36. July 24.—Uncas, 1; Union, of Morrisania, N.Y., 51. August 14.—Uncas, 33; Oceanic, of Mystic Bridge, 51. September 1.—Uncas, 61; Enterprize, of Danielsville, 20. November 1.—Uncas 57; Pequot, of New London, 48. November 10.—Uncas, 26; Pequot, of New London, 90.

Recapitulation: The Uncas Club has played nine (first nine) games, winning six, and losing three. The Uncas won from the Oceanic twice; Enterprise, twice; Pequot, once, and Adelphi once, The Club was defeated once each by the Union, Oceanic, and Pequot Clubs.

At a meeting of the Uncas Base Ball Club, held on the evening of May 4, 1866, amendments to the constitution were adopted increasing the number of active members to thirty-five, making the election of members possible at the meeting at which they are proposed, unless objection is made; and making the election of officers for one year, instead of six months, from May. The following officers were chosen for 1866: President, General Edward Harland; Vice-President, W.H. Whittemore; Secretary, H.P Goddard; Treasurer, Luke Hillard; Board of Director, D. R. Tice, G.E. Palmer, S.T. Holbrook; Delegates to National Association, Colonel J. P. Ward and H. P. Goddard. The latter gentleman is connected with that excellent paper the Norwich *Bulletin*, as local editor.

CHESTER CLUB

The Chester Base Ball Club, of Norwich, Conn., was organized June, 1865. The officers of the club for 1866, are: E.G. Selden, President; C.G. Rawson, Vice-President; Geo. T. Backus, Secretary; S. A. Gilbert, Treasurer.

The club grounds are at William's Park, which is also occupied by the Uncas Club.

The uniform consists of light blue pants, white belt with Chester in red, red and white check shirt, cap of same, white front. Active member, thirty-two; honorary, twenty-one.

GAMES PLAYED BY THE CHESTER CLUB.

September 6, 1865.—Chester and Uncas. Won by the Chester, by 29 to 15.
September 7.—Chester and Uncas. Won by Chesters, by 40 to 39.
September 12.—Chester and Uncas. Won by Chester, by 37 to 31.
September 27.—Chester and Uncas. Won by Chester, by 47 to 33.
July 25, 1866.—Chester and Union, of Morrisania, at Norwich, Union, 45; Chester, 25.
September 29.—Chester and Charter Oak, at New Haven. Score, 39 to 22, in favor of the Charter Oak. Home-and-home game, each having one game previously.

OLYMPIC CLUB.

The Olympic Ball Club, of Philadelphia, was established by the union of two associations of Town Ball Players in the year 1833. One of these associations began playing at Camden, N.J., on Market street, near or upon the ground where the Episcopal Church stands, in the spring of 1831. On the first day there were but four players, and the game was "Cat Ball," or what is called in some parts of New England, "Two Old Cat." The players, who were then over 25 years old, told some of their younger friends of the pleasure and advantage they found in resuming their boyish sports, and invited them to join and make up a number large enough for a game of Town Ball. This was soon done, and a party of fifteen to twenty regularly went over to Camden on Saturday afternoons, in a horse ferry-boat, and played the game of Town-Ball. So great was the prejudice of the public against the game at that time, that the players were frequently reproved and censured by their friends for degrading themselves by indulging in such a childish amusement, and this prejudice prevailed to a great extent for many years. Its existence is shown by the fact that so few persons were found to join in the play, and by the long period that elapsed before any considerable number of ball clubs formed in Philadelphia, or any of the neighboring cities. Their first Association had no constitution or by-laws, or elected members, but the absence of these formalities was not felt, and was no disadvantage; for there were no quarrels or disputes among the players, who always found the principles of good-fellowship and gentlemanly intercourse a sufficient rule for their guidance, and what the Society of Friends call the "weight of the meeting," a sufficient authority to restrain any inclination to a breach of good order. Camden was then a very small village, comparatively little resorted to by Philadelphians, the means of communication with the city limited, slow, and imperfect, consisting mainly of two or three small horses ferry-boats, which left the wharf at the north side of Market street at intervals of about half an hour, and occupied about fifteen minutes in crossing. The ground on which the play began and continued for several years was common and open to the street on which it bordered: no rent was paid for it, and no permission given or asked to use it. The players made their own bats and balls, and kept them at one of the public gardens on Market street, the keeper of which sent out a pail of ice-water to the ground, and supplied the ball players at his garden when the game was over, about sunset, with a bowl of lemonade, etc., at a very moderate charge.

The other Association, which first assumed the name of the Olympic Ball Club, was originally formed for the purpose of playing Town Ball on the 4th of July. They met occasionally at other times by appointment, but had no regular days or established ground for some years. Two or three members of this club began playing regularly at Camden with the first named party, and after a time induced all the members of the Olympic to go to Camden regularly on Wednesdays and on the ground occupied on Saturday by the other party. A match

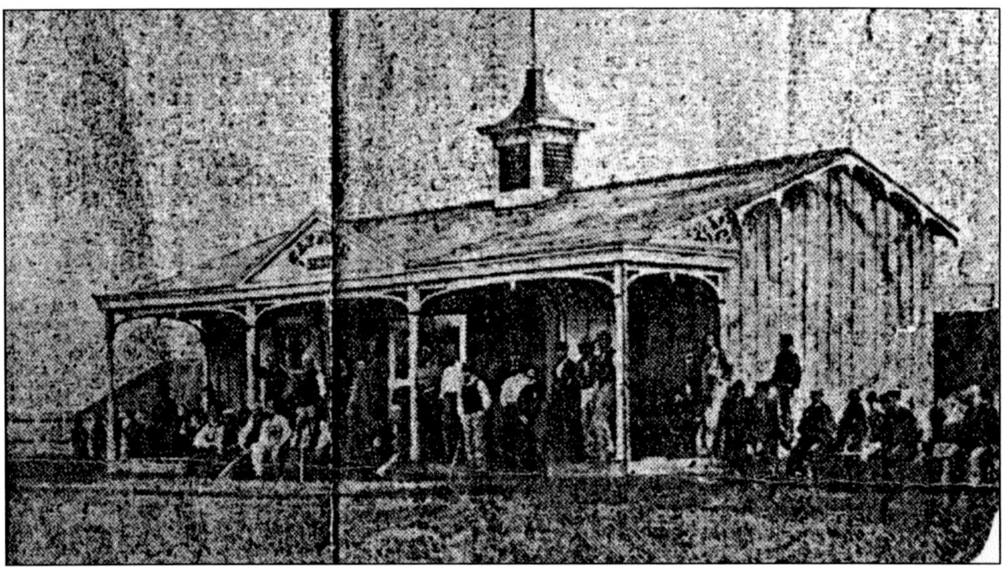

OLYMPIC 1860 PICTURE. *This image comes from an article that claims that a man had a photo of the Philadelphia Olympic team from 1839. That'd be a neat trick, because cameras were not developed enough to take an outdoor picture in 1839. It is probably from the early 1860s, maybe 1860 or 1861. Notice the primitive look of the uniforms, long pants, and cumbersome shirts. It is likely that this is the base ball club, not the town ball club that the Olympics are famous for. They played a far different game than their ball playing brethren from New York. (Source: Priscilla Astifan.)*

TOWN BALL BOXSCORE. *Here is a rare look at a townball boxscore c. 1860. It is curious what "no ball" means in the boxscore, maybe being plugged between the bases. (Source: Charles "Newt" Weaver.)*

TOWN BALL IN PHILADELPHIA.—The match between the Olympic and Excelsior first eleven was played on the 12th ult., on the grounds of the latter. The Olympic Club dates its existence back to the year 1832, so that properly speaking it is the parent Town Ball organization in the city of Philadelphia. It is not to be wondered at, therefore, that it numbers amongst its membership some of the very best players in the country. Against such players on Thursday, the 12th of July, did the Excelsiors contend. Play commenced at 2¼ and ended at 6¼ o'clock. The contest was conducted in the most friendly spirit. The Olympics all played well, McHaines, Warner and Paul making their mark at the bat, and scoring between them 36 runs. The fielding of Richards, Paul, Elkington, and Zimmerman, behind, was very good. The Olympic played their first innings with ten men. The batting of the Excelsiors, considering the superior fielding pitted against them, was excellent; Ridgway, Hayhurst and Conard distinguishing themselves at the bat, and scored 35 runs. In fielding, Hurley, Ridgway, Conard, Bradbury, and Read, behind, won laurels; Hurley especially won the applause of the spectators. Hayhurst and Raiquel, usually good fielders, played miserably in this match. The score was as appended:—

BATTING.

OLYMPIC. Names.	No Balls.	Runs.	EXCELSIOR. Names.	No Balls.	Runs.
Smith	0	7	Bradley	0	7
Payne	1	7	Kline	1	6
E Bomiesler	1	9	Sellers	2	5
Elkington	0	8	Read	1	8
Weeks	0	7	Ridgway	1	16
Warner	0	11	Conard	1	8
Richards	1	5	Hayhurst	0	11
Paul	1	10	Matthias	0	2
Zimmerman	0	8	Hurley	0	6
McHaines	0	15	Bradbury	0	2
C Bomiesler	1	0	Raiquel	1	5
Total	5	87	Total	7	71

RUNS MADE IN EACH INNINGS.

	1st	2d	3d	4th	5th	6th	7th	8th	9th	10th	11th	
Olympic	6	3	9	9	5	20	5	9	6	10	5	87
Excelsior	7	9	10	1	12	1	13	5	1	4	8	71

FIELDING.

	Fly.	B'nd.	Beh'd.		Fly.	B'nd.	Beh'd.
Smith	1	1	0	Bradley	1	0	0
Payne	4	3	0	Kline	8	4	0
E Bomiesler	1	3	2	Sellers	2	3	0
Elkington	5	5	0	Read	0	0	32
Weeks	1	8	0	Ridgway	1	13	0
Warner	6	0	0	Conard	12	2	0
Richards	11	3	0	Hayhurst	4	2	0
Paul	10	0	0	Matthias	3	3	0
Zimmerman	0	1	36	Hurley	15	0	0
McHaines	7	2	0	Bradbury	7	1	0
C Bomiesler	2	1	0	Raiquel	4	0	0
Total	48	27	38	Total	52	28	32

HOW PUT OUT.

	Fly.	Bound.	Behind.	No Balls.	Stakes.		Fly.	Bound.	Behind.	No Balls.	Stakes.
Smith	5	3	2	1	0	Bradley	3	1	6	0	1
Payne	4	2	4	0	0	Kline	4	2	4	1	0
E Bomiesler	8	0	2	1	1	Sellers	5	1	3	2	0
Elkington	7	2	2	0	0	Read	5	1	4	1	0
Weeks	5	3	3	0	0	Ridgway	2	5	3	1	0
Warner	1	7	2	0	1	Conard	2	0	8	1	0
Richards	2	2	6	1	0	Hayhurst	5	3	3	0	0
Paul	6	2	2	1	0	Matthias	6	4	1	0	0
Zimmerman	6	1	4	0	0	Hurley	9	2	0	0	0
McHaines	3	4	3	0	0	Bradbury	2	4	2	0	0
C Bomiesler	5	2	2	1	0	Raiquel	4	4	2	1	0
Total	52	23	32	5	2	Total	48	27	38	7	1

There were from six to eight players upon each side, the latter number being considered a full complement.

The two best players upon each side—first and second mates, as they were called, by common consent—were catcher and thrower. These retained their positions in the game, unless they chose to call some other player, upon their own side, to change places with them.

The following diagram will show the position of the players:

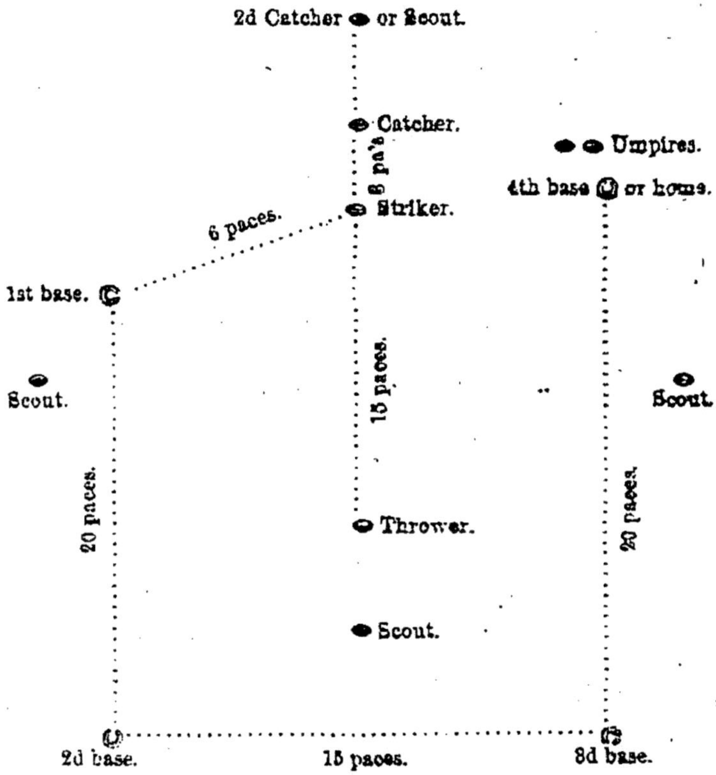

TOWN BALL DIAGRAM. *From* Wilkes Spirit of the Times, *1856, this is a diagram of the game of town ball. Town ball differed from the game of base ball in several of ways. First, the field is a little smaller, with 40-foot base paths as opposed to 90 feet; and an even number of players could play on a side, sometimes as many as 15 per side, in casual contests. The field was square instead of a diamond. Players were also put out by being plugged or thrown at between the bases. That last point alone helped bring on the development of a more civilized game of ball that the Knickerbockers helped hone. Town ball developed in Philadelphia and Camden, New Jersey, as early as 1831. Players began playing "Cat Ball" or "Two Old Cat" at the beginning with four players. The numbers grew when players would come by horse ferry to the field on Market Street. They paid no rent for the field and the owner of the property would sometimes bring out a bowl of lemonade for refreshment, at a nominal fee. The Olympic town ball club of 1833 was primarily a group of students from the Central High School in Philadelphia. That team lasted into the late 1860s and disappeared when the National Association took things over in 1871. Town ball lasted in popularity in Philadelphia until 1860 when it was felt that the New York game was the way to go. (Source:* Vintage Ballist.*)*

between the two parties was proposed and played before their union, and this is believed to have been the first match between two clubs or associations of ball-players in Pennsylvania. No record of this match has been preserved, but it had the effect to make the two parties acquainted with each other, and soon led to a fusion of the two into one. Several years before the club left Camden, a third association, which had been playing for a short time in the neighborhood of the Olympic ground, united with and was merged in the Olympic Club, and afterwards a fourth Town Ball party, consisting principally of graduates of the Philadelphia Central High School, who had met in Camden for a single season, also gave up their organization and joined the Olympic.

As would naturally be expected, many members of the original associations which formed the Olympic Ball Club thirty-five years ago, have ceased to play or to frequent the meeting of the club, but comparatively few of those who were active members have died. Several of them, who were weak and sickly when they joined the club twenty or thirty years ago, recovered their health and strength, and any Philadelphian who will look over the Olympic's early scores and records, will be surprised at the number of the survivors, and their vigor and activity.

In May, 1860, they adopted the National Association game of base ball, setting aside their time-honored play, endeared by the memories of thirty years, to press on in the race of progress. An honorable retirement of most of their old members was, however, the immediate consequence. Mutterings both loud and deep were freely heard at the innovation. Three hundred and sixty feet, compared with the old Town Ball circle of eighty feet, was enlarging their sphere of action with a vengeance. We append a summary of the Olympic Club's games since 1860.

July 24, 1860.—Olympic and St. George's Cricket Club, at Camac's Wood; 25 to 17, in favor of Olympic. October—Olympic and Hamilton; score, 18 to 16, in favor of Olympic.

June 28, 1861.—Olympic and Athletic; score, 25 to 20, in favor of Olympic. October 12.—Olympic and Adriatic; score 25 to 17, in favor of Olympic. Nov.12.—Olympic and Athletic; score, 34 to 18, in favor of Olympic.

October 4, 1862.—Olympic and Athletic; score, 19 to 18; won by Olympic. October 31.—Olympic and Athletic; score, 19 to 10; seven innings; won by Athletic.

August 27, 1863.—Olympic and Mutual, of New York; won by Mutual, by 10 to 7.

July 30, 1864.—Olympic and Resolute, of Brooklyn; score, 24 to 23, in favor of Olympic. June.—Olympic and Keystone; 30 to 24; won by Keystone. June.—Olympic and Camden; 28 to 23; won by Olympic.July 4.—Olympic and Star, of Brooklyn; score, 31 to 22, in favor of Star. August 1.—Olympic and Atlantic, of Brooklyn; 58 to 11; won by Atlantic. August 4.—Olympic and Union, of Morrisania; 25 to 13, in favor of Union.

August 10, 1865.—Olympic and Active, of New York; score, 34 to 12, in favor of Active. August 25.—Olympic and Empire, of New York; score, 37 to 17, in favor of Empire. October.—Olympic and Camden; score, 39 to 22; won by Olympic. November.—Olympic and Athletic; 56 to 9; won by Athletic.

June 20, 1866.—Olympic and Camden, at Camden; score, 47 to 26, in favor of Camden.August 2.—Olympic and Camden; score, 28 to 24; won by Camden. Sept.13.—Olympic and Athletic; eight innings; score, 57 to 16, in favor of Athletic.Sept.22.—Olympic and Excelsior; score, 41 to 16; won by Excelsior.

The officers of the Olympic for 1866 are: President, William E. Whitman; Vice-Presidents, C. Eugene Claghorne and F. De B. Richards; Secretary, Benjamin M. Dusenbury; Treasurer, Edwin W. Payne. The uniform is dark blue pants, white shirt, trimmed with scarlet; white cap, with blue trimming, and red morocco belt.

MINERVA CLUB.

The Minerva Base Ball Club, of Philadelphia, was organized June 10, 1857. This club, dating its organization from 1857, is consequently one of the oldest Philadelphia clubs. The unanimity of feeling in this club is manifest when, upon examination, we find *all* the founders of the club still members. From 1857 to 1864 the club was successful in every match except two, which they played with the celebrated Athletic club of the same city.

In 1865, they played the following games: May 30.—Minerva and Enterprise, at Camden. Won by Minerva, 34 to 29. June 1.—Minerva and Active; 36 to 23, in favor of Active. June 20.—Minerva and Hamilton. Tie game; score, 26 to 26. July 4. Minerva and Athletic, Jr. Won by the latter, by 31 to 27. August 1.—Minerva and Athletic, Jr. Score, 30 to 20, in favor of Athletic. September 5.—Minerva and Ontario. Score, 30 to 20; won by Ontario. September 26.—Minerva and Eagle. Minerva won, by 38 to 21. October 3.—Minerva and Hamilton. Score, 23 to 21, in favor of Hamilton. October 21.—Minerva and Columbia. Won by the latter, by 30 to 29. October 23.—Minerva and Everett. Tie game; score, 27 to 27. October 25.—Minerva and First National. Won by Minerva, by 33 to 18. October 27.—Minerva and Liberty. Score, 35 to 23, in favor of Minerva.

On the 4th of October, 1865, at the great Fair for the Soldiers and Sailors' Home, held at the Academy of Music, the Minerva won the prize chair which was to be given to the club receiving the highest number of votes. All the Philadelphia clubs entered in the competition, which was an exciting one between the Minerva, Athletic, and Young America Cricket Club, the vote polled being: Minerva, 607; Young America, 585; and Athletic, 550. The chair was afterwards presented by them to the Everett Union.

On the 18th of January, 1866, the Minerva Club, by unanimous vote, presented to Mr. Isaac Wilkins, the champion short stop of the Athletic Club, a handsome prize bat, valued at $150. This splendid bat was forty inches long; of rosewood; mounted at the base with solid silver, three inches in length; a silver band, ten inches from top, and capped in like manner; a silver cord was attached, and an inscription plate bearing date, name, and cause of presentation.

The practice-grounds are situated at Fifteenth street and Columbia avenue, being the fine grounds owned and played upon by the Athletic Club. The uniform consists of dark grey pants with cord down the side, plaid shirt with rolling collar, leather shoes with spikes, white navy cap trimmed with blue, German-text M on top of cap, and blue silk belt.

The officers of the club elected April 24, 1858, consisted of President, Theo. E. Wiedersheim; Vice-President, Richard M. Newman; Secretary, Isaac P. Taylor; Treasurer, Edward B. Paul. "Mr. W.——, the Minerva Club's present efficient first officer, has filled the position ever since. His reelection for so many terms is a creditable illustration of his popularity and worth. Officers for 1866, to serve until April, 1867: President, Theo. E. Wiedersheim; Vice-President, E. Forry Caldwell; Secretary, George G. Esler; Treasurer, Frank S. Baker.

KEYSTONE CLUB

The Keystone Base Ball Club, of Philadelphia, was organized November 30, 1859; in the following December, Samuel L. Barnes was elected President; F. P Mulholland, Vice-President, Thomas J. Martin; Secretary, Francis A. Frazier; Treasurer, Job T. Williams. Officers for 1861: President, Samuel Barnes; Vice-President, Hugh Barr; Secretary, F.A. Frazer; Treasurer, J.T Williams. Officers for 1862: President, James Duffy; Vice-President, George W. Butler; Secretary, F. A. Frazer; Treasurer, D.F. McCarthy. Officers for 1863: President, James Duffy; Vice-President, H.D. Mulholland; Secretary, F.A. Frazer; Treasurer, D. F. McCarthy. Officer for 1864: James Duffy, President; A, J, McGrath, Vice-President; F.A. Frazer, Secretary; H.D. Mulholland, Treasurer. Officers for 1865: D.F. McCarthy, President; John McGinnis, Vice-President; F.A. Frazer, Secretary; H.D. Mulholland, Treasurer. Officers for 1866: President, J.H.

Mahony, Vice-President, James Duffy; Corresponding Secretary, F.A. Frazer; Recording Secretary, H. N. Graffen.

The following is a summary of the Keystone games:

July 4, 1860. Keystone, 26; Continental, 11. September 15.—Keystone, 20; Equity, 43. September 29.—Keystone, 20; Pennsylvania, 48.

July 11, 1861.—Keystone, 39; Columbia, 21.

June 20, 1862.—Keystone, 18; Adriatic, 44. October 24.—Keystone, 2; Eckford, 26.

September 4, 1863.—Keystone, 5; Athletic, 25. September 17.—Keystone, 13; Eureka, of Newark, 21. September 29.—Keystone, 13; Athletic, 14. November 26.—Keystone, 15; Chippewa C.C., 16.

June 20, 1864.—Keystone, 8; Athletic, 13. July 16.—Keystone, 17; Camden, 16. July 29.—Keystone, 20; Resolute, of Brooklyn, 32. August 9.—Keystone, 10; Atlantic, 65. August 20.—Keystone, 20; Camden, 44. October 6.—Keystone, 15; Athletic, 23.

May 18, 1865.—Keystone, 15; Camden, 17. May 29.—Keystone, 7; Camden, 19. June 8.—Keystone, 12; Athletic, 21. June 15.—Keystone, 44; Satterlee, 6. June 29.—Keystone, 46; Resolute, of Brooklyn, 16. July 5.—Keystone, 31; Star, 32. July 17.—Keystone, 29; Olympic, 19. July 20.—Keystone, 33; Camden, 23. July 24.— Keystone, 11; Eureka, 50. July 25.—Keystone, 12; Mutual, 30. July 26.— Keystone, 18; Eckford, 16. July 27.—Keystone, 30; Resolute, 15. July 28.—Keystone, 34; Star, 37. July 29.—Keystone, 15; Atlantic, 33. August 5.—Keystone 7; Union, of Morrisania, 24. August 26.—Keystone, 45; Empire, 15. September 14.—Keystone, 35; Camden, 19. September 28.—Keystone, 30; Olympic, 24. November 11.—Keystone, 5; Athletic, 49. November 17.—Keystone, 44; West Philadelphia, 8.

July 3, 1866.—Keystone and National, of Washington. Score, 26 to 9, in favor of National. July 12.—Keystone and West Philadelphia. Score, 35 to 28. Won by Keystone. September 21.—Keystone and Excelsior, in Philadelphia. Tie game, 18 to 18; 8 innings. October 2.—Keystone and Atlantic. Score, 25 to 18, in favor of the latter. October 16.—Keystone and National, in Washington. Score, 41 to 26, in favor of the latter. October 17.—Keystone and Union, in Washington; 27 to 20, in favor of Keystone. October 18.—Keystone and Jefferson. Won by Keystone, by 22 to 13. October 19.-Keystone and Maryland, in Baltimore. Won by Keystone, 33 to 13. October 20.—Keystone and Pastime, in Baltimore; 24 to 12, in favor of Keystone. October 30.—Keystone and Athletic; 7 innings. Won by Athletic, by 40 to 16. November 5.—Keystone and Athletic. Score, 27 to 23, in favor of Athletic.

Practice-grounds, parade ground, Eleventh and Wharton streets. Practice-days, Monday and Thursday. Uniform, white shirt trimmed with blue; blue pantaloons; white cap, with Keystone in the centre, and elastic belt.

Number of members: Eighty-two active, seventy contributing, and twelve honorary.

ATHLETIC CLUB.

The Athletic Base ball Club, of Philadelphia , was organized April 7, 1860. Officers of Club, from date of organization to March, 1861: President, Wm. Emot; Vice-President, Co. Thos. Fitzgerald; Secretary, H.W. Karcher; Treasurer, John J. Heiser.

From March, 1861, to March, 1862: President, Col. Thos. Fitzgerald; Vice-Presidents, Chas. W. Bacon and Col. D.W.C. Moore; Secretary, B. T. Croasdale; Treasurer, N. Berkenstock.

From March, 1862, to March, 1863: President, Col. Thos. Fitzgerald; Vice-Presidents, Chas. W. Bacon and D. W. C. Moore; Secretary, Richard W. Benson; Treasurer, N.

Berkenstock. Captain, D. W. C. Moore.

From March, 1863, to March, 1866: President, Col. Thos. Fitzgerald; Vice-President, Chas. W. Bacon and D. W. C. Moore; Secretary, Richard W. Benson; Treasurer, Theo. M. Page. Captain, G.D. Kleinfelder.

Colonel D. W. C. Moore is the present (1866) President of the club.

Sept. 22, 1860.—Athletic and Pennsylvania; score, 27 to 19, in favor of Athletic.
Oct, 6.—Athletic and Hamilton; score, 37 to 51, in favor of Hamilton.
Nov. 12.—Athletic and Equity; score, 17 to 29; won by Equity; score, 17 to 29; won by Equity.
June 19, 1861,—Athletic and Mercantile; 41 to 13; won by Athletic.
June 28.—Athletic and Olympic; 20 to 25; won by Olympic.
October 5.—Athletic and Adriatic; 18 to 17; won by Athletic.
Nov. 12.—Athletic and Adriatic; 34 to 18, in favor of Adriatic.
August 28, 1862.—Athletic and Mutual, of New York; 17 to 10, in favor of Athletic.
October 4.—Athletic and Olympic; 18 to 19, in favor of Olympic.
October 23.—Athletic and Eckford, Brooklyn; 25 to 32; won by Eckford.
Oct. 31.—Athletic and Olympic; 19 to 10; won by Athletic.
March 22, 1863.—Athletic and Nassau; 29 to 18; won by Athletic.

Left for New York in the 8 A.M. train, June 15, 1863. Received by a delegation of New York Clubs. Quartered at Lafarge House.

June 15, 1863.—Athletic and Excelsior, of Brooklyn; 18 to 17; won by Athletic.
June 16.—Athletic and Mutual, of New York; 11 to 17; won by Mutual.
June 17.—Athletic and Eckford; 5 to 10; won by Eckford.
June 18.—Athletic and Atlantic; 13 to 21, in favor of Atlantic.
June 19.—Athletic and Star; 37 to 17, in favor of Athletic.
June 20.—Athletic and Eureka; 6 to 8; won by Eureka.
Sept. 4.—Athletic and Keystone; 25 to 5; won by Athletic.

Left at 10 P.M., Sept.10, 1863, for Altoona, Penn. Received by Mountain Club. Quartered at Mountain House.

Sept. 11.—Athletic and Mountain, of Altoona; 73 to 22; won by Athletic.
Sept. 29.—Athletic and Keystone; 14 to 13, in favor of Athletic.
June 9, 1864.—Athletic and Camden; 21 to 10, in favor of Athletic.
June 20.—Athletic and Keystone; 13 to 8: won by Athletic.
June 27.—Athletic and Mercantile; 68 to 25; won by Athletic.
June 30.—Athletic and Nassau, of Princeton, N.J.; 14 to 9, in favor of Athletic.
July 28.—Athletic and Resolute, of Brooklyn; 29 to 12, in favor of Athletic.
August 11.—Athletic and Atlantic; 16 to 43; won by Atlantic.
August 25.—Athletic and Camden; 42 to 12; won by Athletic.
Sept. 27.—Athletic and Mountain, of Altoona; 63 to 2, in favor of Altoona.
Nov. 24.—Athletic and Keystone; 23 to 15; in favor of Athletic.
May 13, 1865.—Athletic and Camden; 27 to 12; won by Athletic.
May 20.—Athletic and Camden; 24 to 19; won by Athletic.
June 8.—Athletic and Keystone; 21 to 12, in favor of Athletic

June 12, the Athletics left for New York. This trip did much to establish their reputation. They played five games, winning all, viz.: Arrived at Newark, N.J., at 10 ? A.M. Received by Eureka Club. At 2 P.M., on June 12, 1865, played with the Eureka. Score, 12 to 9, in favor of Athletic. Left same night for New York, and arrived there at 11 ? P.M. Received by delegation of New York Clubs. Quartered at Lafarge House.

June 13, 1865.—Athletic and Eagle; 24 to 14, in favor of athletic.
June 14.—Athletic and Union, of Morrisania; 31 to 21; won by Athletic.
June 15.—Athletic and Resolute; 39 to 14; won by Athletic.
June 16.—Athletic and Gotham; 28 to 20, in favor of Athletic.

July 1.—Athletic and Resolute; 46 to 12, in favor of Athletic.
July 4.—Athletic and Star; 25 to 14; won by Athletic.
August 3.— Athletic and Union, of Morrisania; 26 to 13; won by Athletic.
August 8,—Athletic and Eureka; 38 to 28, in favor of Eureka.
August 10.—Athletic and Active, of New York; 13 to 28; won by Active.
August 19.—Athletic and Camden; 16 to 10, in favor of Athletic.
August 23.—Athletic and Empire, of New York; 40 to 28, in favor of Athletic.
Left for Washington, D.C., August 27, 1865. Received by National Club, and quartered at Willard's Hotel.
August 28.—Athletic and National; 87 to 12, in favor of Athletic.
Left, August 29, for Baltimore. Received by Pastime Club. Quartered at Eutaw House.
August 29.— Athletic and Pastime; 39 to 27; won by Athletic.
Sept. 9.—Athletic and Camden; 37 to 11; won by Athletic.
Left, Sept. 18, for Pittsburg, Penn. Received by delegation of Lincoln, Allegheny and Enterprise Clubs. Quartered at Allegheny House.
Spt.19.—Athletic and Lincoln; 88 to 13, in favor of Athletic.
Sept.20.— Athletic and Allegheny; 65 to 15, in favor of Athletic.
Sept. 21.—Athletic and Enterprise; 53 to 6; won by Athletic.
Sept. 22.—Athletic and Picked Nine, of Pittsburg; 41 to 8; won by Athletic.
Sept. 30.—Athletic and National, of Jersey City 114 to 2; won by Athletic.
Oct. 2.—Athletic and Pastime, of Baltimore; 56 to 10; won by Athletic.
Oct.11.—Athletic and Excelsior; 45 to 11, in favor of Athletic.
Left Oct. 19, for Williamsport, Pen.. Received by Williamsport Club.
Oct. 20.—Athletic and Williamsport; 101 to 8, in favor of Athletic.
Oct. 20.—Athletic and Alert, of Danville; 162 to 14; in favor of Athletic.
Left Oct. 28, for Wilmington, Del. Received by Diamond State Club.
Oct. 28.—Athletic and Diamond State; 104-7, in favor of Athletic.
Oct. 30.—Athletic and Atlantic; 15 to 21; won by Atlantic.
Nov. 2.— Athletic and Hamilton; 41 to 17; won by Athletic.
Left Nov. 5, for New York. Quartered at Merchant's Hotel.
Nov. 6.—Athletic and Atlantic; 24 to 27, in favor of Atlantic.
Nov. 11.—Athletic and Keystone; 49 to 5; won by Athletic.
Nov. 18.—Athletic and Olympic; 57 to 9; won by Athletic.
Nov. 25.—Athletic and Olympic,; 93 to 27, in favor of Athletic.
Left Dec. 9, for Burlington, N.J.
Dec. 9.—Athletic and Burlington; 41 to 5; won by Athletic.
Dec. 9.—Athletic and Mt. Holly; 66 to 8; won by Athletic. The last two innings of this game were played in a snowstorm. After the game, they were the recipients of a fine banquet at the Mt. Holly Hotel, tendered by the Mt. Holly Club.
May 9, 1866.—Athletic and Lenapi; at Newcastle; 131 to 8; won by Athletic.
May 22.—Athletic and Quickstep, at Philadelphia; 99 to 6; won by Athletic.
June 8.—Athletic and Tyrolean, at Harrisburg; 101 to 61; won by Athletic.
June 14.—Athletic and Scranton, at Wilkesbarre; 49 to 4; won by Athletic.
June 14.—Athletic and Alert, at Wilkesbarre; 92 to 2; won by Athletic.
June 15.—Athletic and Susquehanna, at Wilkesbarre; 66 to 11; won by Athletic.
June 16.—Athletic and Monocacy, at Bethlehem; 82 to 10; won by Athletic.
June 7.—Athletic and Chester, at Chester; 80 to 12; won by Athletic.
June 23.—Athletic and Hamilton, at Philadelphia; 50 to 5; won by Athletic.
June 26.—Athletic and Union, at Morrisania; 33 to 20; won by Athletic.
June 27.—Athletic and Star, at New York; 37 to 19; won by Athletic.
June 28.—Athletic and Empire, at New York; 64 to 10; won by Athletic.
July 2.—Athletic and National, of Washington, at Philadelphia; 22 to 6; won by Athletic.

July 9.—Athletic and West Philadelphia, at Philadelphia; 44 to 19; won by Athletic.
July 16.—Athletic and Alert, at Philadelphia; 67 to 25; won by Athletic.
July 17.—Athletic and Irvington, at Philadelphia; 77 to 9; won by Athletic.
Hulky 24.—Athletic and West Philadelphia, at Philadelphia; 67 to 11; won by Athletic.
July 26.—Athletic and Enterprise, of Pittsburg, at Philadelphia; 80 to 7 ; won by Athletic.
July 30.—Athletic and Philadelphia, at Philadelphia; 68 to 10; won by Athletic.
August 1.—Athletic and Germantown, at Philadelphia; 79 to 14; won by Athletic.
August 8.—Athletic and Hamilton, at Philadelphia; 63 to 10; won by Athletic.
August 11.—Athletic and Alert, at Philadelphia; 100 to 5; won by Athletic.
August 24.—Athletic and Columbia, at Bordentown; 65 to 6; won by Athletic.
August 27.—Athletic and Eureka, of Newark, at Newark, N.J.; 48 to 8; won by Athletic.
August 28.—Athletic and Irvington, at Irvington, N.J.; 18 to 11; won by Athletic.
August 31.—Athletic and Logan, at Lambertsville; 106 to 10; won by Athletic.
Sept. 3.—Athletic and Olympian, at Philadelphia; 65 to 15; won by Athletic.
Sept. 7.—Athletic and Liberty, of New Brunswick, at Philadelphia; 53 to 9; won by Athletic.
Sept. 12.—Athletic and Camden, at Camden; 49 to 11; won by Athletic.
Sept. 13.—Athletic and Olympic, at Philadelphia; 57 to 16; won by Athletic.
Sept. 19.—Athletic and Camden, at Philadelphia; 33 to 4; won by Athletic.
Oct. 15.—Athletic and Atlantic, at New York; 17 to 27; won by Athletic.
Oct.18.—Athletic and Frankford, at Frankford; 55 to 5; won by Athletic.
Oct. 22.—Athletic and Atlantic, at New York; 31 to 12; won by Athletic.
Oct.26.—Athletic and Mount Holy, at Mount Holly; 71 to 32; won by Athletic.
Oct. 27.—Athletic and Union, of Morrisania, at Philadelphia; 29 to 42; won by Athletic.
Oct. 30.—Athletic and Keystone, at Philadelphia; 40 to 16; won by Athletic.
Nov. 3.—Athletic and Bachelor, at Philadelphia; 50 to 9; won by Athletic.
Nov. 5.—Athletic and Keystone, at Philadelphia; 27 to 23; won by Athletic.
Nov. 7.—Athletic and Bachelor, at Philadelphia; 36 to 15; won by Athletic.
Nov. 9.—Athletic and Columbia, at Bordentown; 63 to 25; won by Athletic.

UNIFORM.—Caps: white, trimmed with blue; blue star in middle of the crown. Shirts: white flannel, trimmed with blue; the letter "A" (German text) in blue, on the breast. Pants: blue cloth, with white cord down outer seam. Belts: white and blue, with German-silver clasps in front, and the word "Athletic," in blue letter on white morocco, in the centre of back. Number of members: honorary, 48; active, 371. Annual Ball held, Feb.22, 1866, at the Academy of Music.

The Athletic Club, of Philadelphia, never went through a season so successfully in winning trophies as they did in 1866. Out of a large number of games played with the strongest Clubs in the country—over thirty games with Association clubs—we believe they lost but two trophies, one with the Atlantic Club, and one with the Union, with both of which they now stand even in winning games this year. Their nine included Dockney, McBride, Berkenstock, Reach, Pike, Wilkins, Gaskill, Fisler, and Kleinfelder. The Athletics have done more to advance the popularity of the game, by visits to towns and villages where base ball was previously unknown, than almost any other Club in the United States.

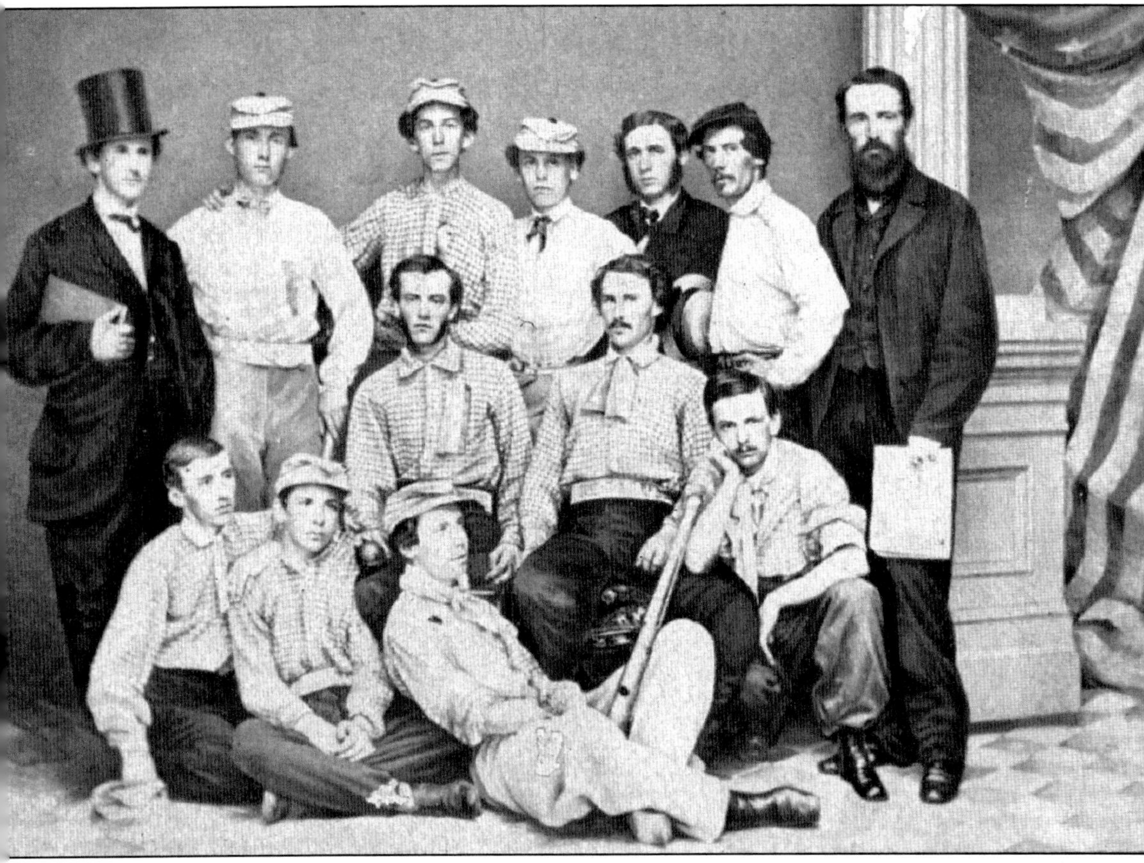

A's Versus Resolutes. *This photo shows a group of players photographed in Philadelphia, composed of members from the Athletics Club and the Resolutes of Brooklyn. Standing with them, top row far right, is the "father of baseball," Henry Chadwick, with his ever present score book. The Philadelphia Athletics, whose name has carried all the way to today's Oakland major league franchise, were the champions of Pennsylvania, and boasted many fine players. (Source: Transcendental Graphics.)*

EQUITY CLUB.

The Equity Base Ball Club, of Philadelphia, dates its existence from April 21, 1860; yielding the precedence of organization as a mere ball club to but two clubs now in existence in Philadelphia, and one (the Winona) long since extinct, it claims to be the Pioneer Base Ball Club of Pennsylvania, as being the first club to play the National Association game. The season of 1860 was the first active ball season in Philadelphia, and the several clubs went to work "with a will," and made the inaugural season of "our National Game" one long to be remembered. The Equity secured the grounds, Ridge Road and Columbia Avenue. They made their "debut" in a match with the Pennsylvania, June 26, 1860, and after a closely contested game, winning their first match, an the first ever played in the State of Pennsylvania. The umpire, upon this occasion, was Mr. T.B. Smith of the Winona. Score, 65 to 52. Their next opponent was the Winona, and the Equity won by a score of 59 to 39. Umpire, Mr. Warner, of Athletic. Their next game was the Winona return, July 19, 1860, resulting in a victory for the Equity; score, 58 to 21. On August 25th, they played with the Pennsylvania a return match, again defeating them by a score of 49 to 23. The following month they were challenged by the Keystone Club, winning this their fifth game played upon the grounds of the Equity. Date, September 19, 1860; score, 42 to 20. On October 23d, they met with their first defeat in a game with the Hamilton Club, the figures standing 15 to 11. The Equity's last match of the season was played November 12th with the Athletic Club. This game resulted in all victory for the Equity, by a score of 29 to 17. In the game played by the Excelsiors, of New York, against a picked nine from our Philadelphia Clubs, the Equity was represented by Mr. W. Fisler, now of the Athletic, and Mr. R. F. Stevens.

In the spring of 1861, just as preparation was being made for an active season, the war drew most of the Equity Club to a different field, and, as a natural sequence, the organization of the club was for the time suspended. In the spring of 1865, endeavors were made to reorganize. About this time, a number of gentlemen connected with the Philadelphia and Reading Railroad, having formed themselves into a kind of mutual exercise club, for ball-playing and general exercise, overtures were made them by the Equity, with privilege of an equal distribution of officers. This proving agreeable, a consolidation was effected, and they once more began to play, securing, temporarily, the grounds attached to the Saunders Institute in West Philadelphia. Subsequently, they secured their present fine grounds at Forty—first street and Lancaster avenue, and several games were played during the latter part of the season among themselves.

THE OFFICERS FOR 1860 were: President, Lawrence K. Mann; Vice-President, Jas. A. Lewis, Jr.; Secretary, J.B. Daniels; Treasurer, J.H. Beitel.

The original first nine of the Equity Club consisted of R.F. Stevens, pitcher; W.H. Litzenburg, catcher; B.F. Shantz, first base; Frank Knight, second base; J.B. Daniels, third base; Harry Shantz, short stop; C. Fackler, right field; Weston Fisler, centre field; B. Loughery, left field.

THE FOLLOWING WERE THE OFFICERS FOR 1861.—President, Lawrence K. Mann; Vice-President, B. F. Shantz; Secretary, Benjamin Tithian; Treasurer, J. H. Beitel.

OFFICERS FOR 1865.—President, Edgar Darrach; Vice-President, H. L. Shillingford; Secretary, W.H. Litzenburg; Corresponding Secretary, E. A. Burling Brown; Treasurer, J. H. Beitel; Captain, Harry Shantz.The Equity was admitted to the National Base Ball Convention of 1860, their delegates being Messrs. R.F. Stevens and B. F. Shantz. The board of officers now stands: President, Col. Thomas Fitzgerald; Vice-President, Harry H. Shantz; Secretary, Clinton G. Hancock; Corresponding Secretary, E. A. Burling Brown; Treasurer, J. H. Beitel.

The club was not engaged in many games during the season of 1866, neither do they claim to be very strong at present; but with Colonel Fitzgerald, of the *City Item*, at their head, united with the fine material of which the organization is composed, they are certain to take high rank at an early day as one of the prominent clubs of the country.

SWIFTFOOT CLUB

The Swiftfoot Base Ball Club, of Philadelphia, was organized July 5, 1866, with the following board of officers: President, Robert E. Lester; Vie-President, Jacob K. Powers; Secretary, John C. Addis, Jr.

The practice-ground of the club is at Twenty-fourth street and Ridge avenue. Practice-days, Tuesday and Fridays. Uniform, blue pants, white shirt, and white cap trimmed with red cord. Number of active members, sixty.

The club has not engaged in any matches of consequence as yet, but anticipate an active season in 1867.

ALLEGHENY CLUB.

The Allegheny Base Ball Club, of Allegheny, Penn., was organized June 8, 1860. First officers were: President, J.J. Moore; Vice-President, J.M. Carrs; Secretary, W.H. Lockhart; Treasurer, Robert Elton.

In this year the club played the following games: June 27.—With Duquesne. Score, 32 to 31, in favor of Allegheny. July 19.—Return game with Duquesne. Score, 27 to 26, in favor of Allegheny. September 13.—With Pioneer. Won by Allegheny, by 28 to 19.

October 31.—Game with Keystone; the latter defeated, by 34 to 22.

July 26, 1861.—Allegheny and Fort Pitt Club. Won by the former, by 50 to 13.

September 9, 1863.—Picked Nine and Allegheny. Score in favor of the latter, by 36 to 22.

July 14, 1865.—Allegheny played with the Enterprise Club. Won by the latter, by 40 to 29.

July 20.—Return game with Enterprise, who were victors again, by 20 to 15.

September 4. —Enterprise and Allegheny. Score, 29 to 24, in favor of the latter.

August 3.—Allegheny and Collins Club, at East Liberty, Pa. The latter defeated, by 45 to 21.

September 19.—Played with the Athletic, of Philadelphia. Score, 65 to 15, in favor of Athletic.

During 1866, the club played the following games: May 11. —With Crescent. Won by the Allegheny, by 97 to 5. June 13.—Game with Enterprise. Won by the latter, by 39 to 27. July 13.—Game with Manchester Club. Score, 46 to 6, in favor of Allegheny. August 5.—With Unknown. The latter lost. Score, 31 to 16. August 17.—Allegheny and Enterprise; in favor of the latter, by 24 to 22.

Officers for 1866; President, A.S. Bell; Vice-President, W. K. Hamilton; Secretary, William Ralson, Jr.; Treasurer, Robert Elton. Uniform, blue pants, white shirt with blue facings, white cap with blue hand. Active members, sixty; honorary, thirty-one.

MOUNTAIN CLUB

The Mountain Base Ball Club, of Altoona, Pennsylvania, was organized in 1862, with the annexed board of officers: President, H. W. Gwinner; Vice-President, L. M. Stewart; Secretary, W. C. Keller; Treasurer, A. Pitcairn.

Game, August 20, 1862.—With Keystone Club, of Harrisburg, at Harrisburg. Mountain, 38; Keystone, 41; ten innings.

Officers for 1863: President, Enoch Lewis; Vice-President, John Reilly; Secretary, W. C. Keller; Treasurer, Robert Pitcairn.

September 11, 1863.—Game with Athletic Club, of Philadelphia, at Altoona. Mountain, 22; Athletic, 73.

Officers for 1864: President, Enoch Lewis; Vice-President, John Reilly; Secretary, J. W. Askew; Treasure, C. L. Kitchel.

September 27, 1864.—Game with Athletic Club, of Philadelphia, at Philadelphia. Mountain, 2; Athletic, 63.

Officers for 1865: President, B. F. Rose; Vice-President, R. Gemmell; Secretary, J. W. Askew; Treasurer, D. T. Caldwell.

September 20, 1865.— Game with Athletic Club, of Philadelphia, at Altoona. Seven innings; Mountain, 16; Athletic, 41.

September 28.—Game with Philadelphia and Erie R. R. Club, of Williamsport, Pa., at Williamsport. Eight innings; Mountain, 47; Philadelphia, and Erie R.R., 35. September 29.—Game with Williamsport; Mountain, 21; Williamsport, 14.

Officers for 1866: President, E. H. Williams; Vice-President, R. B. Gemmell; Secretary, J. W. Askew; Treasurer, D. T. Caldwell.

The Mountain Club played the following games during the season of 1866: May 19.—

With Juniata Club, at Altoona. Won by Mountain, by 65 to 26. June 16.—With Juniata, at Hollidaysburg. Score, 59 to 49, in favor of Juniata. June 23.—Mountain and Bald Eagle, at Altoona. Score, 76 to 27, in favor of the former. July 24.—Mountain and Enterprise, at Altoona. Won by Enterprise, by 55 to 26. August 25.—Mountain and Bald Eagle, at Altoona. Score, 64 to 26, in favor of Mountain. October 11.—With Pennsylvania Railroad Club, at Camden, N.J. The latter won, by a score of 27 to 18, in a game of seven innings.

Number of members, seventy-seven, all active.

ALERT CLUB.

The Alert Base Ball Club, of Danville, Pen., was organized September 8, 1865, and joined the National Association of Base Ball Players at its last annual convention, held December, 1865.

The officers of the Alert Club are: President, Colonel A. J. Frick; Vice-President, W.A.M. Grier; Secretary, O.H. Ostrander; Treasurer, Robert Adams.

The Alerts have never played a regular match. The Athletics, of Philadelphia; the

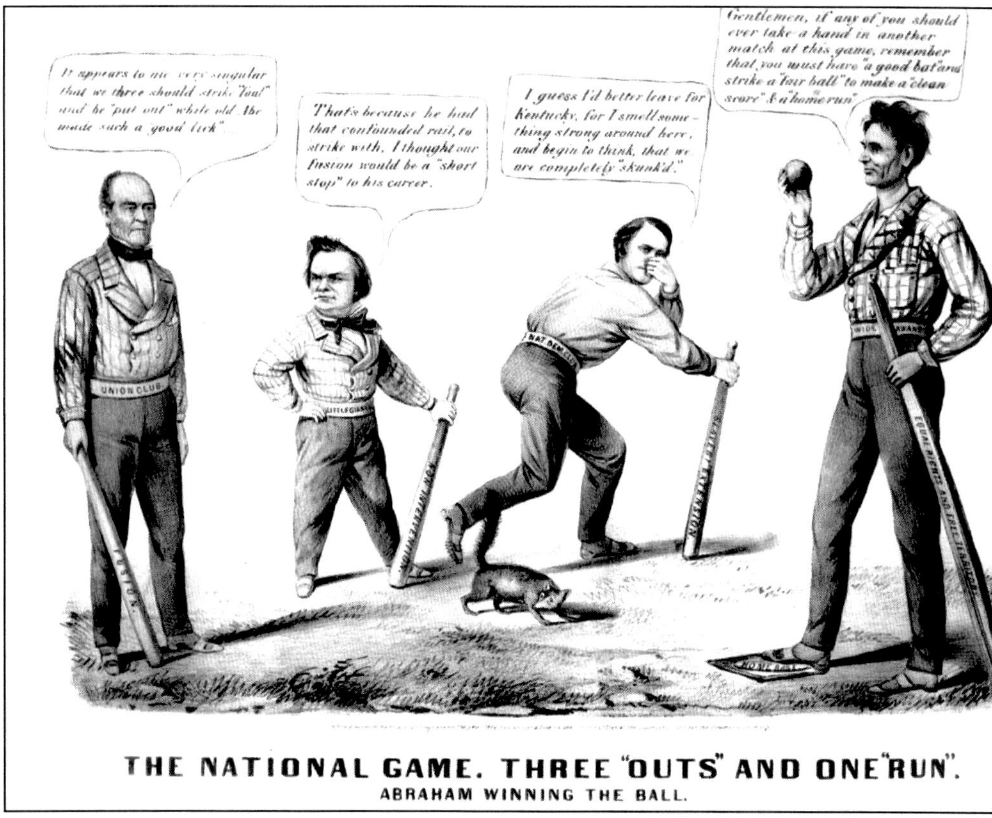

LINCOLN CARTOON. *This Currier & Ives political cartoon promoted Lincoln against Stephen Douglas in the 1860 US Presidential campaign using a base ball theme. Lincoln is said to be a gifted base ballist, a "tall" hitter, so to speak. Early Washington ball clubs used the space behind the Executive Mansion and the Front Lawn of the White House for their ball games. One can only imagine that Lincoln would take in a game, if the opportunity presented itself. I recently found a boxscore between Lincoln and Douglas "staffers" that showed the Douglas staffers winning 18-16. Told by reporters of the outcome of the game, Lincoln is quoted as saying, "Douglas is a weak short stop and will be caught out." (Source: Transcendental Graphics.)*

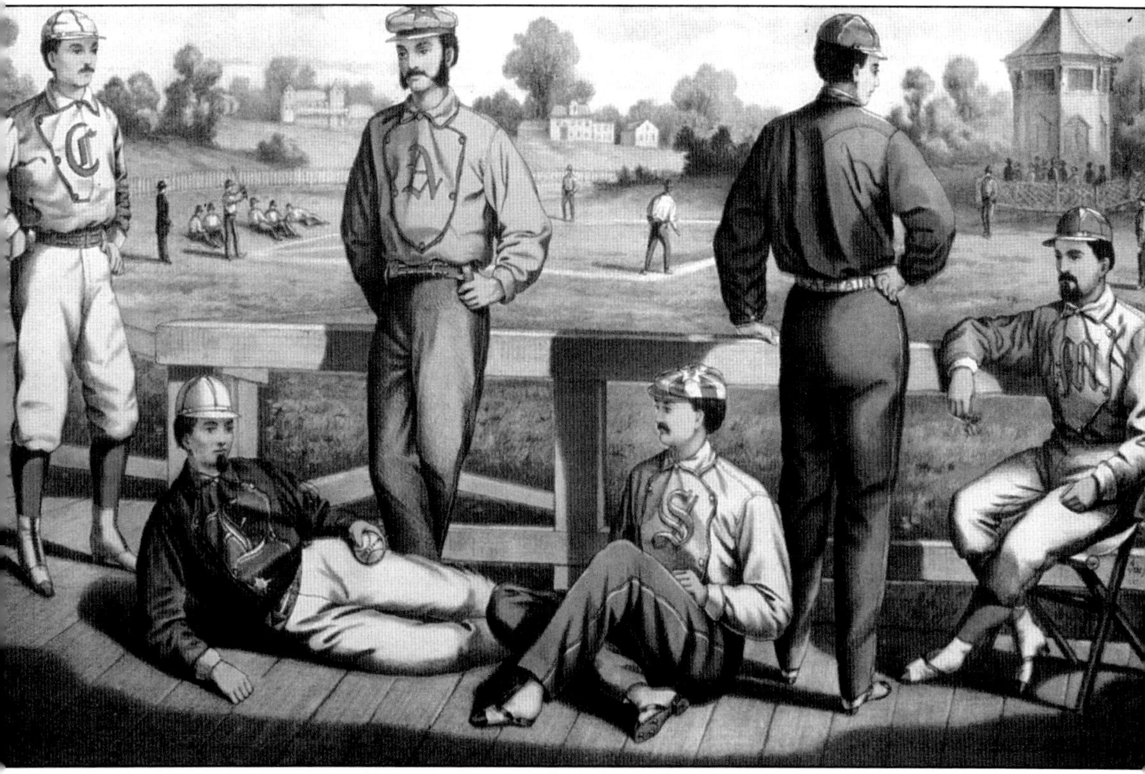

1870s Uniform Fashion. *(Source: Transcendental Graphics.)*

Williamsport, of Williamsport Pa., and the Susquehanna, of Wilkesbarre, Pa., were present here at what was called a base-ball tournament, October 19 and 20, 1865; the Williamsport and our own clubs, each played a game with the Athletic, on the 20th, it being too stormy on the 19th to play. The score of the Williamsport and Athletic was as follows: Williamsport, 8; Athletic, 102; and Alert, 11; Athletic, 162.

The practice-grounds are termed "The grounds below the Aqueduct," Danville. Uniform, white flannel shirt, blue flannel pants, and white flannel cap, with red star in centre of crown. Number of active members, 33. Practice-day, Saturday.

NATIONAL CLUB.

The National Base Ball Club (of Washington, D.C.) was organized 29th of November, 1859. They, however, commenced to play the game in May, 1859, but had no intention of formally organizing, so as to join the Association, until the date of its organization. Nor did it either desire or expect to succeed in any contests with other clubs, as a majority of its members were far advanced in life, only playing ball for exercise, and to have a pleasant time socially. Messrs. Gorman, Morrow and French, who were the founders of the club, became ambitious to have it rank with the finest clubs of the country, and have finally succeeded in gaining for it the acknowledged right to the championship of the South.

The first officers of the club were: President, James Morrow; Vice-President, J. L. Wright; Secretary, A. P. Gorman; Treasurer, A. Dodge.

We append a summary of the games played by the National Club. May 5, 1860.—National and Potomac. Score, 35 to 15, in favor of Potomac. June 2, National and Potomac, won by National, by 46 to 14. September 11, Potomac and National, in favor of Potomac, by 38 to 22. September 21, National and Potomac. Won by the National, by 30 to 25. October 22. National and Pythian. In favor of the National, by 46 to 20.

OFFICERS FOR 1860.—President, James Morrow; Vice-President, J. L. Wright; Secretary, C. C. Ivey; Treasurer, H.H. McPherson.

The first game played by the National Club in 1861 was with a nine selected from the Seventy-First Regiment, New York. Volunteers. July 2, National and Seventy-First N.Y. Volunteers. Won by the National. Score, 41 to 13. October 26, National and Maryland of Baltimore. Won by the Maryland. Score, 17 to 10. This game closed the season of 1861.

OFFICERS FOR 1860.—President, James Morrow; Vice-President, James A. Brow; Recording Secretary, H. A. McCormick; Corresponding Secretary, J.F. Dobbyn; Treasurer, H. H. McPherson.

May 20, 1862.—National and Washington. Won by National. Score, 62 to 22. June 14, Maryland and National. Score, 33 to 31, in favor of Maryland. July 25, National and Union of Washington. National, 39; Union, 15. August 7, National and Seventy-First N. Y. Volunteers. Won by National, by 28 to 13.

OFFICERS FOR 1862.—President, E. F. French; Vice-President, James F. Dooley; Recording Secretary, A. P. Gorman; Corresponding Secretary, G. D. C. Hibbs.

August 4, 1863.—National and Union. Score, 28 to 18, in favor of National. August 6, National and Pastime of Baltimore. Score, 25 to 20, in favor of Pastime. September 1, National and Union. Score, 41 to 10, in favor of National.

OFFICERS FOR 1863.—President, E. F. French; Vice-President, C. C. Walden; Recording Secretary, W. B. Pope; Treasurer, R. A. Cronin.

June 8, 1864.—National and Union. Score, 35 to 27, in favor of Union. June 28, National and Union. Won by National, by 35 to 20. October 19, National and Union. Score, 21 to 11, in favor of National.

OFFICERS FOR 1864.—President, E.F. French; Vice-President, C. C. Walden; Secretary, W. F. Williams; Treasurer, R.A. Cronin.

June 13, 1865.—National and One Hundred and Thirty-third New York Regiment. Score, 26 to 17, in favor of National. July 20, Pastime, of Baltimore, and National. Score, 9 to 35, in favor of National. August 2, Pastime and National. Won by National, by 35 to 22. August 22, National and Jefferson of Washington, D.C. Score, 34 to 13, in favor of National. September —, National and Jefferson. Won by National, by 22 to 10. August 28, National and Athletics of Philadelphia. Score, 87 to 12, in favor of Athletic. August 29, National and Atlantic of Brooklyn. Won by Atlantic, by a score of 34 to 19. September 6, National and Maryland. Score, 38 to 21, in favor of National. September 29, National and Maryland. Won by the National, by 62 to 9. October 8, National and Excelsior of Brooklyn, in Washington. Score, 35 to 30, in favor of National. October 9, National and Enterprise of Baltimore. Score, 59 to 19, in favor of National. October 28, National and Franklin of Washington. Won by National, by 31 to 4.

OFFICERS FOR 1865.— President, E.F. French; Vice-President, A P. Gorman; Secretary, M. A. Tappan; Treasurer, R. A Cronin.

July 2, 1866.—National and Athletic, in Philadelphia. Score, 22 to 6, in favor of Athletic. July 3, National and Keystone, at Philadelphia. Won by National, by 26 to 9. July 4, National and Union, at Morrisania. Won by the latter, by 22 to 8. July 5, National and Excelsior, at Brooklyn. Score, 46 to 33, in favor of the Excelsior. July 6, National and Gotham, at Hoboken. Won by the Gotham. Score, 34 to 24. July 7, National and Liberty, at New Brunswick, N. J. Score, 29 to 9, in favor of National. During this tour the National Club made many friends, and their playing and deportment received commendation and eulogy at every point where they made a halt long enough to become known to the base ball fraternity.

September 18, National and Excelsior, in Washington. Score, 33 to 28, in favor of Excelsior. September 27, National and Potomac. Won by National, by 67 to 19. October 16, National and Keystone. Score, 41 to 26, in favor of National.

OFFICERS FOR 1866.—President, A. P. Gorman; Vice-President, W. G. Moore; Secretary, M. A. Tappan; Treasurer, J. D. Patten. The uniform of the National is blue pants, white shirt with blue shield, and white cap. Their ground is on the "Mall," a portion of the ground surrounding the Presidential mansion.

POTOMAC CLUB.

The Potomac Base Ball Club, of Washington City, was organized September 18, 1865 (originally organized in 1859, but disorganized in consequence of the war). Hon. H. Selden, President; Henry S. Lovejoy, Vice-President; Wm. C. McIntire, Secretary; and R. T. Dodson, Treasurer, for the years of 1865 and 1866.

Owing to circumstances, no record was kept of the very few games played in 1865, and as yet no games (regular) have been played in 1866.

The Potomac practice-grounds are located south of the Executive mansion. Practice-days, Tuesdays, Thursdays, and Saturdays. Uniforms, greyish-blue pants, white flannel shirt, jockey cap with blue trimming, made of white canvas with a long visor, canvas shoes, blue belt; shirt trimmed with blue, and a blue P on the breast. Number of members, fifty; no honorary members.

The Potomac Club was the first base ball organization instituted in the city of Washington, and introduced the National Association, or New York Game, into the District of Columbia.

ALERT CLUB.

The Alert Base Ball Club, of Cumberland, Md., was organized on the 15th of September, 1865.

Their first game was played November 17th, 1865, with the Dexter Club. Score, 40 to 20, in favor of the Alert. Second game, November 25, with Dexter. Won by the Alert, by 26 to 20.

Their first game in 1866 was played in May, with the Antietam Club, whose score was 31 to the Alert's 25. Their second and third games were played on the 30th of June and 26th of July, with the Allegheny Club, both of which were won by the Alert. Their fourth game was with the Antietam, the latter winning, by 59 to 9. The fifth game was with the Advance, of Cumberland, for silver ball and mounted bat. Won by the Alert, by 61 to 25. October 27.—Played with Advance, the score standing 49 to 43 in favor of the Alert. November 3.—The Alert Club played with a picked nine, the result being a victory for them, by 37 to 14. November 10.—Alert and Allegheny. Score, 40 to 16, in favor of the Alert.

The Alert Club played eight games during the season of 1866, ending November 10, of which they won six, and lost two. They defeated the Allegheny, three times; Advance, twice; Picked Nine, once; and were defeated by the Antietam, of Hagerstown, Md., twice. The total runs scored were 359, against 235 by their opponents; average of five runs to an inning, with nine over, or forty-four runs to a match, with seven over. Their highest score in a single inning was twenty-two, and in a match eighty-five; the lowest score they made in a game being nine.

The officers of the Club for 1866 are as follows: President, Charles J. Harrison; Vice-President, Neill Woodrow; Secretary, Joseph P. Knorr; Treasurer, Dwight McCleave.

LOUISVILLE CLUB.

The Louisville Base Ball Club, of Louisville, Ky., was organized April 10, 1865, with the following officers to serve until July of that year: President, Alexander G. Booth; Vice-President, Daniel S. Fullerton; Secretary, Benjamin L. McDougall; Treasurer, Archie M. Quarrier. The club played two match games in 1865 with the Olympic Club of that city. The first came off July 22, and resulted in favor of the Louisville by a score of 55 to 14. The second game was played on Sept. 7, and was won by the Louisville by a score, of 36 to 13. This game was played for the State championship. The Louisville Club's rooms are located on the corner of Main and Bullit streets. Their uniform consists of a grey flannel shirt, trimmed with scarlet: black and white check cap, blue jean pants, and black patent leather belt. Location of ground, corner of Rowan and Eighteenth streets. Officers for 1866: President, Alexander G. Booth; Vice-President, Donald McPherson; Secretary, Barry Coleman; Treasurer, Archie M. Quarrier.

BASE BALL IN CALIFORNIA

Our record of California base ball matters came to hand too late for insertion in this edition. The lovers of the game, however, will be gratified to learn that it is meeting with the same favor and good feeling in the "Eureka State," which is so cordially vouchsafed to it in all of the older States, New Yorkers in particular will be especially rejoiced for its prosperity in California, for they well remember the olden time when that graceful and unsurpassed player Gelston, of the Eagles, left us for the distant sloped of the Pacific. The Eagle Club, named in compliment to his old organization, still flourishes finely in San Francisco. The number of clubs in that city and vicinity now number some seventeen or eighteen, Among them are the Eagle, Pacific, Independent, Empire, Live Oak, Cosmopolitan, Broderick, etc., etc.

BASE BALL IN OREGON.

The Pioneer Base Ball Club, of Portland, Oregon, which, as its name indicated, is the first base ball club ever formed in that State, was organized June 2, 1866, by the election of the following officers: President, F.F. Miner; Vice-President, G.J. Wheelock; Secretary, T.M. Warren, Jr.; Treasure, Joseph Stell. There is also a club at Oregon City called the Clackamas Club. Recently the Pioneers visited Oregon City and played a friendly game with the Clackamas. Score, 77 to 45, in favor of Pioneer. The Pioneer Club joined the National Association at its last convention, held 12, 1866, its delegate being Robert H. Law.

THE FASHION-COURSE MATCHES-NEW YORK vs. ALL BROOKLYN.

This celebrated home-and-home match at base ball between the picked players of the two cities, which came off in the summer of 1858, upon the Fashion Course, Long Island, excited the greatest enthusiasm and spirt among the lovers of the sport at that period ever known in this vicinity. Indeed we question if anything had occurred in base-ball annals since to surpass it. On Tuesday July 20, 1858, the first game was played.

BROOKLYN.—Leggett, c., 5 o. 1 r.; Holder, 2d b., 4 o. 2 r.; Pidgeon, s.s., 4 o. 1 r.; Grum, c.f., 2 o. 4 r.; P. O'Brien, l. f., 3 o. 2 r.; Price, 1st b., 1 o. 3 r.; M. O'Brien, p., 2 o. 3 r.; Masten, 3d b., 4 o. 1 r.; Burr, r.f., 2 o. 1 r. Total, 27 o. 18 r.

NEW YORK.—Pinckney, 2d b., 2 o. 3 r.; Benson, c.f., 3 o. 3 r.; Bixby, 3d b., 3 o. 1 r,; DeBost c., 3 o. 2 r.; Gelston, s.s., 4 o. 2 r.; Wadsworth, 1st b., 3 o. 3 r.; Hoyt, l.f., 2 o. 4 r.; Van Cott, p., 2 o. 4 r.; Wright, r.f., 5 o. 0 r. Total, 27 o. 22 r.

THE FIRST GAME IN OREGON.—Oregon City was lately the scene of a very interesting game of ball, the particulars of which we glean from the Daily Oregonian. The contestants were the Pioneer Club, of Portland, and the Clackamas Club, Oregon City.

The day was very fine, and at 6 o'clock all the party, accompanied by a number of ladies from this city, started out on the Senator. They were met by the first-nine of the Clackamas Club and the Oregon City brass band, and escorted to the Barlow House, where the party did ample justice to a splendid breakfast. They then proceeded to the ground, about a mile from the city, and the game began. A mistake was made in laying out the ground. The pitcher, basemen, and fielders all were stationed facing the sun. This was unfortunate, as the playing was made unpleasant by this disposition of the men. After the game, they returned to the Barlow House for dinner.

The Pioneers returned to Portland on the Senator, much pleased with the courtesy and kindly feeling manifested by the Clackamas Baseball Club. This is the first match-game ever played in the State, and it is a splendid beginning. Much applause is due the Oregon City boys. Their club has been organized but a short time, and they have so well improved their time that we predict that but a short time will pass before they wear the laurels. After the game they offered the winners the ball, which was very properly refused, as the game was a friendly one, and not for blood. The following is the score:

CLACKAMAS NINE.	O.	R.	PIONEER NINE.	O.	R.
Randall, C.	0	8	Witherell, 1st b.	4	9
Pope, P.	4	6	Miner, C.	2	9
Shepherd, 1st b.	2	6	Steel, c. f.	2	8
Briggs, s. s.	3	3	Upton, s. s.	2	8
Hartling, l. f.	4	4	Wadhams, 2d b.	3	7
Barclay, 3d b.	4	4	Quackenbush, P.	4	8
Zigler, r. f.	2	5	Konehtell, l. f.	1	11
Mason, c. f.	3	4	Huff, r. f.	5	8
Charman, 2d b.	4	5	Warren, 3d b.	3	9

INNINGS.	1	2	3	4	5	6	7	8	9
Clackamas Nine	2	7	4	6	1	1	8	11	10—45
Pioneer Nine	26	22	3	7	3	6	6	0	5—77

Umpire.—Mr. Anderson.
Scorer.—Mr. Lewins.
Time of Game.—Two hours and forty minutes.
Flycatches.—Clackamas, 7; Pioneer, 2.
Outs on Fouls.—Clackamas, 7; Pioneer, 4.

FIRST GAME IN OREGON. *This is the actual boxscore from the Henry Chadwick scrapbook of the first game ever played in Oregon, between the Pioneer and the Clackamas. (Source:* Vintage Ballist.*)*

The return game of the selected nines of New York and Brooklyn was played at the Fashion Course, on Tuesday, August 17, 1858.

NEW YORK.—Gelston, s.s., 2 o. 3 r.; Pinckney, 2d b., 2 o. 1 r.; Bixby, 1st b., 5 o. 0 r.; March, 3d b., 3 o. 1 r.; De Bost, c., 3 o. 0 r.; Hoyt, r.f., 3 o. 1 r.; Turner, l.f., 3 o. 1 r.; Davis, c.f., 4 o. 0 r.; Van Cott, p., 2 o. 1 r. Total, 27 o. 8 r.

BROOKLYN.—Masten, c., 3 o. 4 r.; Pidgeon, p., 4 o. 3 r.; Price, 1st b., 3 o. 2 r.; Oliver, 2d b., 3 o. 3 r.; M. O'Brien, 3d b., 5 o. 2 r.; Pearce, s.s., 2 o. 4 r.; Grum, r.f., 1 o. 6 r.; P. O'Brien, l.f., 2 o. 3 r.; Manolt, c.f., 4 o. 2 r. Total, 27 o. 29 r.

The third and final trial between "All New York" and "All Brooklyn" was played on Friday, September 10, 1858, and resulted in a victory for the New Yorkers by a decided majority.

NEW YORK.—Gelston, s.s., 2 o. 5 r.; Wadsworth, 1st b., 5 o. 2 r.; Benson, c. f., 3 o. 4 r.; Pinckney, 2d b., 3 o. 3 r.; Thorn, p., 2 o. 5 r.; Tooker, l.f., 2 o. 3 r.; DeBost, c., 5 o. 2 r.; Burns, r.f., 2 o. 3 r.; McCosker, 3d b., 3 o. 2 r. Total, 27 o. 29 r.

BROOKLYN.—Pidgeon, p., 3 o. 3 r.; Manolt, c.f., 4 o. 1 r.; Grum, r.f., 2 o. 2 r.; M. O'Brien, 3d b., 4 o. 1 r.; P. O'Brien, l.f., 5 o. 1 r.; Price, 1st b., 3 o. 1 r.; Boerum, c., 2 o. 3 r.; Pearce, s.s., 2 o. 3 r.; Oliver, 2d b., 2 o. 3 r. Total, 27 o. 18 r.

THE NATIONAL ASSOCIATION OF BASE BALL PLAYERS.

Prior to 1857, the series of rules prepared by a committee of the principal clubs of New York governed all match games of base ball played by metropolitan clubs; but in May, 1857, a Convention of ball-players was held, at which a new code of rules were enacted; and each year since this code was revised, and the game improved, until its present point of excellence has been attained. At the original Convention, the following clubs were represented by three delegates each, viz.: Knickerbocker, Gotham, Eagle, Empire, Putnam, Baltic, Excelsior, Atlantic, Harmony, Harlem, Eckford, Bedford, Nassau, Continental, Union, and Olympic, all of which were located either on Manhattan or Long Island.

A second Convention was held on the 10th day of March, 1858, pursuant to a call signed by the Presidents of the Knickerbocker, Gotham, Eagle, and Empire Clubs, in which the following clubs were represented by two delegates each, viz.: Knickerbocker, Gotham, Eagle, Empire, Putnam, Baltic, Excelsior, Atlantic, Harlem, Eckford, Continental, Union, Metropolitan, Columbian, Osceola, Oriental, Stuyvesant, Hamilton, Pastime, Liberty, (of New Brunswick,) Monument, Amity, St. Nicholas, Nassau, and Mutual.

At this Convention a Committee of Three was appointed to prepare a constitution and by-laws for a permanent association, and from this the National Association of Base Ball Players came into existence. The rules and regulations of the game adopted at this Convention remained in force until the 9th of March, 1859, when they were amended. The officers elected at the first Annual Convention in 1858 were as follows, and the same held office by re-election until 1860:—W. H. Van Cott, President; J.B. Jones, 1st Vice-President; Thomas S. Dakin, 2d Vice-President; J. Ross Postley, Recording Secretary; Theodore F. Jackson, Corresponding Secretary; E.H. Brown, Treasurer.

At the Convention of March 14, 1860, the following officers were chosen to preside:—Dr. J.B. Jones, President; Thomas S. Dakin, 1st Vice-President; Hervey Shriver, 2d Vice-president; J. Ross Postley, Recording Secretary; Theo. F. Jackson, Corresponding Secretary; E.H. Brown, Treasurer.

In the same year the third Annual Convention was held December 12th, 1860, and since then the meeting has been called each year for the second Wednesday in December., The officers for 1861 were elected at this meeting, and they were as follows:—D. Milliken, President; DeWitt C. Moore, 1st Vice-President; R. Porter, 2nd Vice-President; J. Ross Postley, Recording Secretary; Theo. F. Jackson, Corresponding Secretary; E. H. Brown, Treasurer.

The following are the names of the officers of the Association for each year since 1861 up to the Convention of 1866:—1862—D. Milliken, President; Wm. H. Hegeman, 1st Vice-President; Joseph B. Leggett, 2d Vice-President; J. Ross Postley, Recording Secretary; Z. Voorhis, Corresponding Secretary; E.H. Brown, Treasurer. 1863—Thomas Fitzgerald, President; I.W. Dawson, 1st Vice-President; F.K. Boughton, 2d Vice-President; J. Ross Postley, Recording Secretary; J. W. Mott, Corresponding Secretary; E. H. Brown, Treasurer. 1864.—I.W. Dawson, President; Francis Pidgeon, 1st Vice-President; A. J. Dupignac, 2d Vice-President; J. Ross Postley, Recording Secretary; J. Seaver Page, Corresponding Secretary; P. J. Cozans, Treasurer. 1865—Thomas G. Voorhis, President: D. A. Scott, 1st Vice-President; M. J. Thompson, 2d Vice-President; J. Seaver Page, Recording Secretary; A.H. Rogers, Corresponding Secretary; P.J. Cozans, Treasurer. 1866.—John Wildey, President; Mortimer Rogers, 1st Vice-President; M.C. Sexton, 2d Vice-President; J.S. Page, Recording Secretary; A. H. Roger, Corresponding Secretary; P.J. Cozans, Treasurer.

The number of clubs represented at the above Conventions each year was as follows:—In 1857, 16 clubs; in 1858, 29 clubs; in 1859, 49 clubs; in March, 1860, 62 clubs; in Dec., 1860, 54 clubs; in 1861, 34 clubs; in 1862, 32 clubs; in 1863, 28 clubs; in 1864, 30 clubs; and in 1865, 91 clubs; the number this year (1866) being 202 clubs, exclusive of the delegates representing the North-Western Association of Base Ball Players.

In connection with the National Association there are branch organizations in the form of State National Associations, there being one in Pennsylvania, one for the New England States, and one for the Western States.

TENTH ANNUAL BASE BALL CONVENTION.

Never before, in the history of the National Association, was there such a numerous and influential body of the fraternity gathered in convention, as marked the tenth annual meeting of the National Association of Base Ball Players, held at Clinton Hall, New York, December 12, 1866. The great majority were up to the highest standard of assemblages of the kind, and reflected credit upon the base ball fraternity of the country.

A noteworthy feature of this great meeting was, that representatives from State Associations were present; Messrs. Griggs and Chambers, of the North-Western Base Ball Association, and Judge Rose, President of the Pennsylvania Association, being guests of the National Association on the occasion, and occupants of honorary seats on the platform with the President thereof.

Clubs from Oregon, on the extreme West, to Maine, on the East; and from Missouri, Tennessee, and Virginia, on the South, to Vermont, on the North, sent delegates to this Convention, and the flattering reception given them as their names were announced, and especially the applause which greeted the responses from the Southern clubs, afforded ample proof of the truly conservative feeling which prevailed in the Convention. But if anything more was needed it was presented in the form of the compliment paid the Southern delegation, in the selection of a candidate for the presidency of the association from among their number.

As early as 2 P.M., delegates began to throng the hall of the building known as Clinton Hall, and promptly at the hour of 3 P.M., the President was in the chair and the meeting called to order. The calling of the roll, receiving credentials, and payment of dues of clubs belonging to the Association having been got through with, the report of the nominating committee was received, and the names of the new clubs applying for admission being favorably reported upon, they were all duly elected members of the Association, and as the roll of the new clubs were called, the delegates stepped up to the Secretary's desk, presented credentials, paid their dues, and received tickets to entitle them to seats in the Convention. Nearly three hours were occupied in this business, and on motion, a temporary adjournment was had until 7 P.M.

Annexed will be found a complete list of clubs and their delegates, under the head of the States they belong to.

NEW YORK STATE CLUBS.

Active, New York, J.S. Page, Geo. Ebbets. *Atlantic*, Brooklyn, Thos. Tassic, J. A. Reagan. *Alert*, Elmira, D. B. Hill, C. Hazard. *Atlantic*, Jamaica, A. Hagner, W. J. Lodge. Athlete, Washington Heights, J. M. Cook, V. G. Audubon. Atlanta, Tremont, M. K. Hamilton, Jr., J. McEwen Betts. Auburn, Auburn. Binghamton, Binghamton, D. S. Burr, E. Conklin. Central City, Syracuse, Geo. Barnes, J. W. Yale. Cypress, East New York, G. H. Forbell, P. A. Ralph. *Constellation*, Brooklyn, W. L. Forster, H. W. Redfield. Dictator, Brooklyn, W.H.C. Nagle, E. Storck. *Eagle*, New York, J. P. Cozans, S. Yates. Eagle, Flatbush, H. S. Spofford, J. Stoothoff. *Eckford*, Brooklyn, Frank Pidgeon, John Grum. *Eclectic*, New York, Dr. W. H. Bell, A. H. Wright. *Empire*, New York, T. G. Voorhis, Jas. Cameron. Endeavor, New York, W. G. Ross, C. Lambert. *Enterprise*, Brooklyn, W. H. Murtha, F. P. Albert. *Enterprise*, Clifton, G. W. Dix, W. H. Clark. *Excelsior*, Brooklyn, Dr. J. B. Jones, J. B. Bach. Excelsior, Elmira, H. S. Griswald, L. Rice. Exercise, New York, S. O'Connor, W. Bowers. *Fulton*, New York, W. Campbell, C. C. Smith. *Gotham*, New York, J. B. Mongay, M. J. Kelly. Harlem, New York, G. W. Thompson, A. F. Johnson. Hector, Elmira, G. V. Bainbridge, F. G. Prall. Hope, New York. Hudson, Hudson, Chas. Whitbeck, J. H. Knickerbocker. *Hudson River*, Newburgh, D. A. Scott, J. C. Adams. Idlewild, Cornwall, I.. C. Cleves, S. B. Cocks. *Independent*, Brooklyn, H. H. Beadle, J. F. Pearson. Intrepid, Brooklyn, C. A. Hodges, S. W. Wilson. *Jefferson*, New York, W. M. Richardson, W. Glenn. *Knickerbocker*, New York, Jas. W. Davis, R. H. Hinsdale. *Knickerbocker*, Albany, Geo. H. Turner. F. P. Olcott. Liberty, Jamaica, R. Dunham, C. F. Bennett. Lone Star, Matteawan, D. W. Gitchell, T. G. Featherstone, *Mutual*, New York, John Wildey, S. Burns. Meteor, Addison, J. E. Jones, H. Baldwin. *Monitor*, Goshen, B. R. Champion, E. Dickenman. Monticello, Monticello, C. H. Boyce, R. J. St. John. *Mohawk*, Brooklyn, Hon. A. C. Davis, A. C. Smith. M. M. *Van Dyke*, New York, W. S. Bater, Jas. O'Grady. *Mystic*, New York. C. S. Glover, Jr., Jas. Reynolds. Niagara, Buffalo, no delegates. *National*, Albany, H. A. Carpenter, E. A. Sutter. *New York*, New York, W. Brower, H. C. Weeks. Ontario, Oswego, J. B. Farwell, B. W. Bates. *Oriental*, Brooklyn, W. H. Holmes, A. B. Zobles. Palisade, Yonkers, E. A. Houston, J. G. P. Holden. *Pacific*—New Utrecht, J. Van Brunt, Jr., J. Weir. *Peconic*, Brooklyn, C. Davis, G. E. Van Voorhis. *Powhatan*, Brooklyn, G. N. Dick, Thos. G. Irwin. *Resolute*, Brooklyn, A. H. Rogers,—Lockwood. Sparkhill, Piermont, L. G. Clark, R. W. D. Wood. Sparta, New York, W. Cooper, C. Louck. *Social*, New York, C. W. Travers, J. W. Johnson. *Surprise*, West Farms, B. B. Valentine, J. W. Bolton. *Star*, Brooklyn, W. R. Macdiarmed, J. E. Beale. *Union*, Morrisania, D. Milliken, W. Herring. Union, Lansingburgh, C. S. Holmes, C. E. Twing. Union, Elmira, E. H. Cook, E. S. Scovell. *Unionville*, Gravesend, J. J. Stillwell, J. Morris. *Una*, Mount Vernon, P. Lucas, Geo. Stevens. *Undercliff*, Cold Spring, J. Delany, E. Butler. *Utica*, Utica, L. M. Thompson. *Victory*, Troy, Jos. Wicks, R. V. Freeman. *Williamsburgh*, Brooklyn, D. C. Waring, Jos. Pinkham. Washington, Portchester, Chas. Hilbert, A. T. Brown. West Point, Highland Falls, M. Schneider, E. P. Riordan. World, New York, D. F. Headman, C. Winnacott.

PENNSYLVANIA CLUBS.

Alvin, Philadelphia, P. A. Allen, A. E. Keeler. *Alert*, Philadelphia, A. G. N. Halbeck, A. M. Hicks. *Alert*, Danville, W. W. Pinneo, S. Earp. Alleghany, Alleghany, James M. Carr. Amateur, Philadelphia, James Dainty, Jun., J. H. Kennedy. *Athletic*, Philadelphia, D. W. C. Moore, W. Meiser. Athenian, Philadelphia, J. H. Yearsly, G. W. Shill, Jun. Armstrong, Philadelphia, W. Corson, H. Merlin. Arctic, Philadelphia, A. H. Watt, T. J. Lindsey. Awkward, Philadelphia, W. B. Harman, S. Goomley. Bachelor, Philadelphia, H. A. Macomb, W. H. Pile, junr. Brandywine, West Chester, E. H. Hayhurst, E. Rogers. Chestnut Street Theatre, Philadelphia, H. R. Hellier, E. Sinn. Commonwealth, Philadelphia, E. A. Pharo, J. B. Diehl. Dirigo, Philadelphia, J. R. Caulton, G. W. Allen. *Equity*, Philadelphia, E. A. B. Brown, H. W.

Hancock. Excelsior, Coatesville, J. Stone, J. P. Cromleigh. First Ward, Philadelphia, T. R. Ames, II. C. Gumley. Germantown, Philadelphia, J. Maxwell, Theo. Rufee. Gymnast, Philadelphia, G. A. Kelly, W. R. Murray. Harry Clay, Philadelphia, Daniel R. Kleinfelder, W. A. Hertz. Hiawatha, Kittanning, J. McConnell, J. D. Reynolds. Independent, Johnstown, L. D. Woodruff, J. Riddlesheimer. Juniata, Hollidaysburg, no delegates. Keystone, Philadelphia, J. H. Lynch, W. Deal. Keystone, Harrisburgh, D. D. Downer, B. Frisch. Kensington, Philadelphia, J. Distrech, G. A. Bakhoven. Korndaffer, Philadelphia, G. W. Korndaffer, J. E. Conrad. Kickenepawling, Johnstown, R. W. Hunt, J. M. Bowman. Leisure, Philadelphia, J. Bates, F. E. Gerlach. National, Philadelphia, C. A. Porter, C. F. Berwind. Neptune, Easton, J. S. Mingle, H. J. Rieder. *Olympic*, Philadelphia, J. S. Kuen, A. Thatcher, Jun. *Orion*, Philadelphia, J. R. Reed, H. Disston. Philadelphia, Philadelphia, W. B. Spooner, J. C. Addis, Jun. Randall, Philadelphia, J. Mulligan, H. Donnelly. Raleigh, Philadelphia, A. J. Stief, R. C. Congdon. Rittenhouse, Philadelphia, J. Geraghty, F. Carr. Scranton, Scranton, E. P. Kingsbury, F. L. Hitchesen. Social, Huntington, H. G. Fisher, D. H. Roaker. *Susquehanna*, Wilkesbarre, J. B. Williamson, J. Payne. Tyrolean, Harrisburgh, H. L. Orbs, Chas. Heister. Typographical, Philadelphia, W. Turner, G. C. Stroman. Union, Titusville, no delegates. Unity, Port Richmond, J. R. Beach, W. H. H. Cline. West Philadelphia, Philadelphia, J. R. Smith, G. Young. Western Market, Philadelphia, no delegates. Wild Cat, Brookville, no delegates.

NEW JERSEY CLUBS.

Active, Newark, O. Fitzgerald, W. C. Morton. *Americus*, Newark, D. W. C. Jerolemon, A. P. Mayhew. Atlantic, Trenton, J. H. Stewart, J. Croxson. Bergen, Bergen, J. Winner, J. U. R. Vreeland. Burlington, Burlington, C. H. Schermerhorn, H. Moffett. *Camden*, Camden, H. Graften, S. C. Knight. Champion, Jersey City, H. Davenport, G. Denver. *Columbia*, Bordentown, A. Waterman, T. M. Murphy. Excelsior, Paterson, W. D. Bradley, C. H. Happen. *Eureka*, Newark, C. C. Thomas, E. R. Pennington. Friendship, Beverley, no delegates. *Irvington*, Irvington, J. F. Seymore, J. M. C. Eaton, Monmouth, Hoboken, E. A> Nestlen, W. H. Ostrander. Mohican, Hightstown, no delegates. Kearney, Rahway, J. R. Hanna, S. Marsh. *Liberty*, New Brunswick, J. Van Nest, W. Hatfield, *National*, Jersey City, J. W. Edwards, M. D. Tilden. National, Morristown, F. Child, J. R. Runyon. *Newark*, Newark, E. H. Dawson, *Olympic*, Paterson, S. C. McKeirnan, S. Thorpe. Palisade, Englewood, F. Van Brunt, A. H. Schenck. Princeton, Princeton, L. H. Anderson, W. G. Johnson. Randolph, Dover, M. P. Neff, J. M. Losee. Resolute, Elizabeth, W. H. Woodruff, L. K. Albro, Sea Side, Long Branch, W. K. Bunley, J. B. Conleis, Union, Camden, J. Powell, G. Jones.

CONNECTICUT CLUBS.

Agallian, Middletown, R. N. Crane, C. L. Bonnell. Alert, Hartford, J. V. Slattery, J. Dandon. Alert, Norwalk, J. B. Purdy, D. R. Silleck. Bridgeport, Bridgeport, W. H. Jones, S. M. Cate, Jun. *Charter Oak*, Hartford, G. B. Hubbell, Dr. W. M. Hudson. *Chester*, Norwich, no delegates. Forest City, Middletown, R. W. Newhall, J. Duffield. Howard, Hartford, H. Andrus, F. H. Whittlesey. Hockanum, North Manchester, D. S. Calhoun, P. W. Hudson. Liberty, Norwalk, W. R. Smith, G. E Miller. Monitor, Waterbury, C. C. Commerford, H. D. Boughton. Monitor, Westport, W. Lyon, C. H. Taylor. Marvin, Norwichtown, J. A. Steady, Theo. W. Ames. New Britain, New Britain, P. Corbin, C. S. Lander. Oceanic, Mystic Bridge, S. A. Graves, C. Gleason. Pequot, Fair Haven, W. H. Thompson, C. S. Brown. Quinnipiack, New Haven, S. R. Smith, S. M. Knivals. Waterbury, Waterbury, J. W. Smith, C. E. Smith. *Yale*, New Haven, no delegates.

DISTRICT OF COLUMBIA CLUBS.

Capitol, Washington, H. C. Porter, W. Cunningham. Continental, Washington, W. H. Rhoberts, J. W. Browning. Empire, Washington, C. E. Coon, F. Y. Anderson. Gymnastic, Washington, R. S. Vedder, R. E. Ellenback. Interior, Washington, T. Culver, W. A. Ogden. *Jefferson*, Washington, S. H. Yeatman, G. W. C. Finney. Olympic, Washington, J. Burns, H. W. Dennison. *National*, Washington, W. C. McIntire. *Union*, Washington, M. E. Urell, R. M. Drinkard.

MARYLAND CLUBS.

Alert, Cumberland, S. H. Fundenburg, R. Shriver. Antietam, Hagerstown, H. Kennady, Alex. Null. Enterprise, Baltimore, H. C. Ford, A. S. Houck. Maryland, Baltimore, W. P. Vaughan, J. M. Henderson. Pastime, Baltimore, J. K. Sears, Otto Keilpaltz.

DELAWARE CLUBS.

Diamond Sate, Wilmington, S. H. Edgar, W. D. Mendenhall.

VIRGINIA CLUBS.

Union, Richmond D. B. Parker, A. J. Ankles.

WEST VIRGINIA CLUBS.

Hunkidori, Wheeling, F. C. Winship.

MISSOURI CLUBS.

Empire, St. Louis, no delegates. Union, St. Louis, Thadeus D. Smith.

TENNESSEE CLUBS.

Lookout, Chattanooga, no delegates. Lightfoot, Chattanooga, no delegates.

IOWA CLUBS.

Western, Burlington, George Sunderland. Wahkonsa, Fort Dodge, C. C. Smetzer.

KANSAS CLUBS.

Frontier, Fort Leavenworth, no delegates. Fort Scott, Fort Scott, Capt. J. Smith.

OREGON CLUBS.

Pioneer, Portland, Robert H. Law.

OHIO CLUBS.

Buckeye, Cincinnati, Phillip Lishawa. Capital, Columbus, no delegates. Live Oak, Cincinnati, Dr. John Draper. Occidental, Gambrier, no delegates.

MASSACHUSETTS CLUBS.

Harvard, Cambridge, no delegates. *Lowell*, Boston, Mortimer Rogers.

MAINE CLUBS.

Eon, Portland, J. H. Smith, F. W. Smith.

TOTAL CLUBS REPRESENTED.

New York State, 73; Pennsylvania, 48; New Jersey, 26; Connecticut, 20; District of Columbia, 10; Maryland, 5; Ohio, 4; Massachusetts, 2; Iowa, 2; Tennessee, 2; Missouri, 2; Kansas, 2; and Delaware, Virginia, West Virginia, Kentucky, Oregon and Maine, one each; making a grand total of 202 clubs, representing 17 States and the District of Colombia.

Those in italics are old clubs; all the others are new members of the Association.

In addition to the above list of clubs were present at the Convention, Messrs. Griggs and Chambers of the North-Western Association, and Judge Rose of the Pennsylvania Association, as representatives of over two hundred additional clubs.

The Convention re-assembled at 7 P. M., and the body having become organized, the order of business was transacted in regular form. The report of the Committee on Rules came up for adoption. Below will be found such portions of the report as refers to changes made in the Constitution and By-Laws. Those made in the rules are given in the form of the rules asa they now read, with the amendments introduced.

AMENDMENTS, ALTERATIONS, AND ADDITIONS TO THE CONSTITUTION FOR 1867, PRESENTED BY THE COMMITTEE ON RULES AND REGULATIONS, DECEMBER 12, 1866.

ART. II.—To amend by adding after the word clubs—last line—the words "and State Base Ball Associations."

ART. III. SEC. 1.—To amend by inserting after the word clubs—fifth line—the words "or State Base Ball Associations."

SEC. 2.—To be a new section, and to read as follows:

"Any State Base Ball Association desiring to be represented in this Association, shall present to the Recording Secretary, at least thirty days previous to the annual meeting of this Association, a written official certificate signed by the President and Secretary of each State Association they represent, the number of clubs composing said Association, and their date of organization, names of their officers, and number of members belonging to each club; also the date of organization of the State Association they represent, and the names of their delegates."

SEC. 2.—To be made section 3.

SEC. 3.—Page 10 (second line), to amend by inserting after the word which, "together with all applications from State Base Ball Associations." To insert after the word club (seventh line), "and State Base Ball Association." To insert after the word club (eleventh line), "or State Base Ball Association;" also, after the word club (thirteenth line), "State Base Ball Association."

SEC. 3 to be section 4.

SEC. 4.—To amend by inserting after the word member (third line), "and no State Association shall be represented in this Association, unless composed of eighteen clubs," and by inserting after the word or (same line), the word "either," and by inserting after the word club (fourth line), "or State Base Ball Association."

SEC. 5.—To be a new section, and to read as follows, viz.: "Any club or State Association, organized after the adjournment of the annual meeting of this Association, may be elected probationary members thereof, after conforming to the requirements of sections second, third and fourth, by the Nominating Committee. They shall be subject to the payment of dues and assessments, and be eligible to all the privileges of regular members of this Association until the next annual meeting, at which time they must be duly elected in the same manner as all regular members."

ART. IV. SEC. 4.—To amend by adding after the word organization (last line), "or by a majority vote of the Board of Officers."

ART. VI. SEC. 1.—To amend by striking out the words "in the city of New York," and inserting "at such place as the Association at the annual meeting may direct."

ART. VII.—To amend by inserting after the word club (last line), "or State Association."

ART. VIII. SEC. 1.—To amend by adding to the end of the section, after the word for, "and each State Association shall pay, through their delegates, to this Association, in like manner, the sum of two dollars as an annual due for each club belonging to such Association."

SEC. 2.—To amend by inserting after the word clubs, the words "and State Association."

SEC. 3.—To amend by striking out the words, "a vote by proxy shall not be allowed, " and insert, "Each club who shall have a delegate present at any meeting shall be entitled to two votes, and each State Association who shall be entitled to two votes, and each State Association who shall have a delegate present at any meeting, shall be entitled to two votes for each club belonging to the State Association he represents." Also to insert after the word "club" (third line), the words "or association, and no club shall vote as an individual, and also through a State Base Ball Association." Also to insert after the word "club," (fourth line), the words "or State Association."

SEC. 4.—To amend by adding after the word players (last line on page 15), "And no State Base Ball Association shall be admitted to membership in this Association unless they adopt in their constitution the sentiments or words contained in this section."

ART. IX.—To amend by inserting after the word "Association" (third line, page 150, "and all clubs belonging to the State Base Ball Association."

ART. X.—To amend by striking out the word "immediately," in the first line, and inserting the words, "within one week." Also to insert after the word "members" (on seventh line), "a Printing Committee, consisting of three." Also to strike out the word "and" on the sixth line.
BY-LAWS.

Sec. 8.—To amend by striking out the word "ten," and inserting the word "thirty."

Annexed, we give the rules amended as they now read:

SEC. 5.—*The pitcher's position shall be designated by two lines, two yards in length, drawn at right angles to the line from home to the second base, having their centres upon that line at two fixed iron plates, placed at points fifteen and sixteen and one-third yards distance from the home base. The pitcher must stand within these lines, and must deliver the ball as nearly as possible over the centre of the home base, and fairly for the striker.*

SEC. 6.—*Should a pitcher repeatedly fail to deliver the striker fair balls, for the apparent purpose of delaying the game, or for any cause, the umpire, after warning him, shall call one ball, and if the pitcher persists in such action, two and three ball; when three balls have been called, the striker shall take the first base, and should any base be occupied at that time, each player occupying it or them shall take one base without being put out. All balls delivered by the pitcher striking the ground before reaching the line of the home base, or pitched over the head of the batsman, or pitch to the side opposite to which the batsman strikes from, shall be considered unfair balls.*

SEC. 7.—*The ball must be pitched, not jerked or thrown, to the bat; and whenever the pitcher moves with the apparent purpose or pretence to deliver the ball, he shall so deliver it, and must have neither foot in advance of the line, or off the ground at the time of delivering the ball; and if he fails in either of these particulars, then it shall be declared a balk. The ball shall be considered as jerked, in the meaning of the rule, if the pitcher's arm touches his person when the arm is swung forward to delivery the ball; and it shall be regarded as a throw if the arm be bent at the elbow, at an angle from the body, or horizontally from the shoulder, when it is swung forward to deliver the ball. A pitched ball is one delivered with the arm straight, and swinging perpendicularly, and free from the body.*

SEC. 9.—*The striker shall be considered a player running the bases as soon as he has struck a fair ball.*

SEC. 10.—*Any ball delivered by the pitcher on which a balk or ball has been called, shall be considered dead and not in play until it has been settled in the hands of the pitcher, while he stands in the lines of his position; and no such ball, if hit, shall put the striker out.*

SEC. 13.—*Or, if three balls are struck at and missed, and the last is caught, either before touching the ground or upon the first bound, provided that balls struck at are not those on which balls or balks have been called, or nor those struck at for the purpose of wilfully striking out.*

SEC. 17.—*No run or base can be made upon a foul ball; such a ball shall be considered dead, and not in play, until it shall first be settled in the hands of the pitcher; in such cases, players running the bases shall return to them, and may be put out in so returning in the same manner as when running to the first base.*

SEC. 18.—*No run or first base can be made when a fair ball has been caught without having touched the ground; such a ball shall be considered alive, and in play. In such case, players running bases shall return to them, and may be put out in so returning in the same manner as when running to the first base; but players, when balls are so caught, may run their immediately after the ball has been settled in the hands of the player catching it.*

SEC. 19.—*The striker, when in the act of striking, shall not step forward or backward, but must stand on a line drawn though the centre of the home base, not exceeding in length three feet from either side thereof, and parallel with the line occupied by the pitcher. He shall be considered the striker until he has struck a fair ball. Players must strike in regular rotation, and after the first inning is played, the turn commences with the player who stands on the list to the one who lost the third hand.*

SEC. 20.—*Players must take their bases on order of striking; and when a fair ball is struck, and not caught flying, the first base must be vacated, as also the second and third bases, if they are occupied at the same time. Players may be put out upon any base, under these circumstance, in the same manner*

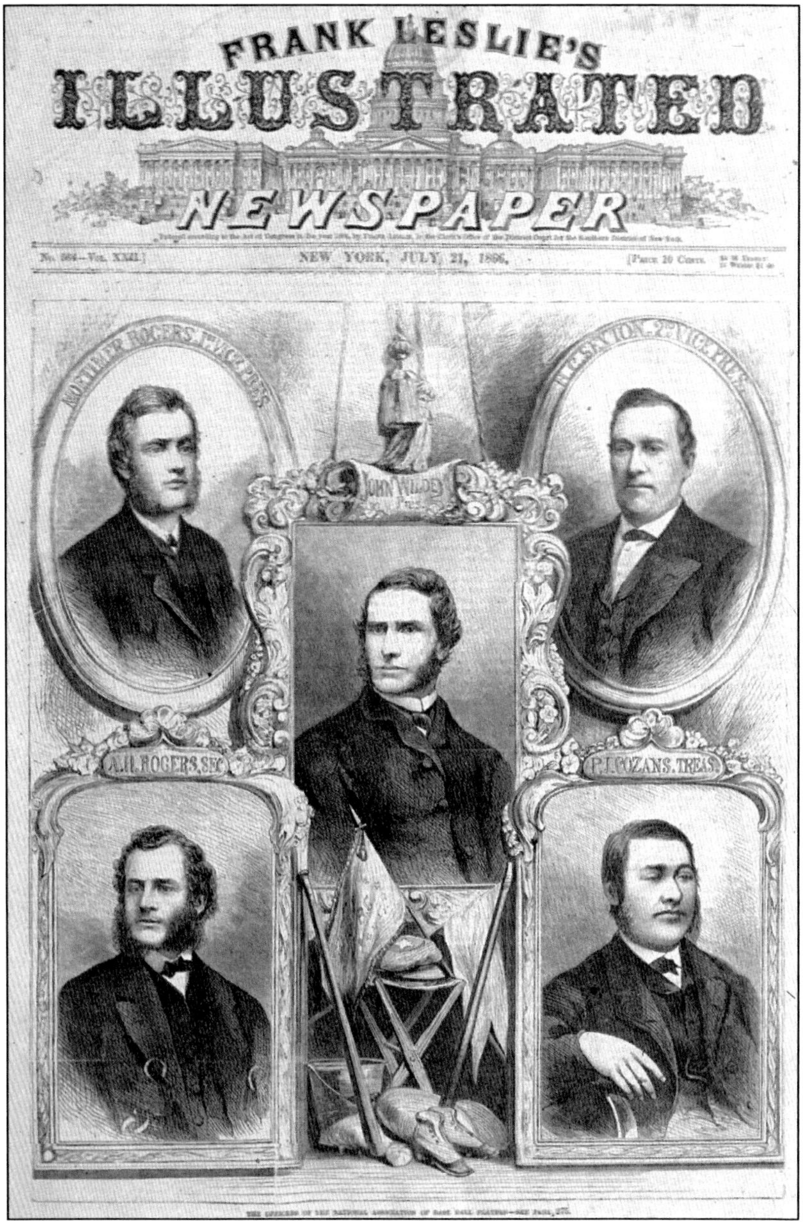

NABBP STAFF. *Pictured are President John Wildey in the middle; 1st Vice-President Mortimer Rogers in the upper left corner; 2nd Vice-President H.C. Sexton is the upper right hand corner; Secretary A.H. Rogers is at the bottom left; and Treasurer P.J. Cozans is in the lower right hand corner. Source: Transcendental Graphics.)*

as when running to the first base.

SEC. 24.—*If any adversary stops the ball with his hat or cap, of if a ball is stopped by any person not engaged in the game, or if he takes it from the hands of any one not engaged in the game, no player can be put out unless the ball shall first have been settled in the hands of the pitcher.*

SEC. 26.—*If two hands are already out, no players running home at the time the ball is struck can make a run to count in the score of the game if the striker is put out by a fair catch, by being touched between home and first base, or by the ball being held by an adversary at the first base before the striker reached it.*

SEC. 29.—*In playing all matches , nine players from each club shall constitute a full field, and they must have been regular members of the club they represent, and of mo other club, either in or out of the National Association, for thirty days immediately prior to the match, Position of players and choice of innings shall be determined by captains previously appointed for that purpose by the respective clubs.*

SEC. 30.—*The umpire shall take care that the regulations respecting the ball, bats, bases, and the pitcher's and striker's positions are strictly observed. He shall be the judge of fair and unfair play, and shall determine all dispute and differences which may occur during the game; he shall take special care to declare all foul balls, balks, strikes, and balls, immediately upon their occurrence; and when a player is put out, in what position and manner, unasked, and in a distinct and audible manner. He shall, in every instance, before leaving the ground, declare the winning club, and shall record his decision in the book of the scores.*

SEC. 32.—*No person engaged in a match, either as umpire, scorer, or player, shall be either directly or indirectly interested in any bet upon the game. Neither umpire, scorer, nor player shall be changed during a match, unless with the consent of both parties, except for reason of illness, or injury, or for a violation of this law, and then the umpire may dismiss any transgressor.*

SEC. 37.—*Whenever a match shall have been determined upon between two clubs, play shall be called at the exact hour appointed; and should either party fail to produce their players within thirty minutes thereafter, the party so failing shall admit a defeat, and shall deliver the ball before leaving the ground, which ball must be received by the club who are ready to play, and the game shall be considered as won, and so counted in the list of matches played; and the winning club shall be entitled to a score of nine runs for any game forfeited, unless the delinquent side fail to play on account of a recent death of one of its members, and sufficient time has not elapsed to enable them to give their opponents the notice before arriving on the ground.*

SEC. 39.—*No person who shall be in arrears to any other club, or shall at any time receive compensation for his service as a player, shall be competent to play in any match. All players who play base ball for money, place or emolument, shall be regarded as professional players; and no professional player shall take part in any match-game; and any club giving any compensation to a player, or having to their knowledge a player in their nine playing in a match for compensation, shall be debarred from membership in the National Association, and they shall not be considered by any club belonging to this Association as a proper club to engage in a match with, and should any club so engage with them, they shall forfeit membership.*

The report of the Committee having been adopted, the next thing of interest was the election of officers, and after quite a busy electioneering time of it, the following officers, were chosen:

President, Arthur P. Gorman, of the National Club, of Washington. First Vice-President, Hon. B. F. Rose, of the Mountain Club, of Altoona, Pa. Second Vice-President, W. H. Murtha, of the Enterprise Club, of Brooklyn. Recording Secretary, A. H. Rogers, of the Resolute Club (address box 6,718, New York Post-office). Corresponding Secretary, C. E. Coon (Address Box 191, Washington, D. C.) of the Empire Club, of Washington; Treasurer, Mortimer Rogers, of the Lowell Club, of Boston.

During the election of officers a vote was taken on the question of the place of meeting of the next Convention, and it was decided to meet at Philadelphia, at the Chestnut Street Theatre, on Wednesday, December 12, 1867, at 11 A. M.

In acknowledgment of the services rendered the Association by Mr. A. H. Rogers, a donation of $250 was voted him. On motion, it was resolved that 5,000 copies of the Convention book should be published. Dr. Jones, on behalf of Mr. Sebring, presented one of the latter's newly invented Parlor Base Ball Fields, and explained to the Convention its features as a means of illustrating the theory of the game. The following are the names of the delegates appointed on the several Committees: Committee of Rules: —J. B. Jones, Excelsior, Brooklyn, Chairman; H. Chadwick, National, Washington; J. Grum, Eckford, Brooklyn; C. E. Thomas, Eureka, New Jersey; J. B. Lynch Keystone, Philadelphia; James Cameron, Empire, New York; G. B. Hubbell, Charter Oak, Hartford, Conn.; G. Ebbets, Active, New York; D. R. Kleinfelder, Harry Clay, Philadelphia, Pa.; Otis Keicholtz, Pastime, Baltimore, Md.; D. B. Parker, Union, Richmond, Va.; Dr, John Draper, Live Oak, Cincinnati; August Waterman, Columbia, Bordentown, N.J. Judiciary Committee: W. Herring, Union, Morrisania, N. Y., Chairman; D. W. C. Moore, Athletic, Philadelphia, Pa.; J. B. Bach, Excelsior, Brooklyn, N.Y.; M. J. Kelly, Gotham, New York; Thomas Tassie, Atlantic, Brooklyn, N. Y.; C. C. Commerford, Monitor, Waterbury, Conn.; S. Yates, Eagle, New York; F. C. Winship, Hunkidori, Wheeling, W. Va.; J. S. Kuen, Olympic, Philadelphia, Pa. Committee on Nominations: Dr. W. H. Bell, Eclectic, New York; J. W. Avis, Knickerbocker, New York; E. Sinn, Chestnut Street Theatre, Philadelphia, Pa. Printing Committee: H. H. Ragen, Independent Brooklyn, Chairman; H. Chadwick, National, Washington; Robert H. Lane, Portland, Oregon.

NEW ENGLAND ASSOCIATION.

At a regular meeting of the Trimountain Base Ball Club, of Boston, held February 1, 1865, resolutions were passed by them, that they would use their influence and endeavors to secure the formation of a New England Association of Base Ball Players, and a committee was appointed to confer with the various clubs of New England to perfect this object. The committee consisted of Frank N. Scott, George Arnold, Edw. A. Saltzman, S. M. Hovey, H. J. Boardman, and W. A. Gammon.

This committee, though its Secretary, George Arnold, corresponded with the different clubs, and in October a call was issued for a preliminary meeting of the Association, to convene at the Hancock House, October 25, 1865. At this meeting the following clubs were represented: Fly-Away and Orient, of East Boston; Orient, of Newton; Granite, of Holliston; King Phillip, of East Abingdon; Harvard, of Cambridge; Lightfoot, of Neponset; Trimountain, of Boston. It was agreed to call a second convention on November 7th, and a committee, consisting of Corliss Wadleigh and six others, were4 appointed to draw up a constitution and by-laws for the Association.

In accordance with the call issued by the preliminary meeting, the convention met at the Hancock House November 7th, and perfected an organization by the adopting of a constitution and by-laws, the electing officers, and appointing the necessary committees.

The constitution provides that the Association shall be called the New England Association of Base Ball Players, with the avowed objects of perpetuating the game, and fostering kindly feelings among clubs, Any club consisting of eighteen active members may be represented by two delegates., The regular meetings are to be held annually on the second Tuesday in March, in Boston. The rules of the game governing the National Association govern the New England association.

The following gentlemen were elected officers of the Association, to hold office until the regular meeting in march, 1866: President, Corliss, Wadleigh, of the Fly-Away; Vice-President, John A. Lowell, of the Lowell; Recording Secretary, Irvin Leland, of the Granite; Corresponding Secretary, Frank N. Scott, of the Trimountain; Treasurer, H. R. Smith, of the Dictator.

After the appointment of the standing committees, Mr. John A. Lowell, on behalf of the committee having it in charge, formally tendered to the Association the silver ball recently given to the New England Clubs as a token of the championship. The ball was accepted, and the following gentlemen appointed a committee to make new rules and regulations governing the playing for the champion ball: F. Wright, of the Harvard; J. A. Lowell, of the Lowell; N. S. Cobleigh, of the Orient.

At this Convention the following clubs were represented by twenty-one delegates: Dictator, of Newton; Eureka, of East Cambridge; Electric, of Bright; Fly-Away, of East Boston; Granite, of Holliston; Harvard, of Cambridge; King Phillip. Of East Abingdon; Lightfoot, of Neponset; Lowell, of Boston; Orient, of East Boston; Trimountain, of Boston.

At the annual meeting held at the Parker House, March 13, 1866, after hearing reports of officers and standing committees, and special committee on rules governing the play for the champion ball, the convention adjourned until Monday evening, March 26. At the adjourned meeting held at the Parker House, March 26, 1866, the principal business was the election of officers and appointment of committees. The following gentleman were: President, John A. Lowell, of the Lowell Club; Vice-President, Frank N. Scott, of the Trimountain Club; Recording Secretary, C. R. Byrum, of the Electric Club; Corresponding Secretary, J. S. Gray, of the King Phillip Club; Treasurer, Wm. G. Kidder, of the Orient Club. The next annual meeting of the New England Association will be held in March, 1867.

NORTH-WESTERN ASSOCIATION.

According to appointment, delegates from various base ball clubs met at the Briggs House, in the city of Chicago, on the 6th of December, 1865, for the purpose of forming a North-Western Base Ball Association. The Convention was called to order by G. Charles Smith, of the Excelsior Club of Chicago, and on motion, R. H. Anderson, of the Detroit Club, was chosen temporary Chairman, and H. G. Teed, of the Elkhart Club, temporary Secretary. The Secretary then proceeded to take the names of delegates present, and the clubs represented by them, as follows: Excelsior, Chicago, Ill.–A. J. Smith, G. C. Smith; Atlantic, Chicago, Ill.,–A. M. Kinzie, Holmes Hoge; Pacific, Chicago, Ill.–J. C. Branick, B. Mackey; Hope, St Louis, Mo.–Jos. Reed. G. Kilpatrick; Julien, Dubuque, Iowa–J. D. Langworthy, E. M. Hodges; Capital City, Madison, Wis.–Geo. Hopkins; Detroit, Detroit, Mich.–R. H. Anderson, H. Burroughs; Forest City, Rockford, Ill. Geo. E. King, H. S. Warner; Sinnissippi, Rockford, Ill.–Elias Nashold; Mercantile, Rockford, Ill.–E. H. Griggs; Western, Indianapolis, Ind.–A. Brewer; Wabash, Lafayette, Ind.–C. F. Howe, Henry Cassell; Elkhart, Elkhart, Ind.–H. G. Teed, N. B. Ridgway; Kenyon, Kenyon College, Ohio–S. R. Huyett.

It was moved and carried that the Chair appoint a Committee, consisting of one delegate from each State, to draft a Constitution and By-Laws, and prepare business for the Convention.

The following delegates were appointed such Committee:–Illinois, A. J. Smith; Missouri–Jos. Reed; Iowa–J. D. Langworthy; Indiana–N. B. Ridgway; Wisconsin–G. B. Hopkins; Michigan–H. Burroughs; Ohio–S. R. Huyett.

Adjourned to two o'clock P.M.

Afternoon session called to order by the Chairman. On motion, members of Base Ball Club present, not delegates, were invited to take seats in the Convention. On motion, each Club represented was allowed two votes in the Convention. The committee on Constitution and By-Laws presented their report, as follows:

Whereas, The prosperity of, and growing interest in, the National Game of Base Ball in the West, and the distance and difficulty of representation in the Base Ball Associations of the East, demand, for the interest of the game, a separate Convention in the West, therefore be it.

Resolved, That we, the Members of Basse Ball Clubs in the various States of the West, organize ourselves into an Association, to be known as the North-Western Association of Base Ball Players.

Resolved, That we adopt the Constitution of the National association of Base Ball Players, as adopted at their convention held in New York City, December 14, 1864, subject to such amendments as the said Association may adopt at their meeting to be held in Buffalo on the 13th of the present month, with the exception of fixing the age at which members may be admitted to clubs, at eighteen years and over. The officers of the Association shall consist of a President, Vice-President, Secretary and Treasurer, to be elected by ballot; and one Vice-President and Corresponding Secretary from each State, to be appointed by the President, who shall hold their offices for one year.

The foregoing report was accepted and adopted, and the Convention proceeded to ballot for officers of the Association of the ensuing year.

The election resulted as follows:—President, G. Charles Smith, Excelsior, Chicago; Vice-President, H. G. Teed,, La Porte, La Porte; Secretary, E. H. Griggs, Mercantile, Rockfords; Treasurer, R. H. Anderson, Detroit, Detroit.

On motion, John H. Gibbons, of the North Star Club, St. Paul, Minn., was admitted as a delegate from said Club. The President appointed the following Vice-Presidents and Corresponding secretaries, viz. Indiana—A. Brewer, V. P.; Lan. C. Patrick, Secretary. Michigan—H. Burroughs, V. P.; Butler Ives, Secretary. Illinois—A. M. Kinzie, V. P.; Geo. E. King, Secretary. Missouri—G. Kilpatrick, V. P.; Jos. Reed, Secretary. Iowa—J. D. Langworthy, V.P.; B. M. Harger, Secretary. Ohio—J. J. McCook, V. P.; S. R. Huyett, Secretary. Wisconsin—N. Treadway, V. P; Geo. B. Hopkins, Secretary. Minnesota—J. H. Gibbons, V. P.; R. C. Olin, Secretary.

On motion, it was voted that it should be the duty of the Secretary of each Club belonging to this Association, to report all matches played by such Club to the Corresponding Secretary for the States in which it is located, and that the State Secretary report the same to the Secretary of this Association.

On motion, it was voted that each Club challenging, or accepting a challenge, bear its own expenses.

The Secretary was directed to write to the Secretary of the National Association, informing him of this organization, and requesting the privilege of representation, by delegates, in the Convention of said Association.

On motion, adjourned, to meet in Chicago, on the third Wednesday in December, 1866.

The Association was duly represented in the tenth annual Convention of the National Association, which was held at Clinton Hall, New York, on Wednesday afternoon and evening, December 12, 1866; the delegates being Messrs. Griggs and Chambers

The North-Western Association of Base Ball Players held their second annual convention at the Briggs House, Chicago, Illinois, on Wednesday and Thursday, December 19th and 20th, 1866. Twenty-five clubs were represented. They adopted the rules of the National Base Ball Players, as amended at the annual convention held at Clinton Hall, New York, December 12, 1866. The following gentlemen were elected officers of the Association: President, J. W. Van Norman, of Detroit; Vice-President, George P. Wells, of Chicago; Secretary, E. H. Griggs, of Rockford; Treasurer, J. E. Hiller, of La Porte.

In concluding our base ball matter, we deem it proper to pay a tribute to our friend Mr. Henry Chadwick, a gentleman who has had a long experience in the reporting of base ball, cricket, and aquatics, for several journals; and whose reports are universally admitted to be a reliable, impartial, and talented character. Mr. Chadwick bestows a care, attention, and pains upon his reports which have won for them a standard reputation and influence with all who take any interest in American out-door pastimes. Knowing and appreciating their worth and value, it affords us sincere pleasure and gratification to add our humble testimony in behalf of their conceded merit and excellence.